Interactive Media
Essentials for Success

Interactive Media
Essentials for Success

Brian Blum

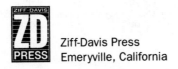

Ziff-Davis Press
Emeryville, California

Editor	Kelly Green
Project Coordinator	Barbara Dahl
Cover Illustration and Design	Regan Honda
Book Design	Paper Crane Graphics, Berkeley
Technical Illustration	Sarah Ishida
Word Processing	Howard Blechman
Page Layout	M.D. Barrera and Russel Stolins
Indexer	Valerie Robbins

Ziff-Davis Press, ZD Press, and the Ziff-Davis Press logo are licensed to Macmillan Computer Publishing USA by Ziff-Davis Publishing Company, New York, New York.

Ziff-Davis Press imprint books are produced on a Macintosh computer system with the following applications: FrameMaker®, Microsoft® Word, QuarkXPress®, Adobe Illustrator®, Adobe Photoshop®, Adobe Streamline™, MacLink®Plus, Aldus® FreeHand™, Collage Plus™.

If you have comments or questions or would like to receive a free catalog, call or write:
Macmillan Computer Publishing USA
Ziff-Davis Press Line of Books
5903 Christie Avenue
Emeryville, CA 94608
800-688-0448

ISBN 1-56276-347-4

Manufactured in the United States of America
10 9 8 7 6 5 4 3 2 1

To Jody—my interactive partner in life

■ Contents at a Glance

■ Table of Contents

Chapter 5:   The Development Process: Production, Implementation, and Publishing 107

Chapter 7:   Emerging Paradigms   161

Interactive Movies and Fiction   162

Interactive Magazines and Books   171

Interactive Media Applications   178

Chapter 8:   The Emerging Language of Interactive Media   183

The 30-Second Rule   184

Click to Stop   185

Click in the Background to Return   186

Continuous Sound Track   186

Friendly Transitions and Waits   188

Let the Cursor Do the Talking   188

Build in Basic Intuitiveness   189

Chapter 9:   Tools You Can Use

■ Credit List for Screen Shots

■ Chapter 1

Figure 1.1
Morgan's Recess in Greece
© 1994 Morgan Interactive, Inc. All rights reserved. Recess in Greece, Morgan, Skatergator, Alicat, Kangaruth, Hip Hop Hippo, and Bernardvark are trademarks of Morgan Interactive, Inc.

Figure 1.2
Material World
© 1994, 1995 StarPress Multimedia, Inc.

Figure 1.3
Electronic Arts' EA Kids Sampler
© Electronic Arts. EA•Kids is a registered trademark of Electronic Arts.

Figure 1.4
A Hard Day's Night
Courtesy of The Voyager Company. Used with permission.

Figure 1.5
Spaceship Warlock
Copyright 1991 by Reactor Inc. "Spaceship Warlock" is a trademark of Reactor Inc.

Figure 1.6
Myst
© 1993, Cyan, Inc. All rights reserved. Myst® is a registered trademark of Cyan, Inc. Screen shot from Myst® used by permission.

Figure 1.7
Manhole
© 1994, Cyan, Inc. All rights reserved. Used with permission.

Figure 1.8
The Eleventh Hour
© Trilobyte, Inc. Used with permssion.

■ Chapter 6

Figure 6.1
How to Shoot Video Like a Pro
© Zelos Digital Learning. Used with permission.

■ Chapter 7

Figure 7.3
The Madness of Roland
The Madness of Roland is a trademark of Hyperbole Studios. © 1994 Hyperbole Studios.

Figure 7.4
Vortex: Quantum Gate II
© Quantum Gate, The Vortex: Quantum Gate II, and Virtual Cinema are trademarks of Hyperbole Studios. © 1994 Hyperbole Studios.

Figure 7.8
Take Control: How to Stay Healthy and Safe from HIV & AIDS
© 1993 InfoUse. Used with permission.

Figure 7.10
Marvin Minsky's Society of Mind
Courtesy of The Voyager Company. Used with permission.

Figure 7.11
Discis Book
© Animation, pictures, music, audio, text and all software Copyright © 1995 Discis Knowledge Research, Inc. All rights reserved.

Figure 7.12
Maus
© The Voyager Company. Used with permission.

Figure 7.13
Cartoon History of the Universe
© Putnam New Media. Used with permission.

■ Acknowledgments

Writing this book has been a remarkable adventure, one that began in Northern California and saw its implementation in the Middle East. I presented the concept of *Interactive Media Essentials for Success* to Cindy Hudson and Eric Stone, formerly of Ziff-Davis Press, on a chilly day in September 1994 at a sushi restaurant in Berkeley. A few days later, I moved myself and my entire family to Jerusalem, Israel.

The offer to write the book arrived through the transatlantic e-mail. Since then, the entire book has been written electronically. I would e-mail the chapters to Ziff-Davis Press, and the edited chapters—all marked up with strike-outs, footnotes, and multiple colors—would be e-mailed back to me. In fact, I never printed out a single page of this book!

That said, I'd like to acknowledge some of the profound help I've received to make the writing of this book from 10,000 miles away a reality: to Cindy and Eric, of course, for believing in me in the first place. To Kelly Green, my Development Editor, who read every word and made it sound even better, not to mention being my tireless advocate for including screen shots at the last minute; to Suzanne Anthony, my Acquisitions Editor at Ziff-Davis, who was there to answer my questions and cajole and nudge me along when deadlines got tight; to Lysa Lewallen, who provided countless hours of administrative assistance and coordinated a lot of the tough job of obtaining screen shot permission; and to Juliet Langley for coming up with not just a name for the book, but an entire series to place it in!

On the home front, I couldn't have written a single word without the unending support and deep "ahava" of my wife, Jody, who put up with my late hours and subsequent morning grumbling. This book is truly dedicated to you. My children's fascination with the writing process has been of great encouragement, too. One friend in particular deserves special mention—Julie Gordon, who took care of cooking, cleaning, and childcare beyond the call of normal houseguest duty in the midst of my most intense writing phase.

To all the colleagues who have followed my progress, know that I keenly appreciate your support, interest, and enthusiasm. The concepts and principles written down here are not just the result of my own thinking, but of the countless discussions I've had with professionals around the world. Just as interactive design is highly iterative, so is the process of putting in words what one knows to be true and effective. For all the good times we've shared over the years, I salute you—and encourage you to keep striving to create the best possible interactive media titles.

■ Introduction

Interactive Media Essentials for Success is unlike any other book on interactive media. Most books on the subject discuss how to use specific interactive media tools—authoring programs, video capture boards, and input and output devices. But this is a book about everything that goes into making interactive media titles—up until the point of actually starting production. You'll learn all the basic essentials for planning and designing successful titles. You might call this book a blueprint, in the architectural sense of the word.

What does an architect do? An architect creates a blueprint that defines on paper what the final structure will look like. It indicates where to start building and hints at the best order in which to do it. An enormous amount of planning goes into the creation of a blueprint. What a blueprint *doesn't* do is specify the specific tools and materials to use. It doesn't tell the contractor how to lay the bricks or wire the sockets. In the same way, *Interactive Media Essentials for Success* will lead you through the interactive media planning and design process.

You'll learn how to think in innovative ways about designing interactive media titles, and how to build a solid foundation without getting bogged down in the details of connecting the wires. You'll even learn when *not* to make an interactive media title. When you're confident that your interactive media project is planned and designed as well as it can be, then you can go out and buy one of the many how-to-do-it books, and you'll know that much better what it's talking about and how to integrate it into your intricately conceived vision. *Interactive Media Essentials for Success* is for you if you're interested in planning, conceptualizing, and dreaming up the best, most successful interactive media productions.

That said, I'll break my own rules repeatedly. Good planning must take into account the functionality—and limitations—of whatever technology you'll be using. But whenever we delve into jargon, it's for the purpose of helping you— the dreamer, schemer, and big cheese behind a project—understand as much as you can about the process so you can talk the talk without looking like a babe in the woods begging to be taken advantage of. Beyond that, I want you to have the tools to create truly unique interactive media titles that go beyond the traps of yesterday's metaphors.

Interactive Media Essentials for Success also tells it like it is. I'm not afraid to say when a title really sucks, or when you should absolutely, positively never do something in interactive media. I'm writing from personal experience, and I'll be sharing lots of real life success (and horror) stories.

■ Why Read This Book?

The bulk of the interactive media development process occurs in production, right? So, why a whole book purposely ignoring what interactive media developers spend most of their time on? The truth is, planning and designing quality interactive media products takes time and hard work, maybe even the hardest work in the whole process. It involves an intense amount of thinking, organizing, and coming to consensus to enhance an original concept rather than minimize it to the lowest common denominator.

At one interactive media job I had, we would hold what we called Pizza Sessions. The goal was to lock everyone on the team in a room for the evening with a stack of pizzas. At the end of a long night, a design and plan for the title would presumably pop out. Inevitably, though, the Pizza Session would turn into the kick-off meeting for a long series of frenetic planning sessions.

You want to know the truth? If you have a six-month project, up to the first two months may be dedicated to planning and designing—that's right, a full one-third of the project! When you stop to think about that, you'll find this book is well worth the read.

■ Who Is This Book For?

The interactive media business has engendered dreams and hopes in the hearts of an ever-increasing number of fellow travelers. In many ways, it's reminiscent of that ever-attainable goal of writing the next Great American Novel. Indeed, in the first session of a class I taught for a number of years at San Francisco State University, I would ask everyone in the room to say who they were and what their dream for entering the interactive media business would be. The ideas presented were as varied as the backgrounds people had—from interactive home improvement titles to standard children's edutainment fare. We even had a digital religion kiosk proposed to help users create a custom faith tailored just for them!

Everyone has an idea that, with the right tools and a lot of late nights, can be turned into a stellar interactive media production, right? Well, yes and no. The days when one person working at a computer could create an award-winning title are, unfortunately, over. Today's interactive media projects require large teams, significant capital, and solid management to be successful. The marketplace is becoming increasingly cutthroat. To stay competitive, you need an edge that sets you apart from the crowd.

Maybe you're the one with the great idea trying to assemble a team to bring it to reality. Or you've just been appointed the interactive media specialist in your company, charged with creating wonderful projects. Perhaps you've even created a few projects yourself, but you've never been exactly sure what you're doing. If any of these descriptions fit, you'll benefit from reading *Interactive Media Essentials for Success.* Above all, this book is for the leaders and future leaders of the interactive media industry.

Who is *Interactive Media Essentials for Success not* for? Well, you're not going to find substantial information about how to "sell" a publisher on your great idea here. Nor will I be discussing how to create a business plan or put together a proposal. My assumption is that you've got the funding (or the wherewithal to secure that funding) to go forward with your project. Now you're interested in finding the most effective way to design and plan for the next however many months you may be ignoring your family and friends. Indeed, working smart will make you popular with both your employees and your psyche.

Beyond that, though, I have one main aim in writing *Interactive Media Essentials for Success.* That's to help people create the best possible titles. I've taught hundreds of people about interactive media, through classes, lectures, and articles, and I have seen a lot of great ideas with lousy implementations. The interactive media industry will not be served by spewing out shovelware, repurposed videotapes and books, and unintuitive interfaces. It will, however, grow and thrive when interactive media professionals push toward using the medium in new, exciting, and above all, appropriate ways.

■ Who Am I?

Why should you believe what I say in this book? My involvement in the interactive media industry began in 1988 when I attended my first meeting of the International Interactive Communications Society (IICS) in San Francisco. I had heard about what was at the time called "interactive video," and it sounded like a way to combine many of the interests I had in one place. Before that, I had worked in audio editing, video production, and as a script and technical writer. I had a B.A. in Creative Writing at the time from Oberlin College, and hoped that someday I might write my own Great American Novel while molding fine young minds as a scruffy professor somewhere in Iowa.

Computers hadn't really entered my world yet. Call me a late-blooming proto-nerd—here I was attending computer society meetings and I didn't even own or use a computer. In fact, my first experience with home computing was universally awful. I had been writing a video script on an old manual typewriter, and a colleague offered to let me use her computer. I had been working for days when, suddenly, a power surge scrambled not only the hard disk file but my floppy back-up as well. I was so frustrated that I defiantly finished the rest of the script on the old typewriter.

A number of years later, I bought a Macintosh SE. It came with a program called HyperCard, which opened my eyes to the power of positive computing (at least compared with my earlier days). I became more and more involved in the IICS, eventually taking on the post of San Francisco Bay Area President in 1992 and International President in 1993. At the same time, I went back to school at night and came out with an M.A. in Instructional Technology. I had a series of jobs, starting with interactive videodisc development for health and education vertical market applications, moving on to one of the top ten CD-ROM publishers, and following that with a stint as Senior Producer for a CD-ROM start-up developer.

Along the way, I really caught the interactive media bug in an even broader sense. I wrote articles for magazines and decided to turn other people on to the field as well. In 1991, I began teaching the Introduction to Interactive Media class at the Bay Area Video Coalition in San Francisco. I moved that class to San Francisco State University's emerging Multimedia Studies Program in 1992.

Interactive Media Essentials for Success is in many ways the culmination of a lot of the teaching, thinking, and writing I've done in the last seven years. I hope that it spurs some of you on to similar flights of interactive career fancy.

■ The Three Businesses of Interactive Media

The broad path that my own career has taken reflects the diversity and scope of the interactive media industry. There are really three types of business under the overarching banner of interactive new media: CD-ROM, hardware and software, and interactive media itself.

- *CD-ROM* is the primary delivery vehicle for interactive media as of the mid-part of the 1990s. Standing for *compact disc read only memory* (the *ROM* part indicates you can play back but you can't record on one yourself), a CD can store anything digital —from crystal clear sound and music to just text. In fact, a suprisingly large number of CD-ROMs are of the latter variety—intended as text archival or library systems devices. On the more visual side, much of what constitutes the 10,000 or so CD-ROM titles in the "consumer" category consists of

  - Clip media—visuals, sound, and increasingly, video bits you can use in your own products, usually rights free.

  - Software applications delivered on CD-ROM—it's cheaper to include a single CD than 16 floppy discs in the package for a new word processor.

  - Shovelware—those annoyingly trashy compilation CDs where a bunch of often unrelated stuff is "shoveled" onto a disc without much thought for creating an integrated interactive media "experience."

  - Pornography—oh yes, one of the biggest and fastest growing categories of CD-ROM is decidedly decadent. Some of it moves into the more creative, interactive areas. But most is an assortment of clips, both still and motion, in various states and positions of undress.

As the industry continues its current focus on building a sizeable installed hardware and software base, the business of selling CD-ROMs as well as CD-ROM drives will be as much a part of the interactive media phenomena as creating quality titles.

- Beyond specific sales of CD-ROM drives, related "hardware and software" sales are perhaps the biggest chunk of the interactive media explosion. This embraces everything from the software programs used to create interactive media titles, to the hardware that is used to run those programs. And, as computers put more and more interactive media features right on the motherboard (or even in the microprocessor brain of the computer itself), the line between interactive media products and just plain computing will be inconsolably blurred. Regardless, it's important to realize that when people talk about the $16 trillion emerging interactive media market (or whatever hyperbolic claim is the latest rage by the time this is published), they're not just talking about interactive media titles or even CD-ROMs with god-knows-what on them, but the whole business of interactive media hardware and software applications.

- The *interactive* in *interactive media* implies that there is a design sensibility active; a push from the stuff you can touch to the more conceptual. Indeed, there's really no such thing as "interactive media" hardware. If it's interactive, it refers to a title and how it's designed. Interactive media is what we're mostly talking about in *Interactive Media Essentials for Success*, and it is rapidly becoming its own legitimate, and unique, new art form.

■ Interactive Media as a Unique Art Form?

While many interactive media projects may bear anywhere from a passing to an overwhelming resemblance to existing media formats—video or text in particular, depending on the project—at its best, interactive media is truly its own emerging art form, one that is slowly but surely defining a unique language and set of conventions. Now, some conventions may be borrowed from the closest applicable "old" media—like interactive screens that look like pages out of a book, or movies with VCR-type control panels.

Indeed, some of the earliest interactive media projects were what we call *repurposed* discs. That is, an existing linear videotape was reworked and reprogrammed for limited interactivity, usually from a videodisc. Before that, interactive programs didn't even have media components. Many were not much more than computer-based versions of the "programmed instruction" booklets many of us suffered through in the late 1950s and early 1960s. (Who remembers programmed instruction? It went something like this—on page 2, you'd have a question: 2+3 = … if your answer is 5, turn to page 10; if your answer is 6, turn to page 11; if your answer is 7, turn to page 12.)

Other interactive media conventions, though, make no sense in any other format—virtual environments where you learn by exploring with your mouse; custom-tailored movie-cum-games where you are the hero. These don't work in any other medium. The most important question to ask yourself when planning and designing an interactive media title is this: Could this content be presented in any other medium, or will it only work if done through an interactive media approach? If the answer to your question is the latter—then you're doing interactive media at its best and most artistic.

There is a precedent for the emergence of an interactive media art form out of an old one. (Please note—being an art form doesn't imply that a given interactive media title is "artistic.") The comparison I'm thinking about is the emerging film industry of the 1920s. Interactive media industry veteran Stan Cornyn asked the question first. What old medium, he wondered, were many of the earliest films based on? The theater.

Many of the pioneering film makers simply trained a camera at the stage and brought the result to the movie house. This didn't require any rethinking of paradigms, metaphors, or artistic conventions. It was only later that a language of film began to emerge. Ironically, one of the most "sophisticated" ways to use video in an interactive media project today is to view the computer display as a stage upon which an actor moves—no changing camera angles or cut-aways.

Beyond the stage similarities, there is an even more fitting comparison with early film. Who was the most important person in an early film project? The director? The actors? The cameraman? No, the most important person was the projectionist—the guy who could fix the machine that played the media. It wasn't until the technology got more sophisticated and broke down less often that artists were free to express themselves. So it is with interactive media. The most important people in our projects are still the programmers, the computer repair technicians, and the toll-free customer service staff.

That's changing fast. Computers are becoming more idiot proof. DOS is soon to be a thing of the past, and slick machines from the likes of Compaq and Packard Bell challenge the Macintosh in terms of ease of booting up. Authoring systems, while still plagued with problems of slowness and incompatibilities, are becoming more robust and cross-platform savvy. This, in turn, frees interactive media planners of dependence on obscure lines of if-then code, and of dependence on the quirky programmers who can say that's the way it is "just because" and you can't argue because you don't know the Lingo.

Chapter 8 of *Interactive Media Essentials for Success* discusses the emerging language of interactive media—the artistic side of the business as we are slowly freed from the shackles of yesterday's General Protection Faults.

■ How to Use This Book

Interactive media is rarely linear. It's hard to pinpoint a beginning, middle, and end to most well-designed titles. In the same way, *Interactive Media Essentials for Success* is meant to be meandered through. Look for what interests you at a particular point in your (and your project's) development, then read that section.

Planning quality interactive media titles involves heavy use of detailed outlines and flowcharts. So, I've chosen to give this book a flowchart metaphor.

At the beginning of each chapter, you'll find a flowchart that shows the subsections in that chapter. Pretend you're looking at a computer screen, and you're clicking a box in the flowchart with your mouse. Then imagine that the flipping of pages is a fancy transition effect. It's the closest thing to "interactive" I can provide in this decidedly linear book format.

Where should you "flip" to?

Chapter 1 presents Guidelines for Interactive Media. Read this chapter to decide whether or not the idea you have for an interactive media project is a good idea in the first place. If it doesn't satisfy certain basic criteria, maybe you should consider either a different topic, or doing your topic in a different medium.

Chapter 2 takes a brief detour into those technological nuances you will need to stay abreast of as you maintain your product's competitive edge. The chapter also includes descriptions of the hottest platforms to develop for, so you can decide where to focus your resources.

Chapter 3 looks into who you'll need to build your project. Who will you need to hire or partner with at each stage of the game? Interactive media is no longer a one-person operation, and planning for collaboration will ensure that at the end of your project, everyone is still speaking to one another!

Chapter 4 discusses the first stage of the development process—Analysis and Design. This is the place to turn to learn more about the steps you'll go through as you plan and design your project. From the initial brainstorm through creating a Functional Spec, it's all discussed (and flowcharted) here.

Chapter 5 goes more into those steps that are beyond planning and design—the production and implementation phases. But it's crucial to know what's coming next as you're planning today.

Chapter 6 breaks new ground with a treatment of Paradigms for Interactive Media. The three basic paradigms are discussed here—the tutorial, the database, and the environment. By learning to categorize products, you can determine where your own leanings are. Like good interactive media, this chapter is as heavy on the "show" as on the "tell," and you'll find plenty of examples, screen shots, and real-life war stories from the interactive media trenches.

Chapter 7 expands on the Paradigms discussed in Chapter 6 and takes you into uncharted territories—interactive movies, books, and even CD-ROM "applications."

Chapter 8 tackles The Emerging Language of Interactive Media head on. Here you'll discover why users turn off and tune out after 30 seconds, how to keep your audience from getting lost by creating a "flat" interface, and how to resolve paradigm conflict.

In Chapter 9, I'll share some Tools You Can Use—useful documents, templates, and formats to get up and running quicker. Look here to see how to create your own interactive scripts, flowcharts, and project management charts.

If your interest is piqued and you want to go beyond this book, the Appendix provides a detailed Resource Listing, divided neatly into Magazines, Conferences, Professional Associations, Books, and locations on the World Wide Web where you can find daily doses of late breaking interactive media news.

I like to refer to the Glossary as our Jargon Watch. Flip here if you're confused or lost by some of the necessary interactive media terminology used in the book. I've provided, if not an exhaustive list, at least a candid approach to the buzzwords of the day. It's all alphabetical, too.

That's what *Interactive Media Essentials for Success* is all about. So go out and start flipping. And plan some really smokin' quality interactive media titles along the way.

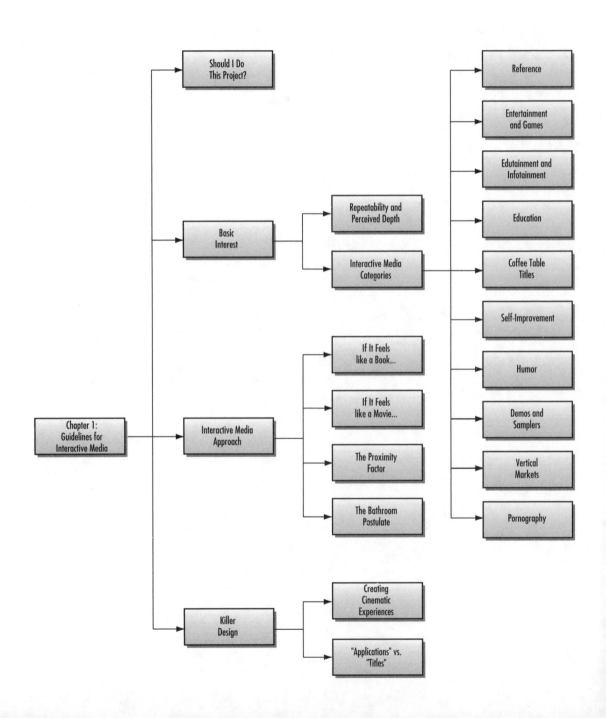

1

Guidelines for Interactive Media

O KAY, SO YOUR NEXT PROJECT IS TO, OR YOU'VE GOT THE BURNING desire to, get started on an interactive media project. Before you jump in, there are some questions to ask yourself. The first might seem basic, but it's important to lay the groundwork: What is this "interactive media" we keep referring to, anyway? And how is it being used in this book?

Interactive media, new media, multimedia—they're all basically interchangeable. When I asked my classes at San Francisco State University to define these terms, they'd usually start off (focusing on *multi*media) by answering, "anything combining two or more media." But that can refer to everything from performance art pieces to a Lotus 1-2-3 spreadsheet with an animated bar chart.

To differentiate what we'll be talking about in this book from the bigger multimedia picture, let's break down the definition into parts.

- *Computer based*—adding this disqualifies the theater performance pieces as well as computer-controlled slide/tape shows where the output comes from a slide projector and is displayed on multiple screens, usually in some living history museum. The stuff we're talking about here is delivered, and viewed, on a computer (or television) screen.

- *Interactive*—the computer doesn't do anything until you do. It's a dumb machine waiting for your input. That also means you control the pace, the flow, and the direction of the experience. In the early days, the computer would sit there silent until you made a choice. Now, computer-based interactive media programs will give you lots of diversion while you're taking a coffee break. They'll play music, cajole you into a preferred interaction, or even make the choice for you if you don't after a certain amount of time.

- *Media*—yes, but how many media do you need to have true interactive *multi*media? Is the aforementioned spreadsheet with a dancing bar chart enough? How about an interactive media slide-show presentation with just text and graphics, where you click a button to show the next computer-generated image? For a project to truly fulfill this part of the definition, it must have "song and dance." That is, there must be some audio—either narration, music, or sound effects; and some motion—either animation or video. And, as they say, if it's got song and dance, that's not just interactive media, that's edutainment!

■ Should I Do This Project?

Once you've got a definition of interactive media that works for you, probably the most important question you can ask—and you better ask it now—is

"Should I do this project?"

Or, put a different way:

"Is this a good idea to do in interactive media?"

Stop right now. Write those questions down on a piece of paper. Or copy this page and tape it to your refrigerator. Ponder the profundity of this conundrum for awhile. Under no circumstances should you do another minute of work on your project if the answer to the question is "no."

Why all the hyperbole? What's the crime of creating an interactive media title that looks and feels like a videotape? Is it so awful if your long-dreamed-of product uses something less than state-of-the-art technology and design? And who's really going to care if the program only interests Tibetan monks with Pentium computers and quad-speed CD-ROM drives?

Look, you're about to spend a lot of time, money, and chunks of soul and flesh making interactive media. You owe it to yourself to make sure you're on the right track—at the very beginning of the project. You can do that by gauging your proposed product with the following basic guidelines:

- **Basic Interest**   Does your proposed title have an intrinsic interest to a wide enough audience, including yourself?

- **Interactive Media Approach**   Is the content of your proposed product appropriate for a interactive media presentation, or would it be better off in a different media?

- **Killer Design**   Can your project surpass or, at the very least, maintain parity with the competition from a design point of view? Does it put the user into a near-virtual environment or provide an almost cinematic experience?

■ Basic Interest

Before you begin any new project, the first question you must ask yourself is, "Does anyone care about my title idea?" Hopefully, you can answer that you yourself care (if you can't answer that in the affirmative, you might as well pack it up right now and move on). If you can count yourself among the caring sort, next ask if anyone else gives a hoot. The Tibetan monks mentioned above is jokey, but you'd be surprised at how narrow some products are targeted. It's like conducting a Boolean search on your computer.

For example, if the user is between the ages of 30 and 40, owns at least a 486 computer with either a SoundBlaster or ProAudio Spectrum card, has an interest in fine French wines and/or the philosophical and historical basis for becoming a pastry chef, and owns a PostScript-compatible printer, then he or she will just love your new title, *From Filo to Flambée—Multimedia Masterpieces of the Great French Pastry Chefs.*

You get the point. Your title needs to have a broad enough interest to grab the attention of not only the buying public, but a publisher willing to fund it. Especially at this point in the interactive media business curve, creating hits with wide appeal is more important than it would be if the industry were more mature. As lauded as the ever-increasing sales of interactive media hardware and software may seem, interactive media just doesn't have the kind of penetration that, say, the videocassette or pre-recorded audiotape industries have. And there's no comparison at all with the book market, where playback hardware, thankfully, isn't even a consideration.

To make matters worse, studies have shown that the average CD-ROM consumer only buys a few titles per year. This is increasing, but it's still not enough to justify niche products like *From Filo to Flambée*. Indeed, targeting teenage boys with their zealous penchant for buying mountains of video games, is about as niche-y as you can get. Just don't expect an interactive Periodic Table of the Elements to be the next killer app unless it's got ninja elephants and snapping turtles with nine lives and a bag of 3D weapons.

Also, at this stage of the industry's development (and I want to stress at this stage that market share, installed base, and suggested retail price guidelines change almost daily), you also need to provide a certain depth to your title. If CD-ROMs were sold at the same prices as audio CDs—$15 and under, for example—consumers could take a chance with a title that might only get used once before hitting the shelf. At today's prices, though—$24.95 to $59.95 at retail—and with no way to preview a title before buying it, consumers become a pretty conservative bunch.

Repeatability and Perceived Depth

What are the biggest selling title categories? By far, it's games, reference, and edutainment. Why? Games can be played over and over again. They provide sometimes hundreds of hours of value for their $50 price tag. Reference titles are used over and over as well, because they provide so much information—from all the animals at the San Diego Zoo to hundreds of thousands of entries in an interactive encyclopedia like Microsoft *Encarta*. Edutainment products are growing more as a reaction by concerned parents to all the games their children are playing!

The need for repeatability in the first two categories has led to a concept I call *perceived depth*. That's where people perceive that a product has depth even if it the average user will never call on that depth. An example of this is the whole series of *Newsweek InterActive* titles, originally published by Mindscape. Each one presents two main feature stories with HyperText and HyperMedia links. They're created by a dedicated editorial team culled from the best of *Newsweek's* ranks. *Newsweek InterActive* is a stand-alone product, not a repurposed version of its print cousin. But who's going to spend $30 for just two articles, when you can buy the print version on the newsstand with tons of articles—even if they're not interactive media–enabled—for a mere $2.95?

So *Newsweek InterActive* added hundreds of audio clips from Newsweek On Air (the publication's radio program), related articles from the *Washington Post* (which owns *Newsweek*), and the text of the last quarter of *Newsweek's* issues. Now you have the ability to do some solid research using *Newsweek InterActive*. And if you buy a whole year's worth of CDs, you'll have all the text of *Newsweek* in a searchable format. How many purchasers of the CD-ROM actually go into that extensive back-end and do research? Very few, undoubtedly. But the perception that the product has depth because it has a deep database of information makes it more interesting—and more saleable.

In a product I produced jointly through Mindscape and Ziff-Davis Press, we did the same thing. *PC/Computing How Multimedia Computers Work* is a 3D look inside your computer. The vast bulk of the program is the 3D animations we created for every part, from mouse to microprocessor. But mentioned prominently in the marketing material is the extra depth we included—such as chapters from other Ziff-Davis books such as *How to Use Your Computer* and *500 Windows Tips*. Including text information is easy, but it's a cheap trick that users won't fall for forever. Milk it while you can.

Creating a once-through title without a huge back-end isn't the end of the world. In fact, some of these titles can be pretty darn impressive. Interactive movies, like Access Software's *Under A Killing Moon*, essentially have a beginning, middle and end—though there's lots you can do along the way. When you've finished the program, though, there's little reason to go back and do it again, unless you're a real technology wonk (and Access Software has provided for that inclination, too, by letting you instantly jump to just the hottest video tricks in the title).

But the once-through on *Under A Killing Moon*—or Broderbund's acclaimed interactive environment title, *Myst*—can last for many, many hours. Indeed, the former is delivered on a whopping four CD-ROMs in a single box. Sierra On-Line's recent interactive movie-cum-game, *Phantasmagoria*, is shipped on a staggering eight CD-ROMs!

How do you gauge interactive media interest? You can pay a market research firm thousands of dollars or more to start. But, in truth, you can learn from a studied "gut" approach. Go to a software store and see what's on the shelves and what's selling. There are currently somewhere close to 10,000 titles intended for the consumer market. The largest new media sections in the largest superstores stock maybe 1,200 titles. It's more common for a mall store to shelve only 300 CD-ROMs. Check out what's on those shelves. The focus on mega-hits to the exclusion of innovative but more narrowly targeted work should be good and depressing. But it will drive home the need for creating broad-appeal titles.

Interactive Media Categories

When you visit your local interactive media outlet, it's very useful to identify what you see by category: It will help you make sense of the variety of titles, as well as to allow you to identify competitive products in order to gauge the basic interest of your own title. Interactive media programs fall roughly into ten categories.

Reference

As discussed earlier, reference titles, along with games and edutainment, are the biggest-selling titles. They have repeatability and usually real (not just perceived) depth—and some are even pretty useful. The sarcasm in the last line is deliberate. I was for a long time the biggest critic of interactive encyclopedias—this despite the fact that for a time I was the in-house product manager for Mindscape's OEM encyclopedia effort.

Why the negativity? Because of the speed, or lack thereof. In the heady early days of interactive media encyclopedias, the technology du jour gave discs a speed so sluggish that it was far faster to go to the shelf, grab the specific volume you wanted, and turn to the right page than it was to wait for the CD to find what you were looking for. On top of that, the information you received tended to be skimpy. To this day, the most popular interactive encyclopedias are based on lesser-regarded print volumes.

However, speed has improved. Content is also improving—Microsoft *Encarta*, for example, has added to and rewritten many of the entries in its original *Funk and Wagnall's*–based offering. And those interactive media bells and whistles are finally adding real value. The ability to copy and paste directly from an electronic encyclopedia into a term paper or report is a distinct advantage over rekeying it yourself. And lately, interactive media reference title prices have fallen to the $50 range in many discount outlets. In the CD-ROM business, reference products constitute the best evergreen titles—the ones that keep on selling, year after year.

Reference titles are also the cornerstone of the interactive OEM business. *OEM* stands for *Original Equipment Manufacturer*. If you buy a computer from Apple but it has a Sony hard drive in it, Sony is the Original Equipment Manufacturer and Apple has cut an "OEM deal" to include someone else's hardware in their box. The same is true for CD-ROM titles.

When you buy a Packard Bell CD-ROM system, for example, you usually get a few CDs thrown in for free. It's good for the hardware manufacturers—state-of-the-art titles help demonstrate what the machine can do—and it's good for the software publishers, who are happier to make a quick buck on a bunch of bundled titles than wait for retail sales to trickle in. Indeed, this "bundle" business was the biggest money-maker for interactive media publishers until very recently, when a viable retail market finally began to take off.

From the financial end of things, it might seem not to make sense: A CD-ROM title may sell for $20 wholesale at retail, while the price for a bundle is somewhere between $5 and $8, even less in large quantities. But the quantities (100–500,000 bundled versus 20–50,000 retail) make up the difference.

What type of interactive products do the best in a bundle? The "must-haves" are those titles with lots and lots of repeatability—that means, first and foremost, the reference category. When you buy a new computer these days, you almost expect a free CD-ROM encyclopedia, not to mention a children's title and a game. The situation is changing, but in the meantime, you can't get away from the OEM influence on the design of your titles.

Entertainment and Games

Blam, pop, pow, slice—look at that head roll down the corridor. Welcome to the decidedly non–socially redeeming world of entertainment titles. About as far from an encyclopedia as you can get, games are what keep the interactive media industry afloat. Your trip to the store will confirm that. So will even a cursory perusal through an interactive media title catalog or an interactive media magazine. To be fair, most entertainment titles offer a lot of good clean fun—who doesn't need a mental break now and then? It's just the highly publicized titles like *Mortal Kombat* and *Night Trap* that have given the genre a bad name.

Games are among the most innovative interactive media offerings. Because sales are so much higher (a hit game sells in the hundreds of thousands, while a "normal" CD-ROM title can qualify for hit status with as few as a 40,000-unit sell-through), more research and development dollars go into making games state of the art than, say, a niche-y piece on Art Appreciation. That means better use of video, 3D scalable environments, attention to detail—the works. If you want to see where tomorrow's interactive media standards begin, look at games like *Under a Killing Moon*, *Dragon Lore*, *Seventh Guest*, and *Myst*.

Edutainment and Infotainment

Probably the most crowded category these days is that of edutainment, and the emphasis here is clearly on the *tainment*. Sold as educational enhancements to a child's afternoon schedule (they're a lot better for you than the aforementioned entertainment offerings, not to mention—gasp—antiquated linear television), these titles have to be as fun, lively, and as MTV-like as possible. High production values, over-the-top humor, and alternative game-oriented presentations convince children ages 3 through 8 to use these purported educational programs.

Purported education? Sure. Look at a series of programs—a true hit—like Broderbund/Random House's Living Books series. Great traditional children's books and stories like Mercer Mayer's *Just Grandma and Me*, Marc Brown's *Arthur's Teacher Trouble,* or Aesop's *Tortoise and the Hare* are adapted to an interactive media presentation. The story is read to you (the text appears on screen, too), then you click around a cartoon environment full of "easter eggs"—unlabeled hotspots that play amusing animations with superb sound. I have no quarrel with these titles; indeed, I own a few of them myself and my kids adore them. But are they educational?

At first, there was the tendency to pitch them that way. They read to you. Kids can click individual words and hear them pronounced. That teaches reading skills, right? Come on. Let's not kid ourselves. Living Books are pure entertainment. They're fun. On a "popcorn to spinach" scale (where spinach is the serious stuff and popcorn is pure fluff), these tend towards the buttery side.

Morgan's Recess in Greece from Morgan Interactive is another title I like (Figure 1.1). It has a similar approach to Living Books—interactive cartoon environments, animation, and humor, but you also learn about Greek mythology through games and characters. It's a little bit more towards the spinach side, but is it truly educational? Nah.

Figure 1.1

Morgan's Recess in Greece is a bit more educational than a Living Book, but still far away from the Popeye grub.

As the age group increases, the debate intensifies. Let's say you're creating a program that mixes serious content on basic chemistry and physics with an irreverent interface and approach. When tough decisions on functionality need to be made, will you sacrifice fun for content and authenticity? Or will you swap accuracy for engagement at almost all costs?

If you're using real actors to guide users through, say, a historical edutainment title, do you want the scripts written to be historically accurate or modern hip and cool? Usually, the *tainment* wins out over the *edu*. That's because first and foremost, most consumer CD-ROM companies are in the entertainment business, not the education business. Education is groovy, but games sell. You want your title to get de-listed after its first dismal month on the shelf? Pass the popcorn and don't look back.

Some edutainment titles use what's affectionately known by many in the business as *stealth learning*. These titles pass themselves off as games and try to sneak their education through the back door. The two best-known examples I can think of are Broderbund's *Where is Carmen Sandiego?* series (Where in the World?; Where in the USA?; Where in the Universe?) and Mindscape's competing *Mario is Missing* series. In the former, you're looking for master criminal Carmen Sandiego and her bag of cronies who have been stealing important artifacts from all over the world. The title plays like a game, but you learn a lot about geography along the way.

Mario is Missing takes the same premise, but focuses on Mario-style arcade action. With your mouse, you move Mario's brother Luigi around a number of cartoonlike environments. Your goal is to return all the historic landmarks that Bowser and his bad guys have ripped off. As you might guess, you pick up all kinds of historical information while you're playing. The PC version is somewhat tame, but using Mario is Missing on Nintendo is not that different from any other Mario game—there are plenty of skill-based challenges to master before you get your information (and, of course, your animated payoff at the end).

Infotainment is not a subset of edutainment. Rather, it suggests a different demographic. Edu-programs are always skewed toward the young. Info-programs target the teenage, young adult and up market. Against All Odds's *From Alice to Ocean* is an infotainment program because it presents solid information in an entertaining fashion—in this case, the journeys of a remarkable woman across Australia by camel and on foot. *Where is Carmen Sandiego?* is edutainment because it teaches things that kids need to learn in school in a fun way.

Education

Educational titles, distinguished from the previous category, are intended for the school market directly. They usually must satisfy local school board requirements and fit carefully into a daily curriculum in order to be put on the adopted list. Education titles have, in the past, tended to be less professional and slick, simply because they could be. They don't have to appeal to the lowest common denominator buyer with four seconds to make a purchase decision in a mall store. Indeed, these aren't the sort of titles you'd find in a mall store. They're not even necessarily on CD-ROM—you'll find a high number of interactive media educational programs available on videodisc and even floppy disk. Some are sold as Integrated Learning Systems (ILSs), where the media is networked in a learning lab set-up.

As you might guess, in *Interactive Media Essentials for Success* I'll hold that education titles can't ignore good planning and design any more than other categories of interactive media can. One education title I worked on was as innovative as the technology allowed us to be. *Ashtown,* from the Institute for the Study of Family, Work, and Community (a division of Info-Use), taught fifth and sixth graders in California about smoking prevention. Delivering it on a 12-inch videodisc and running it in black-and-white Hyper-Card, we still managed to throw in lots of game play and cool engagement. Users could join a TV game show to add up the costs of smoking, then use the same money to buy gifts in a Bob Barker–style shopping spree we called "The Price is High." In another segment, kids made up their own anti-smoking rap song.

Another educational program that pushes the technology bar is *Choosing Success* from Computer Curriculum Corporation. Designed to work in a networked ILS environment, this CD-ROM title helps at-risk teenagers in Florida learn to be make smart choices in some real-life situations. The program simulates the kind of scenarios teenagers find themselves in and lets them role-play their way through.

Coffee Table Titles

I can't really think about coffee table titles without remembering that recurring "Seinfeld" bit a few seasons back about Kramer's coffee table book all about coffee table books—and if you didn't have a coffee table, it had fold-out legs and turned into one for you. Coffee table CD titles are usually a bit less mundane, but the same principle holds: These are light-reading, heavy on the graphics, see it once or twice titles. Their repeatability stems from the fact that they're usually so drop-dead gorgeous, or have grabbed such a particularly fascinating once-through topic, that you just have to show them to your friends. *From Alice to Ocean* (described earlier) was a great coffee table book and it's an interesting CD-ROM, straddling the fine line between info-tainment and coffee table title. *Oceans Below,* from Mindscape, is like a big book of colorful fish—only the fish move. It's lots of fun to look at, but not too deep—except for the water.

StarPress's *Material World* (Figure 1.2), also based on the book of the same name, lets you look at pictures of families from around the world along with their possessions. You would think that the program's interface would let you click on each of the items presented for each family, but that would propel it beyond the quick-view concept. Coffee table titles stay relatively true to their original print-based format. *Material World* adds two things to the pie: an audio narration (from Charles Kurault—a pretty authoritative voice for the title's "On the Road" around-the-world content, wouldn't you say?) and lots more photographs.

Figure 1.2

Material World looks at people around the world through their possessions. The CD-ROM has more media than its book counterpart and an authoritative narrator.

Cramming more media onto a CD treads dangerously into the domain of shovelware. So, while the original book may only have 50 photos, the CD-ROM will have 500 photos—every picture the original photographer took. Some are good, some so-so. If the content is compelling enough, this is a serious advantage for interactive media coffee table titles. But watch out for the flip side: a future of CD-ROM wedding albums where the photographer includes all the proofs—at a price, of course.

Self-Improvement

The self-improvement category stems from traditional educational programs, but it's more on the pop psychology level. It's often closely related to the Tutorial paradigm described in Chapter 6. Examples of self-improvement titles range from CD-ROM workout discs to how to build your own kitchen or carburetor. The best-selling self-improvement titles teach you how to type. Mindscape's *Mavis Beacon Teaches Typing* is the market leader in this category, challenged by *Mario Teaches Typing* from InterPlay. The latter in particular, because of its character license, draws the line between self-improvement and edutainment. Recently, Wilson Learning repurposed a successful series of business videodiscs to fit on CD-ROM and into the consumer market. These discs teach such skills as "Better Decision Making" and "Improved Relationship Skills."

Humor

Most good edutainment programs will have liberal sprinklings of humor—over-the-top jokes and the lighter stuff as well. But there's an entire emerging category of CD-ROMs that is designed specifically to be funny. To date, only one developer has tried to create a completely original comedy CD, with Dennis Miller telling new jokes based on his *Saturday Night Live* Weekend Update shtick (there's also a companion disc full of computer geek jokes). The rest of the titles in this category have been repurposed TV shows or movies—the *Saturday Night Live* 25th Anniversary double CD from GameTek, Voyager's *Funny* (based on the linear movie of the same name).

My favorite is *Monty Python's Complete Waste of Time* from Seventh Level, which serves as a great way to access your favorite clips from that classic British show of the early 1970s in the most surprising of ways. The package includes a screen saver utility—the Desktop Pythonizer—which lets you play Python clips after a certain amount of time or load Python sound bytes in place of standard Windows start-up sounds and beeps.

Demos and Samplers

When you look at lists of top-selling titles (available in most interactive media–oriented publications), in addition to the usual top sellers (games, reference, and edutainment titles) you'll find samplers. *Samplers*, also known as *demos* or *demonstration discs*, give the purchaser little snatches of titles they can buy from a particular publisher, at a low cost. Sometimes these samplers are included for free in the box of a for-sale product (for example, Future Vision Multimedia includes *Galaxy of Stars*, and Dorling-Kindersley packs in their own demo). Other times, they're sold at no more than $7.95 and placed prominently at the checkout counter in minimal packaging—cardboard sleeve and shrink wrap, not even a jewel box. In this case, they become an impulse purchase. Often, the package includes coupons for discounts on future purchases that are worth even more than the sampler itself.

Demos are also used to promote a title before the product is even finished. A demo can be produced early on, even before major production starts, to sell a product or to line up potential distribution partners. Demos can be distributed online (provided that they're small enough) to get buyers hot and bothered months before beta. A more complete discussion of how and when demos fit into the design process is covered in Chapter 4.

Designing demos is an art in itself. You have to go through the same process of planning, but you're basing your final creation on an existing interactive media title. You're usually severely limited by time and money—get it out super fast and don't hire any expensive C++ programmers. Yet, it's crucial that a sampler run fast and flawlessly on every possible computer configuration. Some of the major publishers who are making a bundle on samplers include Microsoft, Living Books, and Electronic Arts (for an example of their sampler see Figure 1.3).

Figure 1.3

Electronic Arts's *EA Kids Sampler* does booming business as an impulse buy at the check-out counter.

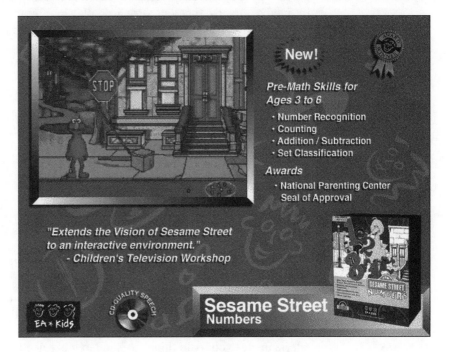

Vertical Markets

The term "vertical markets" refers to the great potpourri known as "other," only in this case the "other" is limited by its decided lack of a consumer market. Like education-specific titles, those products falling in the vertical market category have a narrow focus, usually done on contract with a particular client. Vertical market titles rarely rack up a royalty for the developer. Some examples of vertical markets include

- Health education products done as work for hire for a hospital

- Interactive media presentations for use in corporate board rooms

- Training programs for the MIS department on COBOL programming

- The original Wilson skills training products

- Travel CDs for display in the travel agent's office to entice you with interactive vistas of Rio de Janeiro

- Interactive kiosks intended to sell music, plastic, or even shoes.

All of the above and a whole bunch more are a big part of the interactive media universe that gets very little play in interactive media publications or the interactive media buzz overall. If this is what you're doing in your job, never fear: Everything you read in this book is absolutely, positively as applicable for vertical applications as it is for, say, the following final less-sundry category.

Pornography

Oh, get off your high horse. As with the video business, it's probably pornographic interactive media that drives sales of new hardware more than any other category. Most interactive media pornography is garbage—naked shovelware, really. But, ironically, some of the titles in this category are remarkably innovative from a design point of view. *Penthouse Interactive*, for example, lets you participate in a virtual photo shoot where you decide which shots get placed in the final portfolio. The technology allows simultaneous video windows to play; you then switch between camera angles and choose your best. At the end, Bob Guccioni, print *Penthouse's* publisher, critiques your work.

Another popular title—and one of the first to use a true 3D interactive environment—is *Virtual Valerie*. Created by Reactor, the folks who would later bring us the ground-breaking *Spaceship Warlock*, the synthetic-looking Valerie invites you to do things to her. No more need be said, other than that the title has been so enduring that *Virtual Valerie II* is due out any day now.

Other pornographic titles include interactive strip poker and interactive movies where you decide what happens next. Again, from a design and innovation standpoint, this is much more interactive moviemaking than the average edutainment title, even if the subject matter causes the average interactive media conference goer to flinch. Indeed, at early interactive media shows, the porno offerings were displayed right there on the exhibit floor, next to the Discovery Channel's *In The Company of Whales*. Public outcry has led to the creation of special X-rated tents, where the clientele is mostly male. Still, the very inclusion of these programs at the same shows indicates they're not some alien beast, but a subsegment of the overall industry. And, hey, you gotta laugh—at a recent show, John Bobbit (remember him?) was letting it all hang out to promote his new interactive CD-ROM *A Cut Above*.

■ Interactive Media Approach

Once you've determined that your idea is interesting (to someone), the second crucial question you must ask yourself is—would this be better off in a different medium? Or, put in a different way: Could this project be done in another medium, or is it only possible through an interactive media approach? If your answer to the latter part of the question is yes—this absolutely, positively has to be done in through interactive media, and it wouldn't be the same using any other media or technology—then you can rest easy that you have a product that will pass the interactive media appropriateness test. But it's easy to get tricked up here. Let's look at some examples.

If It Feels like a Book...

So here's the plan: We'll license this great pocket guide to bird watching. It has every bird imaginable—birds of prey, canaries, penguins—you name it. Then, we'll take the pictures and digitize them. We'll create a nice interface, and users can search for the bird they want and see its picture. It'll be a massive hit. No one will ever buy the book again, because it's all on CD-ROM, and that's the medium of the future, right?

What's wrong with this picture? What have the people planning this title forgotten to take into account? Quite simply, they've neglected to ask whetheror not the content they're starting with is appropriate for an interactive media presentation. They've become too caught up with the magic of the technology to realize that the print version on birds is great just because it's a book. It's small and easy to search by flipping the pages—the birds are all alphabetically arranged anyway. And most important, it's portable—you can take it out in the field with you where you're actually bird watching.

The CD-ROM they've proposed blindly repurposes the exact same information, adding no extra value, while taking away the very features that made the pocket guide so popular in the first place. Maybe if they'd added bird sounds, or animations of birds flying or mating or something, the project would make more sense. But that's not an automatic win situation either. Because if a CD-ROM title essentially feels like a book with some interactive media stuff slapped on it (say, a couple of videos of dinosaurs to illustrate 300 pages of text on the subject), it should stay a book. Interactive encyclopedias would fall into this category if it weren't for their sheer exhaustiveness and research abilities. But the bird field guide is too small to get away with it.

How about coffee table books turned into CD titles? I pointed out before that their main advantage is they offer more media than their print equivalent. But if the way all that media is presented is too booklike (that is, forward and backward arrows that let you flip through the title in a totally linear fashion), then the result is going to be pretty boring. It certainly won't be interactive enough to justify the interactive media approach.

In the worst cases, handling large amounts of extra media in a title is accomplished through a computer metaphor rather than a book one. Media is arranged in Macintosh-like folders, which the user hierarchically clicks his or her way through. That sounds like lots of fun, doesn't it? And so engaging! In cases like these, it probably would be better to let the book sit on the coffee table a little while longer.

If It Feels like a Movie...

Here's another scenario. You've obtained the rights to create a CD-ROM version of Ed Wood's original bad movie *Plan Nine from Outer Space*. You figure the film is a classic, so you won't do anything special to it. You'll digitize it, and let the movie play from within a small quarter-screen window. For good measure, you'll throw in a few "chapter stops"—that is, the ability to search for specific scenes. So your users can go right to the scene where Bela Lugosi is replaced by the director's chiropractor after Lugosi dies in the middle of production. Or you can choose seven different flying saucer scenes for the definitive comparative analysis. Bound to be a hit, right?

Sidestepping for a moment the question of basic interest (do enough people care about the movie in the first place? They didn't exactly run to see Tim Burton's take on the subject), this example addresses the question of interactive media approach from a different angle. Instead of starting with a book, the designers here have repurposed a linear movie. The problem with movies is they have a definite beginning, middle, and end. The good ones, at least, tell a story—a narrative—that is meant to be seen in the order the writer or director intended. It is very hard to take any kind of linear media and make it work in an interactive format.

Now, you may have noticed that quite a few linear movies are now available on CD-ROM, particularly in the CD-i format. Indeed, there is a whole new standard (actually two competing standards, see Chapter 2) emerging whose primary purpose is to make it easier to put movies on CD. VCR ownership (in the United States, at least) has reached near the saturation point, so the makers of technology are constantly searching for new ways to sell more hardware. CDs that play movies fit the bill. In this case, though, there's no pretense that these are interactive movies, so the criteria of Interactive Media Approach we've been talking about so far doesn't apply. This is all about the CD-ROM business, and the CD-ROM is just an alternative delivery system.

The quality of the these movies on CD is a little better than what you get on VHS videotape. The biggest advantages are

- You never have to rewind the tape.

- The CD wears down less quickly.

- You can add the aforementioned chapter stops, which work particularly well for specialty movies—say, a music performance where you can go right to the songs you want.

Another thing that sets these special format movies on CD apart from the broader interactive media business is their full-screen full-motion video— which requires special hardware. Today's software-only technology simply doesn't allow for that, generally delivering video filling no more than a quarter of the screen and running at no more than 15 frames a second—usually less. For contrast, regular video plays at 30 frames a second for NTSC (North American and Japanese) systems, and 25 frames a second for PAL (European) systems.

Indeed, a colleague once joked that, in the early days of the industry, he went out and bought a ton of hardware and software so he could play movies or watch TV on his desktop computer. The image was a paltry one-eighth of the screen, and the motion probably no more than 6 or 7 frames a second. And yet, he was overjoyed by his $1,500 investment. His wife came in and took one look at the system and said, "If you want to watch TV while you're on the computer, why not put a TV set next to it?" For less than $200, you can get full-motion, full-screen video at a lot better resolution!

So unless you have the special movie-on-CD full-screen full-motion hardware, the question you're probably asking yourself is: Why would anyone want to buy a linear movie on CD that plays in a tiny window on a desktop computer screen? Right now it's the novelty factor; the type of thrill that technology wonks get off on. But it won't last, and it certainly doesn't translate to the mass market. The truth is, this type of content is just not appropriate for transferring to an interactive media format.

One of the very few linear programs that plays well in non–full-motion, full-screen video is Voyager's *A Hard Day's Night* CD from the Beatles

(Figure 1.4). It's the original linear movie in an oversized postage-stamp video window, with chapter stops. It works because the program's designers added extra goodies—commentaries on the movie by movie and Beatles critics; a gallery of photos; the ability to search for your favorite song; and most importantly, the original script, which accompanies the movie, so you can see what the writers intended John to say and how he mucked it up in his own inimitable way. Because there's video and text on screen, this is a decidedly nonpassive experience.

Figure 1.4

A Hard Day's Night is one of the few linear movies on CD-ROM that plays well in a postage-stamp-sized window.

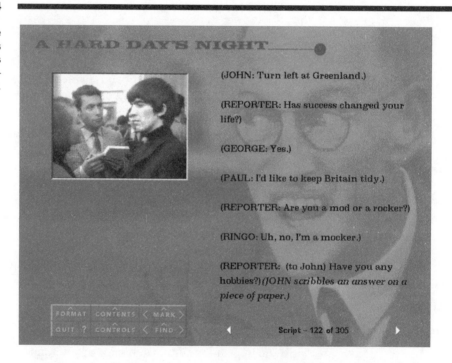

Another movie that made the transition fairly well to interactive media is a "documentary" of celebrities and ordinary folk telling their favorite jokes. Time-Warner's *Funny* chops up what was once a linear laugh riot and lets you choose the jokes by category, performer, or joke title. You can choose Jewish humor, blue humor, or Henny Youngman humor (delivered by the master himself). Because each of the jokes are compact and relatively short, they successfully make the transition to CD-ROM.

The Proximity Factor

How about more subtle shades of interactive media appropriateness? In *PC/Computing How Multimedia Computers Work*, we created a 3D computer you could click on. Really stunning animations would play, explaining how various aspects of the computer worked. We worked on it for a long time, then took it "on the road" to show to magazine editors and reviewers. I remember vividly one writer at a major newsweekly asking, "Well this would make a very nice PBS documentary, but why is it on the computer? What's so interactive about it? Can you play a game with the microprocessors?" I didn't have an immediate answer, and I spent some agonizing sleepless hours trying to respond, if not to her, at least to my own inner critic. I came up with what I call the Proximity Factor.

The Proximity Factor posits that a relatively nonlinear program may benefit from a interactive media approach if getting the user up close and personal with his or her computer screen is desired. For the closer you get to the screen, the more likely you are to interact with it. The further you get from the screen, the more likely you are to sit back on your couch and finger the ol' clicker.

For *PC/Computing How Multimedia Computers Work*, having a user close to those nifty animations is half the experience. A user can stop and start an animation, replay it, and peruse and study it, even if he or she can't specifically "interact" by playing a game with it. If the same program were a PBS documentary, the user—if that term is even appropriate—would be a number of feet away on the couch, watching much more passively. It isn't likely that "user" would be stopping and starting the program, getting up from the couch, and studying a particular image.

The Bathroom Postulate

Related to Proximity is another factor influencing when the content for a particular title is appropriate to the interactive media: the Bathroom Postulate. Not exactly a corollary to proximity, the Bathroom Postulate states, in coarse language, that if the original content for an interactive media title would likely be read in the bathroom, it's better off in its original format. In addition to pricing, probably the biggest hindrance to success for *Newsweek InterActive* was the basic concept. People expect to read *Newsweek* on the toilet! (In more gracious moments, they might read it in bed.)

So, let's say you've got the urge to go and you're looking for some reading material. Are you going to grab your CD-ROM tower computer, power it up, wait for it to boot, start up Windows, double-click the *Newsweek* icon, wait for the program to load, click to stop the opening animation, and settle in for a good read? Nooo!

■ Killer Design

Interactive media is fast developing its own aesthetic and creating its own products to beat. It's not enough anymore to have a great idea and trust that a decent implementation will just follow. As with technology, design must be state of the art. Does your proposed product push the creative/design envelope a notch further than, or at the very minimum maintain parity with, the state of the art in a program on a similar topic? If you use an "old" metaphor of, say, a book with pages and bookmarks and an overabundance of page-turning arrows to structure your title while all your competitors have moved to a 3D virtual space, you're not going to cut it in this third important area.

Creating Cinematic Experiences

In the brief history of interactive media, there have been a few products that have defined, raised the bar, and then redefined, what is state-of-the-art design. Reactor's 1991 release of *Spaceship Warlock* (Figure 1.5) for the Macintosh riveted the still-emerging interactive media community. It may not have been the first title to place the user in a 3D environment where game play is accomplished by moving around and clicking on things, but it did it the best. *Spaceship Warlock* drops users down on an alien planet. You eventually travel to the nether regions of space, fighting bad guys on a pirate starship. But the first thing users experience is a sense of really being in this world. The animation is stunning, sound is used well, and there's a good sense of humor—visit the local bar, and as you drink more and more, your vision—that is, the screen—becomes increasingly blurred.

The successor to *Spaceship Warlock* in terms of design has to be Broderbund's *Myst* (Figure 1.6). The basic metaphor is the same—you're placed on an island (in some strange place, planet, time) and you can go explore at will. In *Myst*, there are games and puzzles to solve, while *Spaceship Warlock* involves figuring out where to go and what to say to that Space Princess. *Myst* uses sound and visuals even more effectively to create a true world. The result is what I like to call a *cinematic* experience, one that is so compelling and complete, that you forget you're using a computer at all. Its akin to going to a dynamite movie and being so drawn in that you forget about the kid in back of you chewing gum or kicking your seat or revealing all the best details because he's seen it before.

Myst, in turn, was based on design work done in the infancy of interactive media by the same developer—Cyan. The product is *Manhole* (Figure 1.7), and I still enjoy playing with my kids. In this floppy disk HyperCard-based title, you go down a manhole and explore by clicking on things. There are no pirates, no puzzles—indeed, the original 1989 version didn't even have color. But the concept of creating a nonviolent, exploratory, and visually rich

Figure 1.5

Spaceship Warlock redefined state-of-the-art design with its riveting graphics and environmental approach.

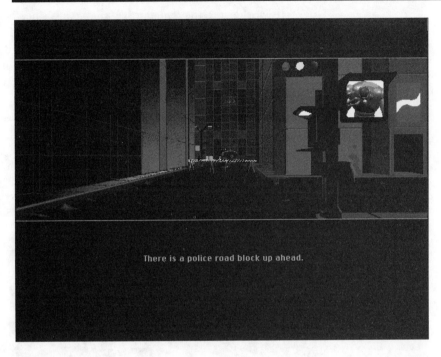

There is a police road block up ahead.

Figure 1.6

Myst creates a cinematic experience, drawing you in like a dynamite movie.

world was pioneered long before CD-ROMs pushed the possibility of 650MB worlds into the vanguard. *Manhole* has since been updated. A new color version with a fully orchestrated soundtrack and voices (the original had mostly text on screen) is now out on—you guessed it—CD-ROM. It's called the *Masterpiece Edition*, and while it's very beautiful, I think some of the hokey charm that was inherent in the original has been lost.

Figure 1.7

Manhole is the interactive-media grandfather to *Myst*. The original black-and-white version was delivered on five floppy disks.

At nearly the same time as *Myst* was hitting the store shelves, so was Trilobyte's *The Seventh Guest* (Figure 1.8). A haunted house story with plenty of puzzles and some eerie transparent ghostlike video, this title's cinematic claim to fame is that when you click to go somewhere, the scene doesn't take you there with some standard wipe effect; rather, the entire perspective changes. You actually feel like you're walking up that staircase or going into that bottomless pit.

Creating a cinematic experience as described in the titles above goes hand in hand with building 3D realistic environments. Indeed, this type of design has almost become the de facto standard in contemporary design. Everyone's using them—even reference products (check out the *Random House Kids' Encyclopedia* or Mindscape's *Complete Reference Library*).

Figure 1.8

If you like haunted houses, you'll love exploring *The Seventh Guest* and its sequel *The Eleventh Hour*—two compelling games set inside an eerie mansion.

3D environments are important to start thinking about now because they're a baby step toward virtual reality.

How so? What is virtual reality, really? It's just a fancy interface to an interactive media core of data. In virtual reality, you access that data by reaching out and touching an object. In a 3D computer environment, you navigate with your mouse through a near-virtual workspace. The feeling is the same, and those developers who can begin to think about how to create these types of 3D spaces in today's 2D limited world will be one step ahead when true virtual reality environments become the norm.

"Applications" vs. "Titles"

In the meantime, the bottom-line question to ask yourself when you're deciding whether to go ahead with an interactive media idea is this: Does my proposed title feel like something new and unique, or does it feel like a computer application? Consumers these days have come to expect their interactive media titles to be intuitive, clear, and as far away from a spreadsheet or word processor as possible. The latter are examples of applications. They have multiple buttons, tirelessly tiled windows and menu bars, and endless hierarchical scrolling lists. They let you get your work done quickly, but they're not as seamlessly user-friendly as a book or a video. They're not an interactive media cinematic experience.

Here's an easy way to tell if you're on the right design track. You're making a program that helps users navigate through, or access great works of art in a museum. You have two basic design choices:

• Create an application look with buttons and pop-up lists so you can quickly find the piece of art you want to find

- Create a virtual museum —a 3D environment where the user navigates the museum with his or her mouse and clicks on paintings on the virtual walls

Which approach do you think would be most appealing to the average consumer? Notwithstanding those buyers who really do want to do hard research on the world of art, the second approach is far more engaging, far more unique, and a more state-of-the-art use of design. Note that a quick-find Index mode should be available too, but it shouldn't be paramount, as it would be in the first approach, which suffers from what I refer to as "button-itis."

Also, don't confuse my prohibition against making interactive media titles that feel too much like computer applications with avoidance of the entire emerging paradigm of Interactive Media Applications. Discussed in Chapter 7, the latter can be totally state of the art, sporting a cinematic feel and everything. They're called applications because, through interactive media, they allow users to "do" or "make" something.

Cinematic environments are not the ultimate cat's meow in interactive media design, and there will be bold new paradigms yet to be dreamed of—probably involving voice recognition and artificial intelligence. Its also important to balance an emphasis on killer design with the interactive media category your title is intended for. The most aesthetically fabulous and theoretically well-designed environment won't fly if your product is an encyclopedia where fast access is truly the goal. Regardless of the category, the key is to stay one step ahead of the status quo. That means keeping abreast of what's out there, and forever thinking about how to push the design envelope that extra inch.

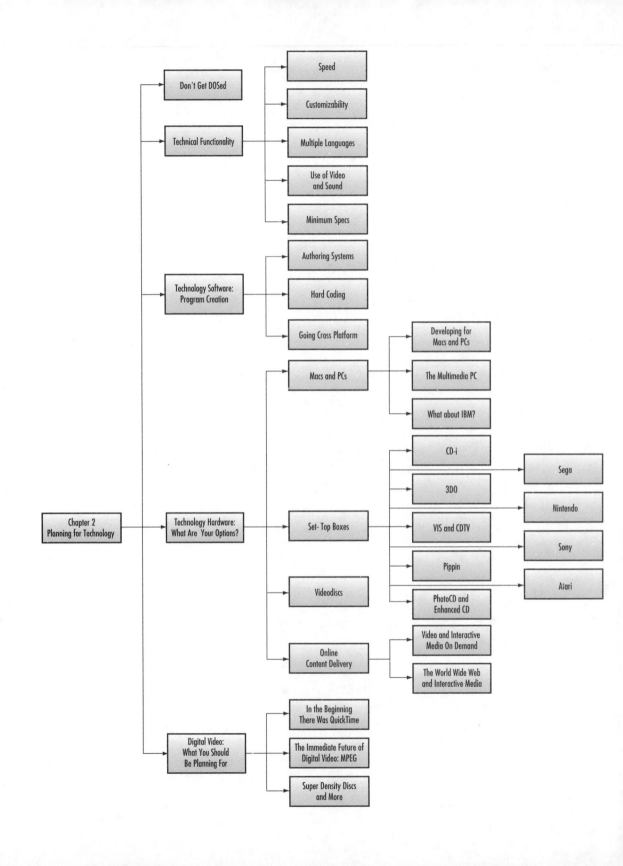

2

Planning for Technology

IN THE INTRODUCTION, I WROTE THAT MOST OF WHAT'S being presented here is relatively "technology neutral." That is, the principles of planning and designing quality interactive media titles should fit whether you're developing for Windows or Nintendo. But the platform you're developing for—and the technology you're using to develop your product—will have a direct influence on many of the choices you make in the planning process. For instance, if you're creating a project to run on an old Nintendo setup, you probably shouldn't plan on including video.

Similarly, there's no point in designing a product that requires heavy-duty animation if the technology you're delivering on can't cut its mustard. (A side note: It's equally important to consider the skills and capabilities of your human resources—if they're not sufficiently talented to create those same high-quality animations, design a product that relies on something else. More on that in Chapter 3.) A successful use of technology is truly no less important than the three design guidelines discussed in the previous chapter. Use yesterday's technology clunker and you'll get ripped by your audience—and the press—as mercilessly as if you'd created a low interest, repurposed video with a button-covered interface.

What factors do you need to consider in keeping your technology as state of the art as the rest of your project? How will this affect your overall planning process? How do you balance technology savvy with very real budget constraints? If you're careful about it, you can avoid getting DOSed.

■ Don't Get DOSed

For those of you who somehow missed the Microsoft 1980s, MS-DOS is the name of the operating system that has run Intel-based, IBM PCs and clones up until the present day. In 1993, it was still okay to produce CD-ROM edutainment titles in DOS. These titles didn't require (and didn't much care for) the Windows application running on top of DOS, instead preferring to boot up directly from the C: prompt. While some games are still coming out in DOS, a competitive edutainment, reference, or coffee table CD-ROM at this point must run under Windows 3.1 at the least, and be Windows 95 compatible to boot. The equivalent on the Mac side would be ensuring that new titles run on everything from System 7 for 680x0 machines to the PowerPC chip. Creating a title today that is optimized for the older System 6 would be near suicidal.

I learned the dangers of designing for yesterday's technology the hard way. In 1993, my company signed off on production of a DOS edutainment CD-ROM title. It seemed like an okay bet. The developer promised it fast and cheap. But the title took longer to complete than expected, so that when it did come out, the market had shifted to Windows, Windows, Windows. When the title finally arrived, it looked pretty lame next to its souped-up Windows companions. For the technically minded, the graphics on our title were 320 by 240 rather than 640 by 480, and the program would crash if you tried to use the DOS shell from Windows. We had used yesterday's technology, and it contributed to the market's lukewarm response to the title.

■ Technical Functionality

Now, all this talk about DOS illustrates the importance of staying up to date technically with something as basic as your operating system. But there are plenty of other factors to stay on top of when planning your product's competitive functionality from a technical point of view.

Speed

While it has never been pleasant to sit and wait for a program to boot up or an encyclopedia to conduct an extensive search, we accepted it in the earlier days of the industry because everything was slow. But nowadays, crack programmers are coding super-fast search engines and custom animation routines that get things up on the screen in a jiffy, even on slower machines. If you get used to the speed of a fast program and then pop in a slower CD, the difference will be much more agonizing than it ever was before.

Customizability

The interactive media equivalent to What You See Is What You Get used to be What You Get Is What You'll Take. Programs installed on your system in a particular way, and that's all there was to it. No more. Programs usually give you options on how you want to alter your hard disk—from letting you choose the amount of space the program will take up to politely prompting you before a program goes and messes with your AUTOEXEC.BAT or CONFIG.SYS. And the way that you use a program now usually includes a large degree of customizability. This includes

- Setting sound levels on the fly.

- Determining whether or not introductory movies and transitions play every time.

- Determining whether or not "discretionary" images are available (A.D.A.M. Software's journey-around-and-into-the-body product, *A.D.A.M.—The Inside Story*, has a customizable fig leaf that can lock out the youngest children. So does Mindscape's *How Your Body Works.)*

- Determining which images or functional tools will be displayed at startup. (This refers more to encyclopedia entries and interactive media applications than other categories.)

Multiple Languages

The market for today's interactive media programs goes far beyond the United States, and the most successful developers begin planning for this inevitability from day one. There are both technical and design strategies to keep in mind as you plan for seamless localization. These include the following:

- Plan for two-byte characters (a single letter or character takes up one byte of information; Japanese and Chinese take up two whole bytes).

- Make sure your CD itself has enough room for more than one language on a single disc, if that's how you hope to sell it.

- Build and plan your movies with multiple soundtracks if you want on-the-fly switchable language capability.

- Allow enough screen space to account for more character-intensive languages, in particular German, which always takes more room than English.

- Keep your soundtracks and visuals separate, even in video, so that dubbing becomes rather than an arduous task. Same goes for text—make sure the text and visuals are on different levels of a graphic, or the text is stored as a font, not a bitmapped graphic.

Use of Video and Sound

Putting actors, videos, and music in your program is not as simple as writing a good script and shooting. You need to know the limitations of the technology, in terms of how big a video can be on screen and even how much an actor can move within his or her own video window. If the window is matched to the background—a common technique that makes an actor or object in a movie appear as if it's really on the background—you need to take special care in the filming process that nothing goes "out of frame." You'll also need to keep track of how big your files are getting, know the best compression technology to use, and bone up on strategies for psychologically minimizing preloading times. Indeed, all of these factors may scream to you: Keep that video short… or at the very least, small.

Music is a whole different ball game. Technological considerations here include the following:

- Creating cross-platform formats so your files will play unconverted on any of the top platforms (the same goes for video)

- Using the right compression techniques so you don't have noise, distortion, or delay

- Devising techniques for creating a continuous soundtrack, if that's what you want, or knowing your limits in terms of mixing music in different sections

Minimum Specifications

What does your program need in terms of the user's hardware and software in order to run properly? This, too, will affect the design and plan of your program. Nowadays, it's acceptable to design a program to run well on an Intel 80486 computer with a speed of 66MHz, as long as you know it will run without crashing on even a 386/33. (Mac equivalent: Design for a Quadra, make sure it barely runs on an LC.)

To accomplish this, you must become minimally conversant with an ugly concept called *data rate*. This mostly has to do with how fast you can get your data from the CD to the computer. It affects search speed and, more importantly, how well a movie or animated sequence plays. There are single-speed, double-speed, quadruple-speed, even eight times normal speed drives on the market now, so which do you plan for? The lowest common denominator? Or do you raise the technology bar just high enough to sneak in some extra performance for your title, but not too high to scare away parents who bought their kids a fairly low-end computer? All of this has a big impact in planning, because it makes no sense to try to teach lip reading if your program is going to skip every other frame.

■ Technology Software: Program Creation

What technology you use when you actually sit down and create a program depends on time, budget, and scope. To brazenly minimize a complicated subject, it basically breaks down into whether you use an authoring system, or go for hard coding in C++, Visual Basic, or some other programming language.

Authoring Systems

Authoring systems are supposed to make it easy for laypeople to create interactive media programs without having to write a word of esoteric code. They're not as simple as they used to be. Now they have their own coding languages, but the coding is usually somewhat English-like, with commands such as "Go to the next screen" rather than "IF Screen 1 contains 'yes,' AND the day of the week is 'Thursday,' THEN skip 3 screens forward, put the coordinates of x,y into p,q,z, subtract the user's IQ and display the results." (The latter was loosely translated from the original Klingon.)

What authoring systems really do is provide tools to perform actions that would be very difficult in other situations. For example, to define a clickable hot spot in an authoring system, you usually just drag a square around the area you want and that's it. The same action in a classic code environment requires typing in the coordinates of the box and adding lines of program code for each type of functionality desired. In an authoring program, the same is done with a standard dialog box.

Here are some of the more popular authoring systems.

Macromedia *Director* is the most popular and popularly priced authoring system on the block, and it has some very sophisticated capabilities to boot. Originally developed as an animation creation tool, Director has evolved into the pre-eminent cross-platform development environment. (More on Director later.)

Apple's *HyperCard* was probably the first authoring system to really speak to the masses. In 1988 it nearly single-handedly jump-started the then-nascent interactive media industry. HyperCard stacks can be created entirely by navigating through relatively intuitive dialog boxes. Knowing how to do a little programming in HyperCard's proprietary scripting language, Hyper-Talk, adds significant interactive media muscle to the mix.

Alleigeint's *SuperCard*, a superset of the original HyperCard, extends HyperCard's basic language and calls it SuperTalk. For a long time, Super-Card's ace in the hole was that it offered color support while HyperCard was decidedly black and white (HyperCard 2.2 finally introduced integrated color). SuperCard sadly languished in the basement of Aldus until it was recently spun off to a third party.

Apple's *Media Tool*, a more robust authoring system than HyperCard, has two components. One is run entirely by dialog boxes. The other requires real C++ coding to sing. Media Tool makes cross-platform development easy, but it runs very slowly.

Asymmetrix's *Toolbook* was supposed to be HyperCard on the PC. The original even let users port their HyperCard stacks into Toolbook "books" with the click of a button, but the result usually required a lot of cleanup. Toolbook was renamed *Multimedia Toolbook* in 1994.

Oracle's *Media Objects* is a very powerful tool that works on Macs, PCs, and even set-top boxes. It's touted as being HyperCard-like in structure—with a similar authoring language—but adds the ability to tap into the power of Oracle's world-class database technology.

AimTech's *IconAuthor* is a a high-priced authoring system that only runs on Windows. IconAuthor offers a very intuitive flowchart metaphor for program creation. At $4,000-plus to buy the development system, this has been a favorite mainly among corporate CBT developers.

Macromedia's *Authorware Professional* is also pricey (it originally sold to corporations for $8,000, with a "discount" for educators down to "only" $4,000). Authorware uses a flowchart metaphor similar to that of IconAuthor. It's one of the industry's most powerful tools—great for educational answer analysis—but up until the most recent release, it's been dead-dog slow and out of the question for consumer uses.

The first version of **Quest 5.0**, a veteran DOS CBT tool, was recently released for Windows. It's not cross platform yet, and it's a bit pricey, but it does have lots of nice features.

Voyager's *Expanded Books Toolkit* is a focused authoring system that lets users create interactive media versions of traditional text-based books, with such high-tech goodies as electronic bookmarks, places to write in the computerized margins, and sophisticated search capabilities.

There are lots more—including presentation programs masquerading as authoring systems, such as Macromedia *Action*, and kids' authoring programs such as *Magic Theater* from Knowledge Adventure. A new tool, *mTropolis* from mFactory, is rumored to be the hottest thing out since sliced cheese. And then there's *ScriptX*—a promising language, long in development, that would be used by existing authoring systems in place of their own proprietary languages to provide easy cross-platform title development. There's also a ScriptX Media Player, which will allow titles created in ScriptX to be played back on machines of multiple platforms. ScriptX from Kaleida is one of the results of Apple and IBM's once-shocking decision to actually talk to one another.

Hard Coding

Coding in C++ or Visual Basic offers the developer a lot of flexibility and a lot of speed. An authoring system may limit you to a particular look or a specified number of transitions. With enough time and resources, you can do just about anything in C++. In addition, programs written this way usually run faster because there's one less layer in between the computer and you. (With an authoring system, you have a complete program with all its overhead running in between your computer's operating system and the title you're creating. That slows things down, sometimes interminably.)

There may also be incompatibilities between your particular authoring system and certain computers, and you may not be able to fix those incompatibilities yourself (unless you're a crack programmer, and then what are you using an authoring system for anyway?). Finally, most authoring systems start to choke on large databases of information. That's why you won't find any interactive encyclopedias written in Macromedia Director.

So why doesn't everyone code in C++? There's a simple formula:

- **Custom Code = Costs More, Longer to Develop, Runs Faster**

- **Authoring System = Costs Less, Faster to Develop, Runs Slower**

The bottom line is that it takes longer to write custom code than it does to navigate through the dialog boxes in an authoring program. And the industry professionals who specialize in C++ programming charge a whole lot more than the graphic artist fresh out of school who you can train to use your authoring system. If you want to get it done fast and (relatively) cheap, you don't really have much of an alternative to using an authoring system.

But you can work around some of those disadvantages by hiring the best authoring system "programmers." Director, for example, has a simple scripting language called *Lingo* that can be optimized by smart team members. Even more important, most authoring systems allow you to "extend" the programs' functionality by adding XOBJECTS or XCOMMANDS. These extensions, ironically, are written in traditional coding languages, usually C++. But they let you get away with a little concentrated C effort, rather than an entire project written from scratch in ancient Sumerian.

Going Cross-Platform

The authoring system versus C++ debate has particular ramifications if you're trying to develop—as you should be—for playback on a variety of platforms (see the next section for details on the platforms you have to consider). Until recently, unless you were writing custom C++ code, it was pretty much impossible to develop effectively for multiple platforms. But custom code that is written properly can work on Macs, PCs, and set-top boxes (souped-up game machines that connect directly to your television) with only moderate changes. Authoring systems, on the other hand, were by and large platform specific.

Now, there have been authoring programs with cross-platform capabilities—Authorware Professional has done it for years—but as I said before, it's always been a sluggish boor, more appropriate for closed corporate environments where you could fix the delivery platforms' specs (a fast hard disk rather than a slow CD-ROM, please). Macromedia Director 4.0 has changed things significantly.

The product is now much more smoothly cross-platform. You can develop on either the Mac or PC, and play it on the other platform with a minimum of effort. Before version 4.0, however, you could only develop on the Mac and port it to the PC using a special playback program. Want to go beyond the PC? There's now a special Director Player that will run Director-created titles on the 3DO platform, OS/9 DAVID (which works on set-top boxes), and even the World Wide Web. Macromedia's stated philosophy is "Author Once, Play Anywhere."

■ Technology Hardware: What Are Your Options?

Cross-platform. Portability. Multiple channels. With so many computer standard wannabes out there, it's become a major headache just to keep up. While most developers focus on the Macintosh and PC-compatible subsection, it's not fair to ignore set-top boxes and game machines that also include CD-ROM drives. And what about online content delivery and the World Wide Web? How do you choose which platform, or platforms, to develop for? Here's a brief guide to platforms and their relative advantages for the developer.

Macs and PCs

The largest installed base belongs to the Intel-based Personal Computer standard running Microsoft Windows (dubbed *Wintel* by some), so understandably, this is where most developers target their release products. Developing for the PC actually usually involves developing at least somewhat on a Macintosh because the PC is a bear of a machine to use. True, Windows has made life a little more consistent and user-friendly for most applications, but there's nothing like a Mac for out-of-the-box get up and go.

The reasons for this are legendary: Apple insisted on keeping its box "closed" and not sublicensing the operating system, a practice that has relegated its flagship machine into near-marginality as Microsoft pushed its operating system further and further into the mainstream. But keeping control of the technology meant that Apple could ensure that things worked with each other. A new board installed in a Mac usually works as soon as you turn on the machine. Most new programs boot up the first time, and can trade data seamlessly. Macs also have built-in audio. And all new Macs can read PC programs.

"Open standard" PCs, on the other hand, can contain a nightmarish mish-mash of potentially incompatible components. You can buy a PC from a single manufacturer—say Compaq, Leading Edge, or Packard Bell—and be relatively confident that the sound card will work with the video card and the settings will be preset correctly at the factory. But many buyers shop at "build your own"-type shops, where you put together your own computer (or the reseller does it for you). Because the PC has this open architecture, you're never sure what's going to be in your computer—whether it will be a SoundBlaster or a ProAudio Spectrum sound card, for example, or which type of BIOS chip it will have. Then, each time you add a new device, you have to make sure it will work with your particular configuration, and it can be a 50-50 bet sometimes.

Developing for Macs and PCs

For the interactive media developer, this means that you must develop—and test—your product on a staggering range of different machines, and while your title may perform beautifully on a Dell Pentium, it may crash in an instant on a Digital 486/33. Tracking down where the incompatibilities lie, and how to fix them, takes up an inordinate amount of a developer's time. What can you do about it? Right now, not much. You could develop just for Macs, but first of all, they're not immune to compatibility problems—Apple has both regular Macs and "PowerMacs" (based on a faster, and totally different, breed of RISC chip). There are faster and slower Macs, just like there are tortoise and hare varieties on the PC. And Apple has opened up its universe to Mac clones, too. More importantly, though, the Macintosh installed base is just too small. If you're going to make a profit, you have to develop for both platforms, with an aim of getting the PC version out first.

To make matters worse and even more confusing, you need only look as far as the recent introduction of Windows 95, the successor to Microsoft's runaway best-selling Windows 3.1. Microsoft has extended Windows's functionality to include many Mac-like features and to add some improved ones. Plug and Play should eliminate many of the hardware incompatibilities. And, through another feature called AutoPlay, CDs will automatically boot up when you insert them in the drive (all you have to do is add a text file called AUTORUN.INF). Finally, Windows 95 is a full-fledged operating system in its own right, doing away with the dastardly DOS once and for all. All this is fine and dandy, but for the interactive media developer, it's yet another potentially incompatible system you must have a version of your product ready for.

Still, developing first for the PC and Mac (and in that order) is the smartest bet for the interactive media developer. Authoring systems are readily available for both PC and Mac, channels to distribution are clear, and the market is growing rapidly. The great variety of titles discussed in this book are for these two platforms. Developers should strive for cross-platform development, branching out to the set-top boxes discussed below as time and resources allow.

The Multimedia PC

While Macs are all basically interactive-media ready (provided the chip speed is fast enough), PCs have adopted a special moniker to indicate their willingness to do interactive media. "MPC" machines have minimum specifications as required by the Multimedia Marketing Council. These include a minimum of a CD-ROM drive and sound board. Any piece of MPC-labeled hardware supposedly will run with any other MPC-branded part. The strategy has largely been successful. There was even a magazine out called *MPC World* (before it was renamed *Multimedia World*).

Of course, the original MPC spec was really too slow, and so there's now MPC2, which requires 16-bit sound and an even faster (double-speed) CD-ROM drive. It won't be long before quad-speed drives become part of the standard, and that's okay—they're all just trying to get the data to you faster. Right now, an ordinary CD-ROM drive transfers its data to your computer at a staggeringly slow speed, something like 15 to 30 times slower than the average hard drive. For now, you should still aim titles for original MPC compatibility, but make sure you've got an easy port to MPC2. Be sure to save all your original files so that when swifter hardware is available, your stuff will run and look better.

What about IBM?

IBM, never content to follow Intel or Microsoft, decided to go its own way in the PC wars. Its UltiMedia solution for interactive media delivery incorporates a high-powered PC running OS/2 and features a dedicated hardware solution called an ActionMedia board. The latter uses its own proprietary compression algorithm based on a standard called DVI, originally developed at the David Sarnoff Labs in Princeton, New Jersey, sold to RCA and then to Intel.

Once upon a time, DVI was the only solution for putting motion video on a CD-ROM. The problem was, the boards that did the capturing could easily set a developer back $15,000 (and that was after the price came down). In addition, you had to send the raw data to an Intel-sponsored compression facility, and they were charging something ridiculous like $100 for every compressed minute of footage.

DVI lives on in the UltiMedia system, but its bastard child—the lower-quality version of the algorithm using software-only (not hardware) compression—has made solid inroads into the digital video community. It's called *Indeo*, and you can read all about it in the section on digital video below.

Set-Top Boxes

A lot of the excitement and buzz in interactive media has been centered around creating a faster, stronger, cooler game machine. The game world has been owned almost exclusively by Nintendo and Sega, battling it out in a duel between a plumber and a hedgehog. But those machines are old, with hardware that was designed many years ago when cartridges, not CD-ROMs, ruled. There's nothing wrong with that. Just ask the millions of mostly teenage boys who remain addicted to even the simplest of systems. But as technology advances, so does the desire to do more.

The term *set-top box* comes from the fact that systems in this category tend to sit on (or under) a TV set, and don't require a separate personal computer. All-in-one and easy to set up, most of the hottest systems have CD-ROMs in them. While games will ultimately make or break which systems sell through to long-term success, nearly all these companies have edutainment aspirations way beyond kill 'em, crunch 'em, nuke 'em.

Here's a brief look at some of the systems that hope to be the next big Nintendo or Sega.

CD-i

CD-i was the first true set-top box out of the gate. Not really a game machine by design, this system from Phillips established its technology as early as 1986 and, unfortunately, is now stuck in is own imminent obsolescence. CD-i is a proprietary (not open) format that can play back interactive media titles. The system sports decent animation, sound, and—with an extra video cartridge—full-screen, full-motion video on an ordinary TV monitor. It's an all-in-one solution that on paper sounds extraordinary. Just connect the wires to your TV, pop in a CD-i disc, and you're ready to play or learn. No set-up anxiety, no Windows, no DOS

In practice, the clunkiness of the system and many of its early titles has had pundits clamoring for CD-i's demise nearly from its release. To the surprise of many, the system has taken a decent foothold in Europe. Some of the earliest CD-i titles included a tour of the Smithsonian; a Time-Life-produced tutorial teaching users how to take quality photographs; and some decent children's titles, including licensing agreements with Sesame Street and the Berenstein Bears. But it's the games that keep the system going. One title in particular, *Voyeur*, is one of the most innovative "adult" games out on any platform, featuring real actors (Brian Keith and Margo Kidder) and a spicy mystery to solve by you, the Voyeur.

CD-i was released at a $699 price point, which made only the early adopter hot and bothered. It's since dropped to half that price or less. For an extra couple hundred bucks, though, you can add an MPEG-based digital video adapter, which lets you play back full-length feature films from disc on your TV (see the discussion below for more details on MPEG). Proponents claim that image quality is at least as good as VHS. You can only fit 70 minutes on a single disc, though, which means you have to have two discs in the box and change them in the middle of the movie. Still, the format lets you search for exactly the scene you're looking for and never have to rewind.

Full-motion video notwithstanding, one of the neatest tricks CD-i did was release a variety of different machine configurations. While the consumer excitement is all about the basic game machine sold in Circuit Cities across North America, corporate training departments have benefited from two alternate arrangements: a professional machine with a mouse and floppy-disk drive for saving student data; and a portable "CD-iMan," which has its own color LCD screen—very useful for taking training or interactive presentations on the road. You don't even need to connect it to a TV monitor, though if the CEO you're meeting with has that available, it makes for a better, bigger picture.

If you're thinking about developing for CD-i, unfortunately the very propietariness that promised to make the system easy to use and ever so intuitive means that development is also proprietary. Most developers write their own custom C++ code. There are authoring systems—notably MediaMogul from OptImage—but it's nothing you'd want to write a high-powered game in. And there's still no decent way to port an existing Mac or PC title to CD-i.

3DO

3DO charged into the foray with a deafening roar and a call to arms. Founded by Trip Hawkins, who took computer software maker Electronic Arts to star status, 3DO's media-saturated intention was to create a state-of-the-art game machine that would have better video, more effects, faster processing (with two separate processing systems), more pixel power—the works. The machine uses a standard double-speed CD-ROM drive.

The initial price—like CD-i—was too high, though, and title makers couldn't spit out quality product fast enough. The first Christmas season was pretty much a bust, and insiders jumped on a bash-3DO bandwagon as quickly as they lashed out at CD-i. The system, however, has held on, and new technology promises to make it faster and cooler, upping its 32-bit processing power to a killer 64-bit (what all that means is less important than the basic concept: bigger is better and faster). Decent titles have finally appeared, and the system now features the same digital video card option that CD-i offers.

For the developer, 3DO was supposed to be a simple port. Change a few lines of code and you could extend your title to another platform. I worked with a developer trying to do this, and their "simple" 3DO port was long delayed in release and pretty slow running once it did ship. There are no easy-to-use 3DO-specific authoring systems at all, though there are tools developers can use to create their titles on a Macintosh with a 3DO emulator card. Macromedia now has a version of their Director Player for 3DO, but it's still too early to tell how well it works, or how many people are using it. For most, it's back to the old C++ grind again.

VIS and CDTV

VIS and CDTV are two now-defunct systems that also vied for the crown of set-top kingdom. They're worth mentioning for what they did wrong and the implications they have for future manufacturers looking for a fast buck. VIS came from Tandy—the Radio Shack folks. It ran a system called Modular Windows, a subset of Windows for the PC, and the goal was to let developers just click a few buttons and—voilà—their Windows-compatible CD-ROM titles would run on a self-contained set-top box. Right.

The reality was that the VIS systems had an Intel 80286 processor (the world has since moved on to 486s and the Pentium chip), and the Modular Windows that was supposed to work so well ran slowly and looked worse. The system made even the paid help hired to demonstrate it at interactive media conferences wince. It was embarrassing and, fortunately, it died before doing any serious damage to interactive media's credibility with the impressionable consumer and cynical press.

CDTV, from Commodore, does not, as you might suspect, stand for Compact Disc Television. No, its an acronym for *Commodore Dynamic Total Vision*. The problem here wasn't bad porting, as with VIS. CDTV simply looked and felt too much like a computer playing back on a TV. It didn't feel like a consumer "appliance." There was blocky text, poorly digitized sound, even a dastardly DOS-like feel to the thing. To top it off, consumers had to put their CDTV discs in a caddie before inserting them, rather than popping them in a tray. If the average Joe knows audio CDs, he'll expect a similar pop-it-in-and-go experience. CD-ROM caddies are part of the computer, not consumer world, and lately, most computer manufacturers have switched to the caddieless drive.

Pippin

Pippin is the latest attempt at following in the footsteps of VIS. This time it's Apple's turn to either shine or make a fool of itself. Pippin, according to the early reports, will be a Mac on steroids—faster processing and a quadruple-speed CD-ROM drive—but without a keyboard or monitor. Macintosh titles are supposed to run on Pippin with just a few modifications; Pippin titles will run on Macintosh with no modifications at all. The Enhanced CD format (see below) will be supported.

If the machine really works, it gives Pippin hundreds, if not thousands, of high-quality proven titles right out of the gate. Why Apple wants to price it at the same high price range of $500-plus that nearly killed both 3DO and CD-i, only Michael Spindler in his infinite and very precise wisdom knows. Will it work? Can it compete with 3DO, CD-i, or more importantly, the upcoming souped-up game boxes? Stay tuned.

PhotoCD and Enhanced CD

Kodak's PhotoCD for still photos and the more generic Enhanced CD audio format are examples of emerging standards without actual standalone machines. Kodak, however, initially hoped to make it big with PhotoCD set-top boxes. The idea seemed brilliant: Consumers would go in to their local photo finisher, who would ask "Would you like prints, slides, or a CD?" For only

$20, you would get all your photos transferred to a CD-ROM. The images would be stored in multiple formats and resolutions so they would look good whether on a computer running Photoshop or an NTSC monitor. PhotoCDs might not replace 3-by-5 prints entirely, but they would be far superior to slides and slide trays.

Kodak produced a number of different PhotoCD set-top boxes that would connect directly to one's TV. The PhotoCD format was also made standard in most everyone else's set-top box—3DO and CD-i in particular. Both PCs and Macs could easily read PhotoCDs inserted into at least a double-speed CD-ROM drive. Sounds like a hit.

What happened was that the set-top box failed as a consumer choice, but PhotoCD has become an international success with professional interactive media developers. The public hasn't exactly been racing to its local photo-finisher to request PhotoCDs or to an electronics retailer to shell out $400 for the accompanying player. But developers quickly realized that creating PhotoCDs directly from 35mm film would save them the expense of purchasing costly slide scanners or frequent visits to the service bureau.

Practically overnight, the industry converted to PhotoCD. Now, almost all images that are used in interactive media titles start out on PhotoCD. This holds for original footage shot by the developer and material received from photo acquisition sources, which readily deliver on PhotoCD.

Very few consumer titles ever appeared in classic PhotoCD format—and most of those could be played directly on a 3DO or CD-i player (so why buy the more limited Kodak PhotoCD player, asked the masses). The best-known PhotoCD title is probably *From Alice to Ocean* from Against All Odds Productions. It's a very good idea for a PhotoCD because it's composed primarily of still images linked together with narration and a search mechanism. But most people who've seen the title have bought the PC or Mac version, which adds motion video through QuickTime.

The Enhanced CD format, like PhotoCD, is finding its way into lots of systems, though there's no standalone Enhanced CD player. Now known officially as *CD Plus*, these are audio CDs with some interactive media extras on them. Any CD-ROM drive that can read a PhotoCD disc can read a CD Plus disc—they both use "multisession" CD-ROM technology. CD Plus discs play back crystal clear sound on a normal audio CD player as well as on most CD-ROM drives. But on computer systems that are CD Plus ready, these same CDs also allow users to scroll through liner and track notes, band photos, maybe a video here or there. It's like bringing back the elaborate inserts of early 1970s progressive rock albums using state-of-the-art technology. Now, who could fault a baby boomer with 1970s nostalgia (and a 1990s wallet)?

Sega

Sega has enough different CD-ROM game machines lined up that something should presumably click. It started with SegaCD, which was the first of the classic game machines to add CD-ROM to the traditional cartridge delivery system. It branched out to such new-fangled names as *32X* and *Saturn*. All of the new ones are CD based; the main differences lie in processor power and who Sega can recruit to develop titles. Sega titles fall decidedly in the game camp, but a few edutainment developers, such as Mindscape, have been trying to port titles like *The San Diego Zoo Presents the Animals!* to SegaCD. No authoring languages are available to ease the transition, but if your company is hot on the custom code route, it can be done.

Not content to rest on propagating multiple species of CD-ROM machines, Sega is also hyping a bizarre little toy called PICO. It's a cartridge-based system, which means that development is more like traditional Sega coding than CD-ROM programming. The actual system has a little five-page plastic book attached to the cart and a stylus. You connect it to your TV. The young kids Sega is targeting turn the pages to see different screens on the monitor. They can interact with them in a very simple way.

Surprisingly, PICO sold decently during its first Christmas, so some title makers might be interested in creating very stripped-down versions of their more complex children's CD-ROM titles for PICO. Sega was offering some decent development money to seed early titles—check whether that's still around by the time you read this.

Nintendo

Nintendo's answer to Sega's CD push has been to eschew CD-ROM entirely. Their upcoming Ultra 64 machine, a collaboration between Nintendo and 3D powerhouse Silicon Graphics (SGI), won't include a CD-ROM drive at all, but will stick with cartridge. Nintendo's logic makes a certain sense: As fast as CD-ROMs can spew out the info, they still are a decidedly slow beast. Cartridges have always been faster. Nintendo certainly knows how to make cartridges. Plus, Nintendo is probably quite pleased to continue their lucrative licensing fee structure, where developers pay Nintendo (or Sega for that matter) a tidy sum on each cart shipped. Interestingly, 3DO tried to lure developers by promising a much lower licensing fee—$3 versus $17. As 3DO hit harder times, they upped their licensing fee, though not as high as Nintendo.

Nintendo development is as proprietary an affair as it comes. Plan on committing significant, highly trained, and dedicated resources if you'll be developing for Nintendo. But with the company's marketing muscle, if you create a hit, you'll be able to coast for a short while.

Sony

The Sony PlayStation (originally code-named *PSX*) has hit the shelves and I can report is that the specs are good, and the developers are coming out in nice numbers. Sony hasn't been as successful in the interactive media arena as it was with TVs and Walkmans, though they've kept up the image of the golden boys of Japan. They came out with a machine called the Data Disc-man, which played mostly text-based CDs on a self-contained LCD screen. You don't hear a lot about Data Discmans anymore.

Then there was the MMCD player, which brought visuals and sound to a Data Discman type of layout. Another turkey for Sony. Newsweek InterActive was developed on both the MMCD and PC formats, but never shipped more than a few thousand units in MMCD format. Now there's the Multimedia Discman—don't ask me what it does! So, when Sony introduces a new strictly gaming machine like the PlayStation, the reaction remains mixed. For developers, it's new enough that there are no cross-platform tools out yet.

Atari

Atari has been around since the beginning of video games. They've teetered on the edge of extinction, and now are trying to make a comeback with the Jaguar. A game machine, it boasts the increasingly important 64-bit architecture found in Nintendo's Ultra 64. The basic unit runs cartridges, but the machine has an add-on option to beef it up to CD-ROM power. It was only test-sold in a select few markets for Christmas 1994, so the jury is still out on whether or not this is a good bet to develop for. As with its compatriots in gamedom, development is strictly a proprietary, C++ affair. This is getting to sound like a broken record, huh?

Videodiscs

Almost forgotten in the interactive media shuffle, the trusty videodisc is like an old friend to veteran interactive media developers. Many of us cut our teeth creating interactive applications long before CD-ROM existed as a viable consumer alternative. Our titles were expensive and played before decidedly small audiences, but they were innovative in their own way. We didn't even use the term *interactive media* or *multimedia*. This was the day of "interactive video."

A videodisc is a like a big LP record, only it can play pictures as well as music. And it's read by a laser, so there's no physical stylus touching the disc itself. Videodiscs, unlike CD-ROMs, are analog, not digital. A videodisc, like an LP, records its video in a line, albeit a curved one. The disc starts at point A, and ends at point B (interestingly, videodiscs start on the inside and finish at the outermost part). Contrast this with CD-ROMs, which record all their data in bits and bytes, ones and zeros, offs and ons.

The advantages of CD-ROM are that you can do anything you want with the information—store it here, store it there, manipulate an image, flip it, distort it, add 15 soundtracks to the same image if you want. Videodiscs can only play video with accompanying sound (stereo or two switchable mono soundtracks) in linear order.

But (and here's the big but) videodiscs have superb image quality, rivaling broadcast television quality, while the CD-ROMs of today, as we've discussed, sport herky-jerky puny images. To this day, if you want to create a program on nuclear power plant training, which seems the better choice: the tiny ¼ screen image, or the beautiful full-screen 25-inch TV playback?

Videodiscs can hold either exactly 30 minutes or 60 minutes of video maximum per side. Which it is depends on whether the system is counting seconds and minutes (these discs are called *CLV* for *Constant Linear Velocity*) or individual frames (these are *CAV* discs, standing for *Constant Angular Velocity*). The latter is more accurate and so is used when a videodisc is connected to a computer for an interactive program. The former is used primarily for movies, which you can buy in your local videodisc specialty store.

In either case, the advantage of a videodisc over, say, a videotape, is you can very quickly search to up to 54,000 frames on the 30-minute version. You can program the videodisc to then play back a single frame or a particular video sequence. Videodiscs today are used extensively in schools, where they're in all practicality being substituted for slide trays—it's a lot safer to carry around a single disc than an armload of slide carousels that could spill out at any moment. Videodiscs are also found in corporate sites, where a substantial infrastructure of machines still exists from the heyday of the laser, about three or four years ago (how time flies when you're fast becoming obsolete).

There are three ways videodiscs are classified, and they have their own code words:

1. Level 1 refers to videodiscs that are played back by themselves. This disc itself is "dumb." You connect it to a monitor (any old TV monitor will do), and use the remote control to determine what you see and when.

2. Level 2 refers to discs that have their own built-in programming. A press of a button on the remote won't just play the disc from beginning to end, but will go a certain number of frames before stopping. Some of the first videodisc entertainment titles, the "Mystery Discs," allowed you to solve a crime by skipping around a disc with your remote.

3. Level 3 discs are also "dumb," but this time it's the computer that controls them. The simplest way to have a videodisc provide really serious interactive value is to hook it up to a computer—the Mac, as always, is

the easiest—and have what's known as a "two screen" title. You place a computer screen and a video monitor side by side. You look at the computer screen to interact with the program. At various points, the computer will trigger the videodisc to play back a specific video sequence.

The advantage to this setup is that you don't need any additional hardware in the computer. Instructors and relative laypeople can create simple programs using the HyperCard authoring system, even in black and white, to control a video sequence, and the result can be quite compelling. I did that with a smoking prevention program aimed at fifth and sixth graders created in 1992 at the Institute for the Study of Family, Work, and Community, a division of Berkeley-based interactive media developer InfoUse, and we won both a silver and gold medal at different interactive media festival competitions.

Now, you can certainly put video directly on the computer—this just requires a video digitizing board inside the computer. This type of setup is very common in publicly accessed kiosks—it's used for everything from tourist information to selling shoes.

In 1994, Pioneer, one of the prime makers of videodisc players, introduced a new consumer-oriented format called LaserActive (Pioneer trademarked the term *laserdisc* for their variety of videodiscs). This new machine combines videodiscs, CD-ROMs, and even a plug-in Sega cartridge to create an unwieldy interactive media monster. Its roll-out price was equally monstrous—over $1,000 for a fully configured system. As we discussed before, consumer standalone machines don't move much merchandise if the price is over $300. Clunk. Double clunk.

Online Content Delivery

Online delivery of interactive media has focused on two different scenarios. One is an extension of the set-top boxes we just discussed, often known as *video* or *interactive media on demand*. The other is the emerging interactive media capabilities of the Internet, in particular the World Wide Web. Currently, both are delivered on standard phone lines, but that may change in the future with higher capacity cable TV lines bringing more data more of the time right into your home. Let's start with the more tangible black boxes, rather than the black void of CyberSpace.

Video and Interactive Media on Demand

The interactive media industry and its pundits in print are a fickle lot. They jump from one hot technology buzzword to another, looking for the scoop or some magical defining moment. First, CD-ROMs were hot. Then it was set-top boxes that would deliver content—especially video—direct to your TV through telephone or cable lines whenever and wherever you wanted it. Now it's back to CD-ROMs again. But the online content delivery boxes aren't dead; they're just dormant until the technology catches up with the initial hype.

The idea behind video and interactive media on demand set-top boxes is that these devices will be capable of downloading entire interactive media programs or linear videos from a central digital storehouse, letting you rent a title for a certain period of time without ever having to leave your house. The concept is still a sound one. It's just that the technological hurdles are formidable. Hundreds of megabytes of information need to flow across great distances, instantaneously and simultaneously, for hundreds, if not thousands, of users.

There are still a number of tests around the United States and Canada trying to gauge both what works technically and what users really want (online voting or online shopping?). There are two basic ways to deliver online content:

1. The set-top box receives the interactive media program, or movie, in real time. It's as if the computer is in one room and the monitor is in the other, and the two just have a long cable in between them.

2. The set-top box is designed to very quickly download the entire contents of an interactive media program into temporary storage. Then the user can interact with the title as if she or he had his or her own CD-ROM at home.

Interactive play between gamers in different cities would be possible in both scenarios. Online delivery will never replace ownership of CD-ROM titles—people like to build a collection, just like they rent and buy videotapes—but someday this will be a viable alternative, despite the problems of today.

For the developer, there shouldn't be too much of an upward programming curve. Whether a title is simply downloaded to a user's home set-top box or used interactively in real time, the very same product that worked on a CD-ROM should work without too many fundamental changes. The main concern for developers then becomes a distribution one—is it a better deal for a small number of people to buy your title, or a larger number rent it? Games, obviously, will benefit the most since they can be replayed, whereas coffee table titles—with their once-over nature—might suffer if people paid less to see their title a single time.

Online delivery is often confused with Interactive TV, where Joe Couch Potato gets to predict the answers to Jeopardy or the results in this week's football game. These systems use regular broadcast television as a base, and let you play along either tapping into a subfrequency being broadcast along with the TV signal, or through radio waves. A colleague of mine once commented that if "interactive" ever came to mean guessing the color of Vanna White's dress, he was getting out of the business. Marty—your future is safe for a while—Interactive

TV hasn't caught on big-time, and the original players are starting to lose their techno-shirts.

The World Wide Web and Interactive Media

When I first got my hands on Netscape, a browser that lets you surf the World Wide Web, I was totally and completely blown away. And hopelessly addicted. My work suffered. My family suffered. I was plugged in to the worst of pop culture, the fastest breaking news, a world community of fellow travelers. Forget about TV—the Web is the mind candy of the digital generation. I have since recovered. I can suppress a desire to read this morning's *Dilbert* until, maybe, lunch time. I even play with my kids sometimes. But the power of those initial experiences on the Web will never be lost on me.

So what is this World Wide Web, anyway?

The Web is basically a way to hyperlink information from all over the world in almost real time. Unlike standard e-mail—where you send a message, it's received, and a reply is sent—the Web lets users connect to faraway computers without delay. If, for example, I want to read this morning's New York TimesFax, I simply type in the location of that page on the Web, and my computer connects to the Times's computer, and displays the news on my screen. If I want to read David Letterman's Top Ten List from the night before, or two weeks before, I simply connect to the CBS home page and up comes the list on my screen.

Here's where it starts getting fun. On the CBS page are other *links*—words and phrases and sometimes graphics shown in blue. Clicking a word takes me to a different page, maybe on a different computer, maybe in a different country. Pages get linked with other pages, and before you know it, you're discovering things you had no intention of finding in the first place. There's SpellingLand—home of all-you-wanted-to-know about "Melrose Place," "Beverly Hills 90210," and other shows from the demented mind of Aaron Spelling. There's Multimedia Wire on the Web—a daily update of interactive media news. And then there's The Dilbert Zone—daily updated comics from the Scott Adams computer nerd classic. Oh yeah, there's lots of pornography too, but we won't mention that.

The Web is great for research. You can connect to university libraries all over the world and do serious searches on everything from warplanes to medical discoveries. You can find out the e-mail addresses of just about any interactive media company doing business. You can even track the status of your Federal Express package.

What does all this have to do with interactive media? The Web is beginning to get new-media savvy. Already it can show graphics. And you can always download QuickTime movies and more from a Web site to play on your home computer. Recently a product called RealAudio became available. It allows you to listen to sound and music off the Net without downloading any-thing except for the RealAudio player. Let's say I'm writing this from Jerusa-lem (which I am), but I want to hear Bob Edwards on Morning Edition. I just go to the NPR home page, and—click!—it's playing on my computer.

Macromedia will soon make a version of its Director Player Web-friendly (officially to be integrated into the Netscape Navigator program), so you can watch a video or animation in real time coming over your computer. This, of course, assumes you have sufficient bandwidth—that is, the data is coming fast enough over either phone or cable wires into a modem or other type of receiving device in your home.

The World Wide Web thus has the potential for becoming its own interac-tive media playback device. Certainly, CD-ROM products will increasingly tie in with their publisher's Web sites—Microsoft is already doing it with Microsoft Baseball, which lets you go online to get the latest stats. Medio (de-scribed more in Chapter 7) is linking its CD-ROM publication, Medio Maga-zine, with its online counterpart, MedioNet. The technological hurdles here are equally as formidable as those in video on demand, but the payoff may be far greater—and uniquely interactive.

■ Digital Video: What You Should Be Planning For

At first, video in interactive media titles was more gimmick than substance. A text-based encyclopedia instantly became an interactive media classic by the simple addition of a couple of video clips. Digital video, in contrast with the analog video that has been used on videodiscs for years, has come a long way since it was first introduced. And it's going even further. First, here's a quick digital video primer.

In the Beginning There Was QuickTime

Introduced by Apple in 1991, QuickTime represented a way to "toss around" video as easily as one uses other file formats on the computer. While people sometimes refer to QuickTime as a program, in reality it's just an extension to the Mac's operating system. This extension lets the computer understand a new file format, the MOOV (pronounce it ten times slowly—you'll get it) in the same way that computers understand formats like BMP, WAV, EPS, TIFF, PICT, or TEXT.

With the QuickTime extension installed on your machine, your com-puter can copy and paste MOOV files from one application to another (appli-cations must be rewritten to understand the file format, but by now, most have). So, you can have a picture appearing in a WordPerfect document that looks like an ordinary PICT, but when you click on it, it comes to life. That exact same file can play from an interactive media authoring program.

What's truly remarkable about QuickTime is that it plays movies without any additional hardware. You can copy files on floppy disk or send them across your network, put them on any other machine with the appropriate digital video extension, and it will play—no expensive hardware required.

Putting movies on the PC may be a technological achievement, but as we discussed earlier, the overall effect for the user can be decidedly underwhelming. QuickTime started out just on the Macintosh with a maximum screen size of about ⅛ of the screen and no more than 12 frames per second. It's improved by QuickTime 2.0 to ¼ to ½ of the screen and up to 30 frames per second depending on processor power. That same functionality, more or less, is available on the PC through both QuickTime for Windows and Microsoft's own competing Video for Windows (with the extension AVI instead of MOOV).

Why have QuickTime and Video for Windows movies been limited to such small windows and such spotty playback? It's all about compression. Let's try a quick calculation. If you work with Adobe Photoshop or other full-featured painting programs, you know that a single 24-bit color image can easily take up a megabyte or more. Let's use this as an average for this example. Now, North American NTSC video runs at 30 frames per second to give the illusion of motion. Doing the math, you can see that 30MB fill a second, and 1,800MB are needed for a single minute of video (1MB × 30 frames/second × 60 seconds/minute = 1,800MB). Since CD-ROMs can hold a maximum of 650MB, uncompressed video won't go very far.

So let's start to compress. First, let's cut down the frame size to a quarter screen from a full screen. Divide by 4—we're down to only 450MB for a minute of video. How about if we start dropping frames—so that only one of, say, three frames gets shown (that would be ten frames per second)? Now we can divide by 3—around 115MB per minute. It's all there in Figure 2.1.

Still not there. Hmmm…So let's start compressing. *Compression* is the process of running the data through an algorithm to take out any wasted or duplicated material. There are a plethora of different compression schemes, ranging from lossy to lossless. You may have heard of some of the names: *Cinepak, Indeo, Video 1*, to name a few. The best ones can compress at a rate of over 100 to 1 (see Figure 2.2). Do that arithmetic, and you're down to only about 1MB per minute—and that's for the dinky frame.

You can start to increase frame size and frame rate, and eventually, with all conditions being optimal, you can get up to 70 minutes of full-screen, full-motion compressed video squeezed into the 650MB of a CD-ROM—but not without a hardware hit. To get the maximum, the computer's software is just not strong enough. A separate hardware component—a board—is required.

Figure 2.1

Getting video to fit on a
CD requires some heavy
slicing and dicing.

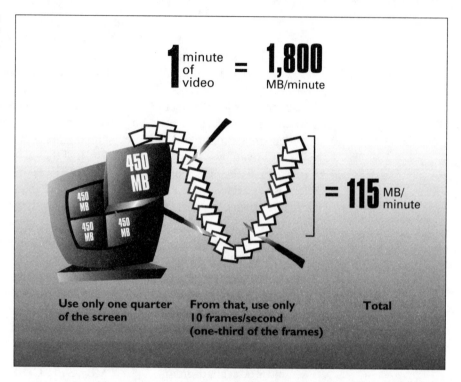

But that hardware is becoming increasingly cheaper. In the PC world, you
have to add in the costs of a video card anyway, so the equation is looking
brighter.

The Immediate Future of Digital Video: MPEG

The most popular up and coming standard for putting full-motion, full-
screen video on the computer is called MPEG. Standing for *Motion Pictures
Experts Group*, MPEG is an internationally developed standard that plays
back video at approximately VHS videotape quality. It does its compression
by looking at one frame of video and comparing it with the next frame. The
computer then only saves the pixels that have changed, not the whole frame.

This makes for great data savings, though it's a little harder to fast forward
as you would with a videotape. Indeed, for editing purposes, you need something else called *JPEG*—for the *Joint Photography Experts Group*—which
saves each frame in discrete, though compressed, information blocks. You can
then find the frame you want quickly and clearly.

MPEG add-in boards are all the rage and have come down in price to
only a couple hundred bucks. And for once, the same standard is being used

Figure 2.2

A good compression
algorithm is your final
step.

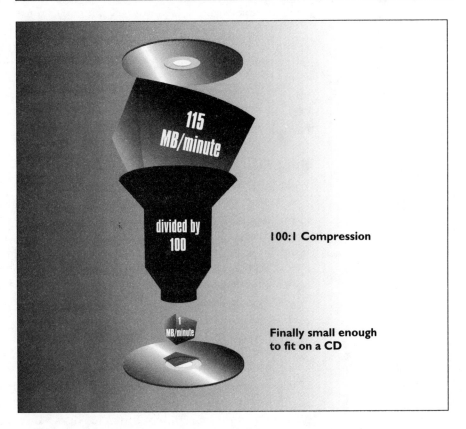

on PCs, Macs, 3DO, CD-i, and others. As a developer, you definitely have to keep your eye on where full-motion hardware-assisted video is going. Can you just port your titles over with a click of a button? Probably not. But if you've created video in a window, as long as you have the original file, you can recapture the video and include it on a new disc in MPEG format.

If, however, you've integrated video or animation into a title using the Theater in a Box metaphor (described more in Chapter 5), so that the placement of said video is fixed to interact with a 3-D or photographic background, increasing the video size isn't going to work for you. About the only improvement you'll see is an increase in the number of frames per second.

On the other hand, if you made compromises in your original design—say, you wanted to have your video actor shown in a full-screen long shot, but had to settle for a partial screen medium shot—you may be able to restore your starting concept as the technology improves. Always save your original work. Shoot or create in the highest possible standard, and later on you'll be able to upgrade your work if it makes sense.

A final note on MPEG: As with MPC, there's more than one MPEG to keep your eye on. MPEG1 is what's finding its way into the low-cost boards today. But watch out for MPEG2, which will provide better quality soon. And MPEG3, with even greater compression, will probably be most useful for online content delivery. And just when you get comfortable with MPEG, there will likely be a completely incompatible, but superior proprietary compression technique just waiting to jump into the fray.

Super Density Discs and More

What MPEG will do for digital video quality, the Super Density Digital Video Disc will do for storage capacity. There are actually two contenders in this field—one from the Sony/Phillips juggernaut, the other being spearheaded by Toshiba and backed by Time-Warner, Hitachi, and half of Hollywood, it seems. In both cases, the idea is to increase the amount of data a CD-ROM can hold. Sony/Phillips can cram 3.7 gigabytes (yes, gigabytes) onto a single-sided CD-ROM, or 7.5GB on a double-sided one. Toshiba can fit a whopping 10 gigabytes of digital data on one of their Super Density (SD) discs.

The SD format will support MPEG2 digital video, and lots of it—with that much room, you can fit several movies on a single disc. MPEG2 guarantees that the video quality will be superior to today's VHS videotapes. An SD disc, of course, won't run on today's double-speed CD-ROM drives, but hopefully, the reverse won't be precluded. And there's still the related compatibility issue—Sony/Phillips-formatted discs won't work on Toshiba machines and vice versa.

That seems partly because the Toshiba machines, with their strong Hollywood connection, are aimed more at the set-top market, while the Sony/Phillips format is positioned as a computer CD-ROM upgrade. At this early stage, it's difficult to predict whether one or the other of these two heavyweights will emerge victorious from this all-out celebrity slugfest, or if there's a future of happy coexistence in store for us all.

Still, the possibilities raised by breaking through the storage barrier are truly boggling—SD CD-ROM drives begin to replace VCRs as high-quality video playback machines. The machines give the average consumer access to state-of-the-art interactive technology, which can deliver enormous interactive content in the highest resolution. Released from its shackles, CD-ROM is seen as an empowering media by artists from all walks of life. We all make buckets of money. Now, isn't that a fairy tale ending to our discussion on technology? At the very least, it should give us something to dream about as the technology makes its mass-market debut as early as Christmas 1996.

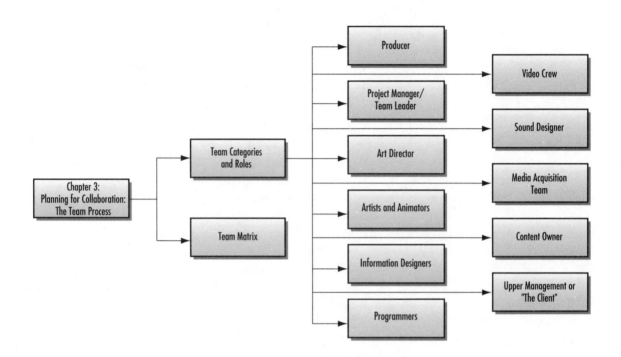

3

Planning for Collaboration: The Team Process

IT'S THE GREAT AMERICAN NOVEL PHENOMENON ALL OVER AGAIN. Anyone with a good idea, the right skills and training, appropriate equipment, and a high threshold for sleep deprivation can create a best-selling epic in print. So why is it not the same in interactive media? The "novel" is redefined as "computer software," but the principles are eminently familiar. Except for one: Interactive media requires a team. It is a decidedly unindividualistic endeavor.

It wasn't always this way. In the earliest days, a solitary hard-working individual with HyperCard could create some serious interactive media. Many teachers and professors in high schools and universities did just that. Robert Winter is probably the most famous. He created a series of music appreciation "stacks" in HyperCard, and through collaboration with The Voyager Company and later Microsoft, these CD-ROMs have become classics as brainy-yet-accessible education titles for the masses.

Today, however, the technology has gotten sophisticated enough—and the competition sufficiently fierce—that unless you are Joe Sparks, the single-minded genius behind Pop Rocket's interactive rock 'n' roll CD, *Total Distortion*, you're going to need a decent-sized team to get up and running to create your interactive media masterpiece. Even the aforementioned Sparks has a small team working in his garage.

Who are the team members you'll need to create a interactive media project? How do they relate to each other? What can you do to define their roles early on so that by the end of your project, everyone is still speaking to one another?

■ Team Categories and Roles

Whether you're hard at work on an interactive movie two years in the making or a small training project due in six weeks, there are always the same basic "categories" of responsibilities that need to get done in a project. For smaller, quicker projects, jobs are often combined. The writer doubles as the Producer and maybe even the graphic artist. The sound person also shoots video and does a little Lingo programming on the side. The same doubling up of roles holds in smaller companies—especially start-ups, where a clear corporate deliniation of responsibilities is nearly anachronistic. But the categories of the people you want on your team remain the same. They are

- Producer
- Project Manager/Team Leader
- Art Director
- Artists and Animators
- Information Designers (Writers)
- Programmers
- Video Crew
- Sound Designer
- Media Acquisition Team

- Content Owner

- Upper Management or "The Client"

Producer

The Producer is the big cheese, the head of the team, and the person responsible for balancing overall vision with technical and content considerations. Good Producers are sticky like glue—they hold everything together. If you asked me to describe my role as Producer in past projects in 25 words or less, I'd probably say the Producer is the person who takes a project from conception on through implementation and marketing. In some cases, a Producer comes up with the idea him- or herself and sells it (internally or externally); in other cases, some basic project parameters are given to the Producer, who then fleshes things out.

Most teams have a single Producer at the helm, but in larger companies, there may be both Executive Producers and Line Producers (the term "line" probably comes from being on the "factory line"). In your organization, this may be worded as *Senior Producer* and *Producer*, or *Producer* and *Assistant/ Associate Producer*. However it's termed (I'll stick with the first way), the Executive Producer will handle high concept, strategy, and business aspects of a product or product line, while the Line Producer covers day-to-day project management.

The Executive Producer leads the way in the early design meetings, ably complemented by the Line Producer, who consolidates the results of brainstorming sessions into a *Functional Specification*—the document that serves as the real blueprint for a project (more on this in Chapter 4). Producers of both ilk take a leading role in look and feel as well as interface issues. In general, the Executive Producer tries to create the overall product vision, while the Line Producer tries to maintain that vision.

Beyond vision and design, the Executive Producer assembles the design and development team, leveraging his or her knowledge of both internal and external resources. If a proposal needs to be written (or funded) to get things going, the Executive Producer is first in line. The Executive Producer also negotiates contracts (with a little help from the lawyers), sets budgets, and initiates timelines. Once the everything is in place, the Executive Producer continues in a less active role, attending weekly status meetings, approving milestones, maintaining relationships with third-party developers, and making the hard calls of when to slip (a deadline) and when to drop features.

The Line Producer is charged with serving as the down-in-the-trenches traffic manager, communicating with the wide variety of talents needed to put together a interactive media project. Whether that means coordinating to get sound files to the Team Leader, managing outside audio and video contractors, or getting scripts and content approved, the Producer is in the thick of it. See the section "Team Matrix" at the end of this chapter for a more detailed look at the intricate interrelationships between team members, and you'll see that the Producer touches everyone.

Once a title is full swing into production, the Line Producer's role shifts to coordinating with the marketing and PR people. This aspect of the job varies, depending on whether the company the Producer works for is a publisher or a developer. Good Producers, however, are at least consulted on how the packaging and documentation should appear. They need to get screen shots out to the appropriate departments. They will summarize the products' hottest features to help with the back-of-box and PR copy. They may even get to go on the road to sell the product to magazine editors. By this time, the product is probably ready for Quality Assurance checking, so the Line Producer puts the development hat back on and serves as liaison between the programmers, artists, and Quality Assurance staff.

All through the process, the Line Producer is responsible for keeping the Executive Producer in the know, and the latter, in turn, keeps upper management (or "the client") informed. Indeed, Producers of both types prepare budget amendments, argue for more money, make hard recommendations on resources and deadlines, and prepare many, many reports.

What should you look for in hiring a good Producer—Executive or otherwise? The best Producers are those Renaissance men and women who have done a little of everything and now want to focus on managing. It's crucial to be able to "talk the talk," to understand about palettes and class libraries from the development side, and about price protection and SKUs from the marketing and sales side.

If the Producer has ever used an authoring tool, he will understand the frustrations programmers have. If she can write, she'll quickly know when she's got a bad script. If he's spent time digitizing QuickTime videos, he'll empathize with an artist when she tells him the computer crashed overnight during a batch of compression. Naturally—and perhaps most importantly—good management and people skills are a must.

A solid Producer must also stay up to date on what's out there. He or she has got to know the competition well, and that means attendance at all the big trade shows as well as smaller society and Special Interest Group (SIG) meetings (local IICS meetings are a perfect place to start—see the Appendix for how to contact a chapter near you). And reading…there are enough interactive media magazines out these days to give the average Producer a lifetime of bathroom breaks!

Project Manager/Team Leader

Which title is used here depends partly on how you've structured your team. The way I like to do it is to have a "second in command" to the Producer; a person who takes on responsibility for organizing and whipping into shape those people who are hands-on creating the product. The Producer is naturally involved at this level, but because his or her responsibilities extend beyond the internal organization to external clients and more peripheral team members, there needs to be someone who is in the trenches with the artists and programmers on a daily basis. That's the Team Leader.

Team Leaders can come from a variety of backgrounds—art, programming, video—but they must be people with the hands-on experience to inspire trust and confidence in their teams. They can also be the hardest people to find—those staff members who have technical savvy and who are also good managers. Team Leaders divide up responsibilities—who's doing what and when. They monitor progress, keep the Producer informed, and answer endless technical questions. If a project is being developed in Director, the Team Leader may be the "assembly" person as well, who puts together a project's structure prior to calling in the Lingo programmer.

Within larger interactive media publishing companies, the Producer is sometimes focused into more of a marketing role, with the emphasis on the business aspects of a project—who'll buy it, how to extend it into a line, how to convince sales to sell it and PR to promote it (these kinds of Producers are often called Product Managers). In these cases, the Producer has less time for the day-to-day managing of the project, and the Team Leader transforms into a full-fledged Project Manager, with an almost equal responsibility for creative vision as the Producer. I say almost equal because it's still the Producer's butt on the line if things go awry. They shoot Producers; they only shift Project Managers to a different project. So the Producer must still maintain final veto power if consensus decisions can't be arrived at.

The term *Project Manager* in many companies has a technical ring to it. At Mindscape, we had both Producers and Project Managers. The latter were also the lead programmers on a project. They had broad responsibilities for the entire title and its development, because they were the only ones who understood the intricacies of the C++ code being developed. However, only the other programmers on the team reported directly to the Project Manager. Any outside writers, artists, or other resources reported either directly to the Producer or the Art Director. This type of arrangement is in some ways akin to a Producer/Director role on a film, where the Director has a more technical hands-on approach, and the Producer is in charge of keeping things on time and on budget.

Art Director

The Art Director sets the artistic standards for a project. Depending on the company arrangement, this person may also be the direct supervisor of the artists working on the team. On most teams, when the Production Phase kicks in, the Art Director, Team Leader, and Producer serve as a kind of three-way management team. Each has his or her own area of expertise, and the effect is one of checks and balances.

But even prior to that, the Art Director may find him or herself part of a different threesome, working with the Information Designer (see below) and Producer to hack out a Functional Specification. In this case, the Art Director takes on responsibility for honing a project's Interactive Design. The Art Director must have a keen sense of interface design and interactive media navigation.

The Art Director must also be someone who can do mundane things such as determining the number of colors available in a particular program's custom palette (a thankless job made ever more excruciating by the fact that the artists can see how good their work looks, and then they have to "dumb it down" to a lower number of palette colors to work on the average maximum 256-color machine). If the Art Director manages people, those skills should be part of his or her mix as well.

Artists and Animators

Interactive media projects are heavily dependent on art and animation; it's usually the most intensive—and most visible—element of a title. As a result, the artists you hire for your team will make or break the project. You can have a great idea, but if your artists are not talented, your project will be raked over the visual and visceral coals. Good artists don't come cheap. Splurge here. It will make a difference.

Artists and animators come in many flavors:

- 2D artists focus on two-dimensional images. They use programs like Aldus Freehand, Adobe Illustrator, and most importantly, Adobe Photoshop. They do the bread-and-butter work on a title.

- 3D artists are the most in demand these days. They use programs like StrataVision Studio, Macromedia's MacroModel, and Alias for the Silicon Graphics platform. The software of choice these days is clearly Autodesk's 3D Software—which is as much an animation tool as a 3D still generator. One recent report said that nearly 75 percent of all games using 3D backgrounds were created in 3D Studio. It runs only on the PC. The fastest machine around is the Silicon Graphics, but it's a bear to learn, and the improvements might not justify the expense.

- Animators are that special breed of artist who can make still images come to life. The hottest 3D animation is started and completed using computer software tools, but ironically, the best and most fluid character and human body animation is still done by hand. Images are drawn ink-on-paper, just like in the Disney cartoon studios, then scanned into the computer, where they are digitally inked and painted. This may seem like a chore, but the computer still can't create that Beauty and the Beast look the way a trained, and very highly paid, pen and paper animator can.

As you're searching for the best artists, also consider what your project's needs are. Will you be needing

1. Lots of classic interface design with logically arranged buttons in the appropriate spatial placement? If so, you might want to consider an artist who also has specific experience in interface design. Don't assume that every artist does. Interface design is a whole discipline unto itself; you can even take classes in it now. Some artists are good interface designers. In other cases, you might want to hire someone specifically with that title. Producers and Team Leaders should also have a very strong sense of what works and doesn't work in this most basic of design areas. Art Directors must be been born with good interface sense.

2. Plenty of backgrounds—either 2D or 3D—to create realistic-looking worlds? There are artists who love creating the elements in the back, and not the movable pieces in the front.

3. Tons of clickable objects? Then look for artists who are good with the detail work of creating, and probably later animating, small objects and pieces on screen.

Artists are also called to create prototypes and storyboards—both of which often start out on paper. Prototyping, which is discussed in Chapter 4, can be done both on the computer and quickly on paper with a few sketches. Storyboards—which lay out what's going to happen in an animation or art sequence—are almost always done on paper. Later, they're either redrawn or, occasionally, scanned into the computer. In both cases, you'll want artists who are proficient both on and off the computer.

Information Designers

Information Design is a term that has evolved from Instructional Design. The latter refers to the process of structuring instructional information into a coherently designed program that makes sense from a pedagogic point of view. Instructional Designers are masters of arranging information hierarchically, so it can clearly be seen what information needs to be learned before the next chunk of information is presented. Instructional Designers play truly key roles in educational projects, often serving multiple roles of design, research, and writing.

If a project is not inherently educational, though, I like to use the term *Information Designer*, one that I first heard from colleague Ann Marie Buddrus, who is now with Pacific Bell developing CD-ROM and online-based interactive magazines. Information Designers essentially do the same thing as Instructional Designers—they take an unstructured morass of information and try to make sense of it so it can be used in a interactive media program. The process usually begins with research and, depending on an Information Designer's particular skills, concludes with writing the scripts for the project itself. That's why the term *Information Designer* is often used as a synonym for *writer*.

This final step is a tricky one, though, because good researchers sometimes, but not always, make good writers. You should carefully determine your writing needs. Do you need someone who can write

- Factual but lively copy?

- Over-the-top humor?

- Dialogue for on-screen video characters?

- Short animated cartoon bytes?

- Technical material for a Help section, User Guide, or manual?

Identifying the right person is crucial, and it's one of the biggest determinants of whether your project will really sing or stink. How many CD-ROMs have you either seen or read about where the acting, dialogue, or narration was criticized as bad, boring, or hokey? Too many, I suspect. Acting or narrated delivery can certainly be at fault, but it all starts with the script, and if the script sucks, there's little even Harrison Ford can do to add the ol' Indiana Jones spark to it.

I have played the roles of the writer and the person hiring the writer. With a B.A. in Creative Writing, I took my pen to paper and wrote six different mini-interactive role-playing movies for InfoUse's *Take Control: How to Stay Healthy and Safe from HIV and AIDS.* The program was designed for people with mental retardation, a population sorely at risk from contracting HIV through both sex and intravenous drug use. The writing job called for scripts that were simple and clear, while at the same time not condescending. I'm proud of the job I did—except in one place. I tried a little humor.

In one of the vignettes, "Bill and Barbara" want to have sex together for the first time. But they're all out of condoms. It's Barbara's house and she's sure she has an extra box lying around somewhere. They decide to search for the missing prophylactics, and turn the house upside down, looking in drawers, under chairs, in the fridge, even in the dog's supper dish. All of this is set to a slapstick soundtrack reminiscent of the Benny Hill show. They finally find the condoms in the bathroom medicine cabinet.

I don't know what I was thinking when I wrote this monstrosity. I'm not sure what my bosses were dreaming of when they let me convince them to include it. All I can say is, I was younger and more foolish back then. More recently, I had a writer create some very tongue-in-cheek Groucho Marx-influenced stand-up comedy bits. I'll never know how they would have played on the "small screen," because my bosses this time decided to play it safe and profitable by rejecting it.

The bottom line here is this: You may need a number of people to fill the roles of Information Designer/Researcher/Writer. And you very likely will need a trained Editor to supervise, or at least look over, the work turned in. The Editor may even wind up doing substantial rewrites on work. Never underestimate the value of a second pair of eyes. All this undoubtedly will influence how you structure your project. There are two basic options:

1. You could have your Information Designers/Writers and Editor on-staff as part of an in-house department. This approach means that you'll want to use the in-house staff to the max, doing double duty. These people will design, research, and write the scripts, and become true content experts with a great degree of ownership in the title. For content-heavy edutainment and infotainment titles, this is a good way to go. But you run into the problem that at the end of the writing phase of the project, your Info Design staff may be stuck with little to do unless you have another project waiting in the pipeline. You may even need to lay people off, hopefully only temporarily. It happens.

2. You could hire your Information Designers/Writers and Editor as freelancers whenever you need them in the process. This gives you a lot more flexibility in picking and choosing the best people for the right job, but you may get stuck needing someone when no one is available. Information Designers, in this case, would come in early on, then be replaced a bit later by scriptwriters, who would follow a finished functional specification and plug in scripts when they're called for. For titles that are not information heavy but require lighter writing (such as Living Books click-and-get-a-joke type products), this is a smart direction to take. Freelancers often work out of their homes—they may not even be in the same state or country as you.

By the way, make sure your writer—whether in or out of house—understands that writing for interactive media is not the same as writing for the printed page. Narration that must be spoken is entirely different than a research paper. See the section in Chapter 8 on "The 30 Second Rule" for some guidelines on how to write in short information sound bytes.

On a purely semantic note, be careful not to confuse scriptwriting as part of the Information Design function with writing scripts for authoring systems. There can be confusion because the English-language commands programmers use are often called "scripts," too. Want ads, for example, may say they're looking for a "scriptwriter." They're not looking for an English major who can write for interactive media. They're probably looking for a technical person or someone who knows Macromedia Director.

Technical Writers are a very different beast from the Information Designer/ Writer. Tech Writers are the magicians who can take one look at your product and create the manual or User Guide that will accompany your disc in its retail packaging. Technical Writers are usually freelancers, though not always—it depends on how many simultaneous projects you have in development. Perhaps the clearest difference is that their job starts near the end of the process, not up front in the design phase. Your product must be in a stable enough state to be documented.

Hopefully, the Technical Writer's job is short and sweet. The longer the manual required, the harder your title probably is to use. The best titles are so intuitive they don't need a manual at all. Instead, a QuickStart Card is included, providing a modest dose of help for the totally clueless, as well as pertinent information such as who created the program (yeah, yeah, the credits); what to do and who to call if the program doesn't run on your hardware configuration; and what will happen to you if you try to copy the program and make illegal discs for others.

More and more technical documentation is moving toward online help. The same skills for the Technical Writer are required—an attention to detail, the ability to ask even the stupidest of questions, and a strong sense of organization. But there are some extra software tools you'll need to learn, such as the frighteningly titled RoboHelp, which is used to create Microsoft Help online documentation. Knowing a program like this can make a Tech Writer that much more valuable.

Programmers

Go out and find the biggest nerd in town—that's who you want on your programming team. That wasn't very kind, and it's the kind of broad generalization that's undoubtedly unfair. So some top programming talent can be a little antisocial. That's okay. You're not hiring them for the gregariousness. You're hiring them because they know if/then statements better than they can recite their own name. Next to your Artists, Programmers are the people who make your program work as well as it looks. Bad coders can make the best screens intolerable.

However, it's not always their fault.

Verbum Interactive was an early attempt at an interactive magazine. An ambitious two-CD set from the publishers of the print magazine *Verbum*, the CD-ROM had really quite good information and entertainment value. But the thing was so slow that it took literally minutes to go from screen to screen or section to section. Now, it's true that it was far ahead of its time, released in 1990 and optimized for slow as molasses single-speed CD-ROM drives. And it was based on an early version of Director. But if that product had been custom-coded by the hottest C++ programmer in San Diego (*Verbum*'s headquarters), maybe, just *maybe* I could have shown it to somebody. The truth is, every time I set up a demo of that product, people went for a cigarette break before the opening animation could load.

Programmers have a weird sense of time. It's hard to pin them down to a schedule, and you're probably better off if you don't try. What's the point of insisting that they show up every morning at 9 a.m.? They're the type who will be in the office until 2 or 3 a.m. every night when crunch time arrives. At Mindscape, there were sleeping bags and cots in the aisles. They'll expect their comp time afterwards, of course, but they will have earned it (and they know it). Then they'll lounge around reading the paper, eating pizza, and learning new software tricks until the next programming crunch.

Because interactive media development is divided into the custom code camp and the Director developers, there are two types of programmers you could and should be looking for:

1. Hard-core C++ programmers—that's the *lingua franca* of the interactive media programming world these days. There are a few people coding in Pascal, and Visual Basic is growing in popularity, but for all intents and purposes, it's C++. The powerful extensions to authoring systems—such as XOBJECTS in Director—are usually written originally in C++ as well. Look for programmers with cross-platform experience, too. Just because you have the best Mac C++ coder in Multimedia Gulch doesn't mean he or she can do Windows without some background—there are big differences in the way the code calls the operating system and interacts with the variety of devices and drivers unique to each hardware configuration. Also ask potential hires about their experience in engine development. By building common elements and reusable code, you'll be one step ahead for the next time and won't be constantly reinventing the wheel.

2. Authoring system programmers—these types know how to write for their particular authoring system's scripting language. Not all authoring systems are extensible with scripting languages; those that consist solely of English-language commands and menu choices can be handled by less hard-core types or even artists turned scripters. But even

relatively simple languages, such as HyperTalk for HyperCard, require knowledge into nuance and structure. The best code is written by the best coders, whether of the hard-core or authoring system variety. Sorry, there's no easy (or cheap) way out of this one.

Video Crew

I've lumped together the many talented professionals who make up a video crew—partly because it's not so much a function of the interactive media process as it is traditional video recording. Basically, to create video to use in a interactive media title, you need to record it as you would any other video—direct to tape. Later on you can digitize it and play with it on the computer, but first, you need the traditional lights, camera, and action. So the team members who make up your video crew include the full range of pros—camera crew, director, producer, sound expert, lighting whiz, key grip, best boy, dandy dog…. It's a very rare company that has an in-house video production facility, so most of these team members are part of your "extended family."

Because there are so many computer-specific concerns to keep in mind on the video set, you're going to need a special computer person at the video shoot. This is particularly true if you're shooting blue-screen video to be overlaid on top of animated backgrounds. That's the process that makes it look like an actor is walking around on your computer screen. It's described in detail in Chapter 5. Your computer specialist will need to keep track of such blue-screen specialties as:

- Making sure the actor stays within the parameters of the "box" that defines his or her movements on the computer screen

- Operating the computer so that you can see the backgrounds you brought from your office on the studio's video monitors

- Constantly checking the quality of the blue-screen (or chroma) itself

When you're shooting video for interactive media delivery, there are considerations to keep in mind for sound, and you need a sound professional on the set who has experience in interactive media. Now, it's true that sound on the computer doesn't need the quality that it would on a hi-fi stereo. It's usually playing out of crappy speakers, or even the computer's built-in speaker (more often the case with Macintoshes). But you need a certain flat sound to start, one that doesn't go all over the place in terms of highs and lows. Shakespearean emoting is groovy for the Opera House, but the resulting sound distortion may be more than even the best in-house sound "sweetener" can handle.

Once the tape has arrived back home, you'll need an in-house video crew. This can be a dedicated video person or artist/animator(s) doing double duty. The reason this function can get away without a specifically trained video person is that the process at this point has little to do with video and a lot to do with computer software. Editing in Adobe Premiere (probably the most popular, affordable computer video editing software), for example, is more akin to the cut-and-paste functionality common to all computer applications these days than it is to entering SMPTE timecode in a professional video editing facility.

Sound Designer

We've just discussed the special requirements of sound people in the video recording facility. But back home at the ranch, you'll need an audio person with even more specialized skills. Because when animation fails and video sputters, it's sound that can save the day. In the hands of a skilled Sound Designer, a long animation with a boring narration can be spruced up by a dynamic soundtrack with sound effects and music.

There are really two types of functions the Sound Designer handles:

1. Technical duties—this includes recording narrations and digitizing them, then linking them with animations or videos using computer software tools.

2. Creative duties—this is where the fun is. Sure, recording a good quality narration is creative, but the best Sound Designers are also crack composers and sound effects generators. They operate as if they're scoring a movie. Once you've got enough of the animation or video assembled, the Sound Designer watches and begins creating for the specific scenes in front of him or her.

In both cases, Sound Designers are working with computers. Occasionally, they may bring in a real guitarist for some acoustic magic, but most of their work is creating computer synthesized music and sound effects. No, it doesn't sound like early Pink Floyd Moog synthesizers. But since audio for interactive media titles ends up entirely digital, it's normal to start out creating it in digital format. MIDI (Musical Instrument Digital Interface) is the language of choice for sound pros. WAV and AIFF are the most common file formats when MIDI isn't available. See Chapter 5 for more details.

A Sound Designer is someone who can listen for the best possible sound under the worst possible conditions. They'll probably compose their music in MIDI and play it back on nice big speakers. Sounds great. But by the time it's compressed and squeezed down into a format that will play decently on the largest number of machines out there, it sounds squooshed and hissy. So, the sound person plays around a lot with EQ, and different software methods for removing the noise. Ironically, in one company I've worked in, our sound guy had his own built-in Dolby™ system, but it had nothing to do with his hardware. He wore hearing aids in both ears, and he never heard the hiss the rest of us did. But he was one of the most brilliant composers I've ever met.

Audio professionals and Sound Designers can be in house or out of house. You always need someone to integrate the audio in your project in house, but as with the dedicated in-house video person, an artist, animator, programmer, or even temp can handle some of the more menial technical conversion tasks. The musical and effects composition person is often a freelancer. The advantage here is the same as with scriptwriters—you have a bigger pool to choose from, but the people you want may not be available when you want them. If you have an in-house person, you'll have to build him or her a nice sound studio, probably with a soundproof booth (unless you'll be doing only your narrations out of house). That can add up to tens of thousands of dollars in outlay and overhead.

Whichever you choose—treat your Sound Designer well. A Sound Designer can be your most important asset. Think about the movies or TV. What if they took away the soundtrack—the music, the effects, even the ambient sounds? Here's a better test: Imagine the *Starship Enterprise* without the background sound—slight "whoomping," as I call it. It would be dead as an MIS department in a Muzak-infested office building. That should make you appreciate the value of sound—and the need to find the best talent to join your team.

Media Acquisition Team

Unless you're creating everything in your program from scratch, you'll need someone (or a whole team) to acquire media for you. The Media Acquisition Team, like many of the categories described above, can be in or out of house. If you only need the occasional image or sound, it isn't worth putting someone on staff. And there are plenty of organizations, like Jill Alof's Total Clearance in Tiburon, California, that will be more than happy to take on the job for you. If, however, you're creating image- or music-heavy programs with lots of pictures, videos, or sound to be acquired, combined with a workload with plenty of simultaneous title development, hire the best and put them to work.

Your Media Acquisition people don't have to be lawyers. They just need to be sticklers for the law—to advise you when you need the rights to something and when you don't. And then they need to do all the legwork—the boring paperwork and phone calls—of tracking down and acquiring media.

Detective types, on the other hand, will love a good hunt for the perfect image of a pre-Columbian Aztec temple.

The Media Acquisition Team, as I'm defining it here, are really the people who "acquire" the media, not the group that decides what type of images, videos, and sounds need to be acquired. That's the job of the Producer or Team Leader—to work in conjunction with the Artists and Information Designers to come up with lists and preferences. Those lists are then forwarded to the Media Acquisition Team, who work with archival image houses and clip media libraries to find the most appropriate media, transfer slide material to PhotoCD and get it all sent back to your office. That media is then examined carefully and, once the team has decided what they'll be using, the Media Acquisition Team starts writing letters and getting checks cut. Team members in your Media Acquisition department must be painstakingly detail-oriented and thorough.

Content Owner

As I've said before, probably the most unique, artistic uses of interactive media involve creating entirely new stories, plot lines, and art. But it's still far more common to be using an existing resource and "adapting" or "repurposing" it to the interactive media format—hopefully following the criteria set forth in Chapter 1. Existing content almost always has an owner. I'm not talking about individual photos or videos licensed from an archive house—that's the job of the Media Acquisitions Team. The Content Owner is that person (or corporation) who owns the original resource—the book, encyclopedia, film—that you are using as your base.

Sometimes you get a savvy, sophisticated, hip-but-not-overbearing Content Owner who knows how to work in a interactive media context. More often than not, though, the owner of that very valuable content doesn't know diddly about what you're doing. The Content Owner will probably be very interested in what you're doing and in learning more, but in the end the Owner never really gets it. That can lead to some uncomfortable moments that with tact, patience, and skillful manipulation, you can get around.

I'm not saying you have to mislead and trick your Content Owner. Just massage the ego. Let's say you're doing a interactive media dictionary and the Content Owner—the original print dictionary publisher—doesn't want you to change a word. Well, okay. You have to assume the reason you're paying that Content Owner lots of money or a good chunk of the royalty stream is they have something you want.

But then they want you to include all those ugly line drawings created for the dictionary in 1932 exactly as they are. But they look terrible on CD-ROM. You want to colorize them, push the pixels a little. So what are you going to do? March right into Mr. Big Dictionary Mogul's office and demand? Not. The fine art of diplomacy is a key skill to have here.

Content Owners are not always malicious. They may range from benign to intellectually impoverished. You've got to laugh. You also have to know when to fish or cut bait. There are times—and I've been through them—where you actually have to cancel a project because the owner of content won't let you do what you feel in your heart of hearts must be done to create a saleable product. Don't cringe, don't mope. Know that you've done the right thing—for the good of your project and of all interactive media!

Content Owners are not the same as Content Experts. The latter is someone who you hire to become a part of your Information Design team. Content Experts are simply people who know a lot about a particular subject. They're usually paid hourly.

Upper Management or "The Client"

The final team member you must consider when developing a smooth-flowing product is your boss. Who the boss is depends on the structure of your organization. If you work for a big company and are creating an interactive media project for sales reps, a presentation, or even for commercial sale, your boss is Upper Management. Most people find Upper Management annoying. They're usually not concerned with reaching the same artistic heights as you are. The bottom line—which you should be trying your best to adhere to anyway—is of utmost importance to Upper Management, who in turn are responsible to their bosses—very often the shareholders of the company.

Clients are who you report to if you're an independent developer creating product for a specific someone. Here, you may be Upper Management yourself, but you're still beholden to Mr. Coca Cola, who's paying you to create Coke Kiosks; or Mr. Motorola, who wants a prototype for an interactive cellular phone interface in time to show at the next Consumer Electronics Show. Both clients and Upper Management share a basic similarity with Content Owners (who can double as clients or Upper Management)—they're not usually interactive media experts, but they hold the purse strings. Your role is to keep them informed, convince them that your approach will ultimately be better, and know when to be politically expedient and shut up and do what they say (within reason).

Here's an example of a particularly politically sensitive client. When creating InfoUse's *Take Control* videodisc title to help people with mental retardation stay away from AIDS and HIV, we did our research carefully and determined that we needed to be pretty graphically explicit. This particular population didn't understand vagaries or abstractions of any kind.

The client in this case, however, was the U. S. Government around the time of the raging controversies in the nearby National Endowment for the

Arts. The script, with its call for actual demonstrations of safe sex, not to mention a glossary of sexual slang terms—so that our population would actually understand what was being talked about—was so heavily edited that content areas we felt were crucial got nixed. In the end, our program taught its users everything you need to know about safe sex, including how to buy a condom, but stopped just short of what to do with that condom.

■ Team Matrix

Each team member may have his or her role, but getting everyone to talk to each other at the right time requires careful planning as well. The web of interlinking relationships between team members can be quite bewildering, but once unraveled, it makes sense. Figure 3.1 shows how it works in the average team.

Figure 3.1

This matrix shows how your Team Members are all interconnected.

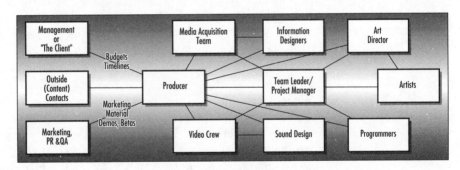

In this matrix, you'll find your two main players in dead center: the Producer and the Team Leader. Arranged around the Team Leader are the roles played by Media Acquisition, Information Design, Art and Art Direction, Video Production, Sound Design, and Programming. The Team Leader receives input from each of these players, since it's the Team Leader who has hands-on responsibility for getting the project completed.

The Producer is slightly off to the side in this matrix. The Producer provides his or her guidance and vision to each of the players, who then provide their input to the Team Leader. The only team members the Producer is not directly involved with are the Artists, who are managed directly by either the Team Leader or the Art Director—notice the line connecting Artists to Art Director. The Producer arranges for the video crew to get going, and gives his or her input to the Information Designers, Programmers, and Sound Designer. The relationship with the Art Director is probably stronger and more direct than this matrix shows.

There are some additional lines drawn between functions. Media Acquisition and Information Designer have a direct connection because the initial lists of what images, videos, or sounds may need to be acquired usually come from those team members closest to the content—the writers. Similarly, the Video Crew and Sound Designer have a close working relationship because there is sound in video that needs to be sweetened and synched up. And of course, the Art Director and the Artists, as mentioned early, are naturally connected, usually in a supervisory fashion.

On the other side of the matrix, the Producer maintains contact with the "outside world." The Producer, not the Team Leader, deals with budgets and timelines and presents timely information to management, who may be either internal or an external client. If there is an outside contact for content, it is the Producer who manages that relationship, although the Information Designers will have plenty of input as well. Finally, the Producer is the person responsible for getting information to Marketing, Public Relations, and Quality Assurance (although the Team Leader—since he or she knows the product so well—may take on more of the connective role to Quality Assurance than the Producer does, depending on the project and size of the company). If you've hired an external Quality Assurance firm, though, then it's the Producer's responsibility to serve as go-between.

This matrix is meant to give an idea of how teams can be structured, but it should also be apparent that the team process is exceedingly dynamic. While the Producer has the final say, when you have so many interconnecting lines, it's difficult to get anything done without building consensus. Some managers prefer to rule with a hard hand while barking orders. I have always felt that getting everyone to buy into a concept, to feel that they have ownership over an idea or implementation—even if it takes longer to get to that consensus—is a more efficient way to keep teams functioning and happy.

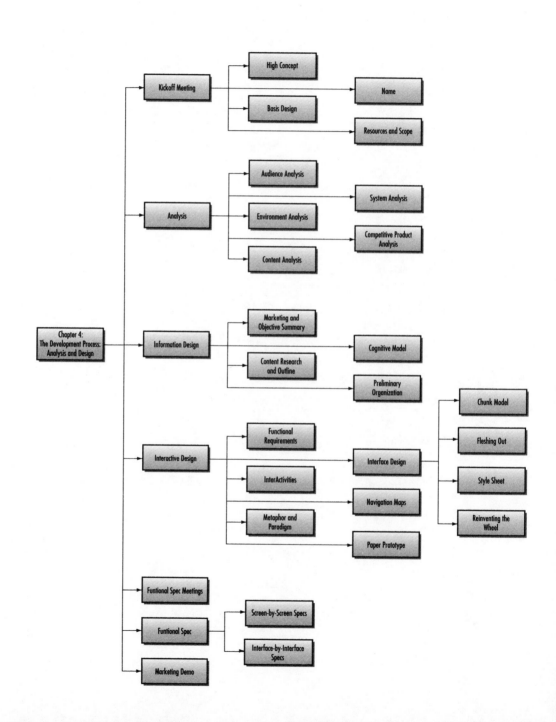

C H A P T E R 4

The Development Process: Analysis and Design

Okay, kids, it's time to rock and roll. You've got the band together. And you've assembled the right instruments. You've brought in a killer song writer. But does she know how to put her thoughts down on paper in a way that everyone can understand? And what kind of music are you going to play, anyway? Can a '90s band really do '50s covers and still be a hit with the prepubescent demographic you've targeted? Maybe you need to cut a demo tape.... Nah, just do it—if you're good, everything will come together.

If anything is clear so far, it's that nothing just comes together. Indeed, here's another tip to clip and post on your fridge:

The word *just* should be banned from the interactive media lexicon.

Careful planning and design is what this book is all about, and there's no place where planning is more crucial than the development process. This process is shown in the interlinking chart that spins its weblike structure in Figure 4.1. In this chart, there are eight distinct "phases" of the interactive media development process. The first four are discussed in this chapter under the broad heading of Analysis and Design. The second four phases are covered in Chapter 5, "Production, Implementation, and Publishing."

Let's take a closer look at the chart. The eight phases are

1. Kickoff meeting

2. Analysis

3. Information Design

4. Interactive Design

5. Pre-Production

6. Production

7. Implementation/Evaluation/Revision

8. Publishing

The chart is read top to bottom, and tasks in the development process should occur more or less in that order. Within a phase, however, tasks can occur in any order, including at the same time. All tasks from a particular phase should be completed before the next phase begins. There are some exceptions, of course, to the rules.

Notice the shaded box connecting Information Design and Interactive Design. In the middle of these two phases is a box labeled *Functional Spec Meetings*. This indicates that the phases of Information and Interactive Design are highly iterative. Information Design necessarily kicks in before Interactive Design, but both must be complete in order to hold definitive Functional Spec meetings.

The Functional Specification that comes out of these meetings, by the way, will be referred to repeatedly throughout this section. It's probably the most important document you'll create during project planning and design. It is, quite literally, the specification that defines how your project will function—what will be in it, how will it look, feel, taste, smell.

Figure 4.1

This Interactive Media Design and Development Methodology has eight distinct phases and dozens of individual tasks.

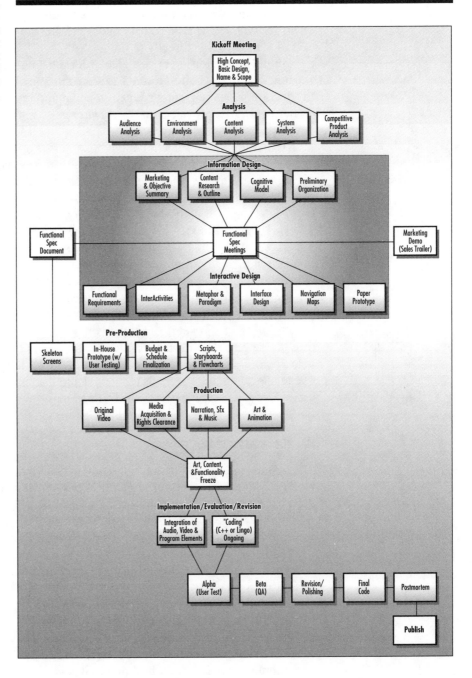

Coming out of the Functional Spec meetings you'll see two boxes that don't really have a home—*Marketing Demo* and *Functional Spec Document*. The Marketing Demo sort of goes nowhere, while the Functional Spec document leads directly to the next phase—Pre-Production. From here until Production, a very specific order must be followed. Only when Scripts, Storyboards, and Flowcharts are complete at the end of the Pre-Production phase can true Production begin and restore the any-order-is-okay pattern that prevails most everywhere else in the interactive media development methodology.

Art, Content, and Functionality Freeze serves as a midway point between Production and Implementation/Evaluation/Revision. It's connected as much to one as the other. Finally, as Implementation is kicking into high gear, there are four final tasks that must go in order—they're milestones, really—culminating in Publishing and its accompanying Postmortem.

This chart is a model scenario. If you followed it exactly as it is presented, you'd probably win awards for your stellar management skills—not to mention the undying gratitude from your staff for adherence to a reasonable development schedule mixing hard work with ample time for a full social life. And I could retire on sales of this chapter alone.

But this is the real world, and nothing ever goes according to plan. You have to try, but don't get frustrated if you have to begin Pre-Production before you've finished Information Design. Or you find yourself finalizing a demo before you've analyzed your audience. That's the way it goes in interactive media when there are bills to be paid and demanding clients to be placated. But you at least have to start with a plan.

■ Kickoff Meeting

Much of the interactive media development process is the same as it would be for any development effort, regardless of the media. Every product requires some up-front planning and analysis, then moves into production and finally involves getting the sucker out the door. And every product begins with some kind of a kickoff. Often, it's the boss and a client, or a few employees, coming up with an idea over beer and stale pretzels—the pizza sessions described in the Introduction. A more formal kickoff meeting, though, is a great way to get everyone on your team—not just the inner circle—on the same page before the process begins.

Kickoff meetings range from brainstorming encounters to presentations of hard work already completed. They should include everyone who's going to be on the team, even if a particular person's role won't become active until months later. I believe that communication must flow openly on a team (and in a company). Trickling out information on a "need to know" basis might work in spy films and the military, but it breeds distrust and rebellion in a team of creative interactive media professionals.

Indeed, the more team members feel there is information being withheld from them (even for legitimate reasons), the less they will feel like this is "their" product. You want team members to believe in your vision as much as you. So, get them involved. Bring them up to date from the very first moment, and you'll set a tone of cooperation that will last your entire project.

Kickoff meetings should be inspirational. But there are four basic pieces of information that must be imparted and defined, whether in cheerleading fashion or something slightly more sedate.

High Concept

What is this thing that we're about to make? Where did the idea come from? Why does someone think it's a good idea, one that will sell? The High Concept doesn't have to be specific. It can be as simple as "We want to create the ultimate nonviolent exploratory game that teaches quantum physics through puzzles and rock and roll." Or you can act like a Hollywood producer straight out of Robert Altman's *The Player*, defining your product by comparing it with existing properties—"It will be a cross between *The Lion King* CD-ROM and *Mortal Kombat II*—something for the whole family." What happens after that is what the development process is all about.

Basic Design

Again, we're talking real preliminary here. If you knew what your specific design was all about, you wouldn't need the ten tasks in Information and Interactive Design. But it doesn't hurt to have some general parameters:

* Will your program be a complete interactive environment or have a control bar? (You don't have define how the control bar looks or even what controls are in it at this point.)

* Will users play a lot and learn a bit, or learn a bunch and play a smidge?

* Can you assign any adjectives to your title's design? Would you describe it as "fun," "scholarly," "offbeat," "beautiful," or "thorough"? Or any combination of the above?

Name

What are you going to call your program? Your marketing and sales people will love it if you can lock down the final name early on, because they can then begin to build early excitement for the program. The worst thing for the sales force is when they hype the heck out of a product and then the name gets changed, so they have to explain to all their buyers and distributors that no, this isn't a new product, it's the same product with a new name, and no, I don't know who's crazy idea this was....

If you're really on the fence about what to call your program, or you're worried that the competition will catch wind of your killer app and try to cut you off at the pass, you can use a code name. Hardware manufacturers routinely do it. This can be as outlandish as labeling a new computer after a well-known scientist (and subsequently getting sued by that very same figure—go ask Apple about their infamous "Carl Sagan" code-named machine) or as simple as using the name of the grant received (InfoUse's *Take Control* was originally known as *AIDS2* because it followed up on the AIDS1 prototype that was funded by the U.S. Department of Health and Human Services).

Resources and Scope

Since you have the whole team together at your kickoff meeting—including the Producer and maybe even his or her boss—you have a great opportunity to determine the scope of your project:

- How big should it be?

- How long should it take?

- What's the maximum it should cost?

- How many people can we dedicate to the project?

- Should it be like any other projects your company, or other companies, have created?

An interactive media project, almost by definition, will take on a life of its own as analysis and design move forward, and certainly it's inadvisable to try to set a firm drop-dead deadline before the Functional Spec is hammered out. But there are general parameters everyone on the team should know clearly—from the top. If you have to ship by Christmas or else the company is out of business, that's going to affect how much content you can cram in. Similarly, there is usually a tight cap on the amount of money you can spend before you're tapping into the private reserve.

There is probably also an upper limit on the number of people you can throw at a project—they may be limited by your physical space or, if you're using freelancers, the availability of certain types of potential team members in your geographic location. And while you haven't conducted a competitive analysis yet, there may be existing products you know off the top of your head that can help guide how big you think your title should be—you can say you want your title to have as many screens as *Myst*, or slightly more entries than *Encarta*.

At the end of the kickoff meeting, don't be sloppy—write up the notes and disseminate them. You'll want to do this for nearly every task or phase.

■ Analysis

In the second phase of project development, you'll be analyzing five discrete areas. When you're done, you should have a pretty good idea of who's going to use your program, under what conditions, on what machine, what they're going to learn, and what they're going to compare your program to.

Audience Analysis

Audience Analysis is probably your most important analysis task—carefully studying who's going to buy or use your product. If you're creating an instructional program for in-house training, you're going to want to ask a lot of questions about your learner's aptitudes, educational background, and why they're interested in—or being forced to participate in—the training. Your information-gathering techniques can range from informally questioning employees at their workstations to developing a written questionnaire that you have filled out, scored, and statistically ranked. There are six basic types of questions you'll be asking:

1. Questions to identify the basic nature of the problem and subsequent need for interactive media training

2. Questions to determine priorities and get at specifics within the problem

3. Questions that require demonstration of skills or knowledge by your learners—so you know exactly what you have to include in your program

4. Questions to determine your learner feelings or motivation—do they care about learning or are they indifferent, belligerent, or worse?

5. Questions to identify causes or to look into the background of the problem—where did it come from? Are there internal politics you should be deft at sidestepping?

6. Questions to procure demographic data—how old are your learners, what do they do in their free time, how educated are they?

For consumer titles, the questions are basically the same, although the focus is more on what unexpressed need (the "problem" above) will be satisfied by spending $25, $50, or more on this title. In addition to the six questions, ask questions specifically about the buyer of your program:

1. Will a parent be buying this for a child?

2. Will a teenage boy be buying it himself to neutralize unacknowledged sexual frustrations?

3. Will the buyer be a baby boomer trying to recapture and relive his or her youth?

Here's another difference about consumer titles: Your buying public isn't as captive an audience as factory line workers or programmers in the MIS department. Hiring an established market research firm to conduct focus tests will give you your most conclusive answers—and the ones the client can't refute if the results don't jive with his or her preconceived notions. But, as pointed out in Chapter 1, you can also go on your gut—visiting stores and talking to friends, colleagues, and potential consumers.

Once you've done your analysis, write it up, then summarize it in three succinct categories:

1. Primary users—your main buying or learning public (for example, children aged 7–11 who want to learn more about frog anatomy)

2. Secondary users—those people who may also be interested, but who you didn't really target (older children 11 and up who really dig the interactive lab dissection feature)

3. Tertiary users—peripheral users who stumble across the program and buy it on a whim or use someone else's copy (the parent who bought the title for his kid in the first place who enjoys the *Sports Illustrated* model you hired to perform the example dissections)

Audience analysis can be as formal or informal as you feel you need it to be in order to gain a solid understanding of who your users are. But please don't skip this phase. Don't assume that because your proposed product interests everyone in the office—or has been the pet project of the client for the last 10 years—that it will grab a sufficient core of real consumers on the street. Too many companies have gotten burned by similar interactive hubris.

Environment Analysis

Where will your product be used, and under what conditions? What does the particular space look like? There are plenty of options:

• In a learning laboratory at the office or in school

• On the user's desk—also at the office or in school

• At home in a private study

• At home in a public place, perhaps connected to the television

• On the "street," say for a public kiosk

- In the air—interactive in-flight entertainment is coming, you know

For each location, write down the features that appear important to you. These might include the following:

- How is the noise level where the product is to be used? Are there any visual distractions in the vicinity? (This one's hard to determine for a consumer product to be used in a multitude of private homes, but give it a whirl anyway.)

- How many users will be involved at once—one on one, groups gathered around the computer?

- When will the product be used—morning, evening, anytime?

- How long will the product be usable before either galloping technology makes it seem obsolete or the information becomes out of date or irrelevant?

- Does the product need "managing"? In a public setting, this might mean maintenance and cleaning. At home, think about software updates as new material or bug fixes become available.

All of this is important in analyzing the product environment. Write it down and summarize.

Content Analysis

Don't confuse Content Analysis with Content Research leading to the creation of a Cognitive Model and Preliminary Outline in the Information Design phase. Content Analysis is the systematic study of what's out there for you to use. If you're going to create a program on medical breakthroughs, what sources can you draw on for your information? Are there profiles of individuals, or does the literature focus only on the technology discovered?

How about media? That's part of your content. If you're creating a program about the Civil War, check into what your image sources are—if it turns out there are only three paintings in existence depicting the entire battle you're planning to focus on, you're either going to have to make up media yourself from scratch or consider a different topic to take to interactive media. After determining who your interested audience is, Content Analysis is the single most crucial step that will tell you if you can actually pull off what you propose to do.

If you have a Subject Matter Expert lined up already, you can call on this person during the analysis task. In fact, the SME may be the person who writes up your analysis. The point is—you want to know what you're getting yourself into before you commit time and resources to do serious Content Research. At that point, you'll return to the sources you identified during

Content Analysis and get way more in depth. By the way, the Internet and in particular the World Wide Web have made doing this kind of preliminary analysis a whole lot easier. You still have to go the library eventually, but you can browse card catalogs all over the world without ever getting up from your chair.

System Analysis

In classic Instructional Design, the designer is not supposed to specify what system will be used to deliver the program until after the needs have been completely analyzed. If the enormous informational title you're planning on *Fire Truck—A Worldwide Companion* turns out to yield only three major truck manufacturers, you might be able to fit your program on a few floppies rather than CD-ROM. But in the real world, decisions about what systems to use are often based on more practical considerations:

- Your company has expertise in Mac and PC development and none whatsoever in Nintendo cartridge production. You're probably not going to develop Mario games, are you?

- Sigma Designs has just given you a half a million dollar advance to develop a version of your title to run on their RealMagic MPEG board. I bet you're going to be developing an MPEG version real soon.

- Your development team insists that they can't create a decent title unless the minimum specs are at least 24MB, a quad-speed drive, and a Pentium processor. Your sales force tells you they can bundle 2 million copies if it will run on a 4MB 486DX33. Your expectations just got lowered.

- You work for Microsoft and were considering developing your next title to come out first for Macintosh, with a Windows 95 version not planned until three quarters later. Chairman Bill is not pleased.

Suffice it to say that, usually, interactive media developers have a pretty good idea of their target system or systems before they ever get started. That may limit creativity and certain ideal tenets of analysis and design, but that's the way it is. Note that related to considerations of System Analysis are the capabilities of your team. If you're planning on doing an animation-heavy title, but your team is weak and couldn't draw a body in motion if their life depended on it, you probably shouldn't go forward with the original concept unmodified.

Competitive Product Analysis

You've looked at your audience, the conditions, and the machine—that's your internal analysis. Now go external—look at your competitors. Find out what they've done and how they've done. This is as true for consumer titles as it is for corporate training applications—if there's an off-the-shelf piece of courseware available at a tenth the price you were planning to spend on development, maybe it's better to recommend the former.

The first thing you have to do is make a list. Write down every possible competitor that pops into your head. Don't limit yourself to the obvious. If you're creating a reference title, write down the top-selling encyclopedias and electronic "bookshelves." Then look through relevant magazines—there is certainly a plethora of CD-ROM quick-reads these days. Perhaps the *SGML Journal* is more your cup of tea. You'll find news of existing products as well as announcements of products to be released in the coming months.

Scour the back pages, too. In between the sex ads are some lesser known but equally relevant titles you'll want to include on your list. Then jog down to the store. See what jumps out at you. See how things are placed, what's getting the most shelf space in your general category. Write, write, write.

Then buy, buy, buy. You want to get your hands on every relevant piece of software you can and analyze it up the wazoo. What does each title do right, wrong, medium? Which features do you see that your competitors have that you know you have to include to stay competitive? What obvious features are your competitors missing that you can capitalize on by including before they do?

Look into both quality and quantity. Count up the number of media elements a competitor has. Forty video clips? You can do better than that. Count the number of hotspots, and if you're really ambitious, the number of clicks a user can perform if he or she wants to see and do everything. This exercise might yield some surprising results. A program with many, many screens but only a few clicks suggests a high degree of passive linearity. A title with only a few screens but an abundance of clicks may reveal the secret to its engagement in a more "scientific" way than the usual gut feeling.

How about packaging? Look at the boxes of the top sellers. Does an octagonal box correlate with more sales? What about an oversized carton with nothing but a CD and a QuickStart Card in it? You're trying to get at what makes some titles sell so well and others get delisted in a matter of weeks. Oh, you don't know exactly how well your competitors are selling? Well, there are plenty of services who would just love to sell you that information, with prices usually starting at a minimum of $1,000 a pop.

These services range from complete marketing reviews with predictions for the future to data in spreadsheet form listing every single product on the marketplace, how many units it's selling at what price, and in what type of store (mall versus SuperStore). One of the best of these comes from an outfit called PC Data. Although this report only measures 23 percent of the marketplace and misses some major retailers entirely, its data is still extremely useful.

Extrapolate the data and you realize that at one point, *Myst* was probably seiling 16,000 units a month at retail. This is in a business when 20,000 units over a product lifetime is respectable. From there, you can create a convincing visual presentation for the sales department of what percent of the market each of your competitors has, and how much you predict (or hope) you should be able to grab.

A couple of final notes: If, in the course of your research, you discover a product either on the market or just about to be released that is nearly identical to yours, don't look the other way. Consider this information carefully and be ready to revise or even drop your title concept. Good planning means designing not only the best titles, but the right ones, too.

Finally, if you're the person in your organization on whose shoulders it falls to conduct a competitive analysis, don't fret. It's probably the best opportunity anyone can get to play with software all day. Enjoy yourself.

■ Information Design

In Chapter 3, we discussed the role of Information Designers on your team. The tasks that these staff members conduct are so crucial to the successful development of your project that they command an entire phase of their own. The Information Design process is not the only place that Information Designers are active, though. They'll be essential when you sit down with your expanded team to hack out a Functional Spec.

Then, wearing the double hats of "writers," they'll continue to play an active role all the way through to storyboarding and scriptwriting. The tasks in this phase, then, are the primary Information Design steps that precede the writing of the Functional Spec. Note that the Producer is an active participant in the Information Design process, though not the main mover and shaker.

How much time should you allot to Information Design? That depends on the project, of course. But here's a good rule of thumb:

At least one third of your total development schedule should be dedicated to planning and design.

That means if you have nine months to ship a product, you'll probably spend three months designing it and six months building it, testing it, and getting it to market. This assumes you have a publisher already. If not, add "shopping your title around" to the end of the nine-month cycle.

Now, of that one-third design time, at least half (six weeks in our example) is dedicated to up-front Information Design, including input from the Interactive Design Team to revise and improve the initial spec. The remaining six weeks is dedicated to finalizing a Functional Spec and getting going on scriptwriting and storyboard creation.

There are four main tasks in Information Design.

Marketing and Objective Summary

The first task in the Information Design phase is creating a document called the Marketing and Objective Summary. It may or may not be conducted by the Information Designers. It's probably a more appropriate job for the Producer, although good Information Designers will want to have their hands in it too since they were probably involved in the Content Analysis task earlier. The Marketing and Objective Summary is the bridge task between Analysis and Information Design. It is firmly grounded in the concept that to properly design the information and interaction in an interactive media program, you have to know your market. Therefore, before any real research begins, there must be a guide, a focus, a gentle push to get the train rolling and then keep it on track.

The Marketing and Objective Summary basically takes the information you gathered so far—by looking at your audience, your environment, the system you've got a strong hunch you'll be developing for, and who your competitors are—and puts it together into a nice, neat report. It doesn't have to be long. It does have to be evocative. It's okay to go even a little overboard on the hype. You want people to get excited. You might have to sell your internal sales staff. Or this document may become part of a proposal to seek outside funding. Don't shy away from thinking like a PR maven.

The Marketing and Objective Summary is a living, breathing, and evolving document. What you write down at this point will be rewritten when you learn more later on. Eventually, this report will form the opening to your Functional Specification, and the complete design you'll have developed by that point will undoubtedly inform and influence your marketing analysis.

When it's ready to be written, the Marketing and Objective Summary should be divided into the following sections:

1. An Executive Summary or Overview—this introduces the reader to the product and starts to build the hype. It should be only a few paragraphs, but should summarize what's to come in the rest of the document. The Executive Summary should never be more than a printed page in length.

2. Your program's Unique Selling Proposition—known affectionately as the USP, this is a one line description of the product from the buyer's point of view. It should describe what an impatient consumer will "get" in a five-second quick look at your product. It's okay to employ a catchy slogan. Here are some examples I dreamed up when I had a little too

much free time on my hands. They're all for products from publisher Future Vision Multimedia:

- For *Leonardo the Inventor*, a tightly focused title concentrating specifically on DaVinci's inventions: "See Leonardo's Inventions Come To Life… in 3D."

- For *InfoPedia*, the latest entry to the interactive media encyclopedia wars: "More Entries, More Media at a Lower Price."

- For *Pathways through Jerusalem*, a virtual tour of the Holy City featuring video actors playing historical characters: "The Ultimate Tour of the Ultimate City with the Ultimate Tour Guides."

3. A Brief Description of the Product—here's where you write up what little you know at this point about the product. Your previous defining of High Concept and work in Content Analysis will be of the most use to you here. Include the following:

- Any initial goals and objectives

- What you're trying to accomplish

- What the basic look, feel, and interaction will be like

- Any existing work you'll be licensing

- Even the reason behind the name

This should be the longest section of your Marketing and Objective Summary.

4. The Results of Your Analysis—target audience and environment. You can show this fairly simply, by listing the primary, secondary, and tertiary users, and the range of environments they might be using your product in. You'll save the results of your Competitive Analysis for the next item.

5. Competitive Analysis—list your competitors, with a brief description of each product and how it compares with what you hope to do. If you've done a spreadsheet or graph looking at the total market and what share you hope to grab, include that, too.

6. Platforms you expect to release for with a description of minimum specifications—if it's going to be out for MPC and Mac, say it. Then qualify that with the minimum megs of RAM, hard-disk space, single- or double-speed CD-ROM drive, and other technical specs you'll need for the title to run properly. List both the minimum and the optimal specs—it's okay to say that your title will run (barely) on a 4MB 386 while it's optimized for a Pentium.

7. Key Features—you've already described the product. Now break out of narrative mode and list, in five bulleted points, the main features that make this the pick-to-click title that everyone's gotta have. This section effectively sums up in an easy-to-grasp format what you've already presented elsewhere in the document.

8. Budget and Deadlines—approximately how much do you think you'll have to spend to bring this title to market? How long do have to do it? What milestones are you hoping to meet? This is where you include the results of your Scope and Resources analysis. Don't feel like you're getting yourself boxed in—you'll refine this later. For the Marketing and Objective Summary, though, you just want to have an idea of the budget range and a ballpark schedule (Christmas 1997, 1998, or 1999?).

9. Project Team—who do you anticipate including on your team? This may be a done deal, or it may be a wish list. For Marketing and Objective Summaries that double as proposals, it's a way to tell the outside world that you've assembled the best team imaginable to create this title.

Content Research and Outline

Here's where the Information Designers take over from the Producer and start the real work of Information Design. At this point, you've already completed a preliminary Content Analysis. Now you'll flesh out that preliminary work and create a much more detailed outline of what information is available. Your Content Research and Outline will be more focused than the Content Analysis that preceded it as well, since now you've got a Marketing and Objective Summary chugging behind the scenes, adding its subtle spin and allowing you to move forward in a narrower direction.

If you used an SME, now's the time to bring him or her back. If you visited the World Wide Web or the library ever so briefly, return now for a more serious second date. When you're done it's time to start parsing.

Cognitive Model

A Cognitive Model takes the information you've uncovered and begins dividing it into categories, related info chunks, and sequenced topics, so you can digest it more easily. (My thanks to colleague Joan Freedman of Johns Hopkins University for some of the following points.) A Cognitive Model groups information according to:

- Information that must be seen in a particular sequence, either chronologically or in order of performance

- Information that can be seen in any sequence—completely nonlinear

- Information that should be grouped together whether it is seen in a particular sequence or not (here, a common heading can be identified for the information to make it easier for the user to grasp)

- Information the user has to see to get the point of the program

- Information the user can skip (optional tangents, See Alsos, and so on)

- Information that is "highly recommended" to see (such info should be strongly prompted in the program's interactivity)

For Tutorial Paradigm programs, some additional groupings are particularly useful (see Chapter 6 for a detailed discussion of Tutorials):

- Information that should be repeated

- Information that will not be a part of the program, but that is a required prerequisite in order to complete the program successfully

- Information organized by Known to Unknown

- Information organized by Simple to Complex

- Information organized from Easy to Difficult to learn

Preliminary Organization

Your research has thus far resulted in a detailed outline and information arranged according to categories. This is all well and good, but it can be confusing and often overwhelming to readers with less familiarity and commitment to the topic than your crack team of researchers. A more persuasive document features the Information Designers' own editorial slant. At this still-early stage of product planning and design, your Information Designers know the material better than anyone, so they're the best candidates to craft a Preliminary Organization of how the material might actually work in an interactive program.

This Preliminary Organization can take several forms:

- It could be a simple outline with some leading narrative comments interspersed at crucial junctures.

- It could be the original outline without any modification, but with a good Executive Summary at the front end.

- Or it could go so far as to include sample graphics, diagrams, and flowcharts.

As long as everyone involved remembers that nothing is set in stone yet, creating a Preliminary Organization document is an important and useful task. The danger arises when Information Designers start to "own" the material too early (this can happen to any member of the team, by the way, at practically any time—don't be surprised if you find your artists getting overly attached to a favorite animation). There's still a lot of crafting to come, and the early research and organization completed here has to go through the full Interactive Design phase next.

■ Interactive Design

Interactive Design begins slightly after Information Design starts, but runs mostly in parallel. Once a Marketing and Objective Summary is complete, the Interactive Design team can begin thinking of innovative ways to structure and present the content of your title. Look at the Interactive Media Design Development Methodology flowchart in Figure 4.1 again. The box surrounding Information and Interactive Design emphasizes the iterative nature of these two phases. The relationship can be simplified as Figure 4.2.

Figure 4.2

Information and Interactive Design operate in parallel with informal Functional Specification meetings occurring throughout the processes.

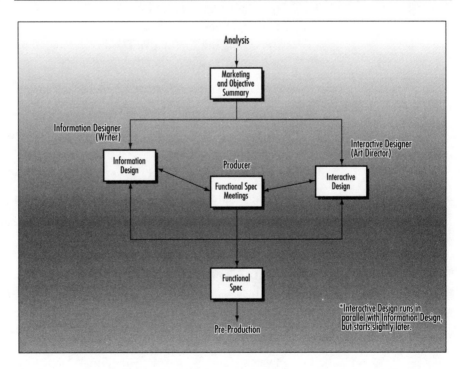

The main goal behind both phases is to hack out a Functional Specification—that's in the center. How the two teams get to that Spec, how often they meet, and how soon they join for formal Functional Spec meetings—that's the job of the Producer, who serves as a go-between, linking the two processes and teams and moderating the Functional Spec meetings as well. So as you go through this section, keep in mind that Interactive Design is not done in a vacuum. The process is much more back and forth, with frequent meetings interspersed throughout.

Let's get real here for a moment. Big formal teams and big formal meetings? Sometimes, maybe. But more often than not, the Information Design "team" is just a single person. Interactive Design—well, that's the Art Director, with a sprinkling of the Producer for extra spice. Functional Spec "meetings" are held in the hallways, over lunch, whenever team members get together to informally brainstorm on the product. When a formal Functional Spec meeting is held, it's more of a friendly get-together of three people who've been working closely all along.

In bigger settings, however, you may indeed have a team of five Information Designers working alongside an Art Director, two artists, an Interface Designer, a couple of programmers, and even the President—who has a strong interest in adding his or her perspective to the product. In such a situation, you'll probably want to follow the model presented here more closely.

However big the Interactive Design team is, coming up with an Interactive Design means considering five main tasks:

1. Functional Requirements—what does your program have to do?

2. InterActivities—what do your users get to do?

3. Metaphor and Paradigm(s)—does your program fit into an already established model?

4. Interface Design—how will your program look and feel?

5. Navigation Maps—how will users get around your program?

When it's all together, you'll want to test your design with a simple Paper Prototype.

Functional Requirements

While the Information Designers are looking at your program from a content point of view, Interactive Designers are thinking about screens: What needs to happen on this screen? How many other screens have this kind of a need? Where did I come from to get to this section, and how do I get back to where I was before? What if I need help? What if I want to quit and go home?

As its name suggests, the Functional Requirements task looks at the big picture questions of what functions your program will require. Functional

Requirements come more from a program-centered, rather than user-centered, sensibility. This can be as simple as defining buttons or control panels (the aforementioned Help and Quit functionality), or a lot more involved, such as specifying a cross-platform model for Hypertext links. Functional Requirements are holistic—you'll be considering groups of screens rather than specific screens (the latter is really the purpose of writing down a Functional Spec document). Functional Requirements help the programmers get going early developing the more complicated sequences

Some requirements you might want to consider when developing your Interactive Design include

- How will the user navigate through the program? By ways of a complete environmental exploration, or will other tools be available—a Return to Previous Menu button, a Return to Main Menu button, a Step-Back button? How about a Map or Index that keeps track of where the user is—a "You Are Here" type of functionality?

- Will the user need to input any data into the program—for example, text into an online notebook or search field? If so, will that be via the computer's keyboard or will the program provide an option for users without a keyboard (by clicking letters on the screen, for example)?

- What input devices will be supported by the program—mouse, keyboard, joystick, remote control, virtual reality headset, voice input, touch-screen, or something even more exotic? What are the limitations and possibilities of the specific target systems in terms of input devices?

- How about output? Will the program be able to export data to the clipboard? Print text and graphics to a printer? What kind of printers and printing will be supported? Color inkjet printers? Plotters? Strictly laserwriters?

- Will there be menus, dialog boxes, or other types of navigable user-controlled functionality? How will these appear? Will menus be pop-up or pull-down on a mouse-click, or automatically appear on roll-over? Once open, will they have multiple hierarchies or always bring up a separate dialog box?

- Will there be Hypertext links in the program? Will these appear with highlighted text, or through separate "See Also" buttons? How much Hypertext do you want—only a few terms or everything in the program (linked to, say, an online dictionary)?

- Can the user save his or her place in the program (especially important for games), or does the program always restart from ground zero each time it's opened?

- If there are buttons, how will they operate and appear? As radio buttons? (Push one in, the others all push out.) As Windows toggle buttons, which gray out when they're not available?

Functionality can be grouped as well:

- *Global Functions* are those that apply to every screen—such as a Help, Map, Quit, or Return button.

- *Regional Functions* are those that apply to specific groups of screens, but not every screen. These can include certain types of text-input fields, "See Also" buttons that only appear on database screens, and the like.

- *Local Functions* are those that apply to individual screens. An activity or interactive requirement that only appears once, or that shows up intermittently on a small number of screens that refuse to be easily grouped, would fit this category.

InterActivities

Once you know what your program has to do functionally, it's time to brainstorm up some true interactive activities (I like to call them *interActivities* for short). InterActivities define not what the program has to do, but what your users get to do. It isn't as daunting as it sounds. A interactive media environment where you click and explore is an interActivity. So is searching for the capital of Zimbabwe in an interactive encyclopedia. The specifications for a puzzle you have to solve in a *Seventh Guest* or *Myst*-like game? You got it. This task is all about defining the specific interactions users will encounter and implement while using your program.

Coming up with interActivities that matter (rather than gratuitous mouse clicks to go on to the next screen) is a challenging task, but one that you should relish—good interActivities will make or break your title. You can come up with great and meaningful activities by basing them on the objectives (marketing or educational) you've set forth in your Marketing and Objective Summary. For example, Table 4.1 shows some possible objectives matched with actual interActivities for the award-winning *Ashtown* smoking-prevention title for fifth graders.

In Ashtown, the interActivities are the entire product. Future Vision's *Explorers of the New World*, another title I worked, embeds its interActivities inside a more linear interactive media experience. A good part of *Explorers*—which chronicles the adventures of Columbus, Cortes, Magellan, and 60 other adventurers who were active from AD 1450 to 1600—consists of narrated animation screens, accessed by clicking hotspots on a particular explorer's route map. But interspersed are three full 3D environments and six interActivities.

ASHTOWN INTERACTIVITY	POSSIBLE OBJECTIVE/TOPIC
"TransOrgan Express"—a trip on a make-believe subway through the body, stopping at various diseased and healthy organs along the way.	What effects do smoking and second-hand smoke have on the body?
"At the Park"—an interview activity where users get to hear teenagers' comments on how "cool" or "uncool" smoking makes you.	What are the social consequences of smoking?
"Ask Blake"—the local advice columnist receives letters from concerned kids—can you help him respond?	What can you do around others who smoke?
"The Price is High"—a TV game show where you calculate costs of smoking for a year, then spend the same money on valuable prizes!	How much does smoking cost—to you and society?
"City Hall"—the City Council must vote on an ordinance banning smoking in public places. You're the mayor. How do you vote?	Can you change society vis à vis acceptance of smoking?

The latter range from a quiz game where you help Cortes escape from marauding Aztecs in Montezuma's palace, to a rather morbid activity where you must "find the hidden food sources"—those less identifiable but entirely edible objects Magellan's crew desperately ate to avoid starvation (yum... rats, rope, and roaches).

Ashtown and *Explorers* are educational programs, but the interActivity development process holds true for other types of titles. Know what you want to accomplish, then figure out the best way to get there. Interactive Designers can start their work with just a Marketing and Objective Summary, but it's better to use what the Information Designers have come up with—that's why the Information Design process begins slightly before Interactive Design.

Your Information Designers will have set their own Preliminary Organization ideas down on paper, which you should pay good attention to. But ultimately, the onus of creating killer interActivities is on members of the Interactive Design team, who have the experience, and sometimes even training, specifically in interactive media (a good researcher is a good researcher, regardless of his or her familiarity with state-of-the-art interactive media design). Once interActivities are brainstormed and somewhat decided upon, they are fed back to the Information Design team, where they are refined even further. InterActivities then help further focus the Information Designer's research.

Metaphor and Paradigm

Because interactive media is so visual, choosing a metaphor and paradigm for your program is a unique task to the interactive development process. Metaphors place your goals and information in a familiar context. They are a shorthand that makes things easier to deal with. Compare the DOS directory structure with the Macintosh or Windows 95 metaphor of a desktop with files, folders, and a trash can (or recycling bin in Windows 95). It may be just as fast or efficient to use a command-line interface, but which one makes more sense from the get-go? Which is more familiar?

Now look at Bob, Microsoft's interface for computer novices, which extends the metaphor even further. The file folders reside in a "real" filing cabinet. The calendar program looks like a calendar on a desktop. The clock program is a cartoon ticking clock. These are examples of metaphors—they're not real, but they feel real enough to bridge the conceptual gap. While there are plenty of metaphors you can think up for making your title's contents more accessible (a "book" is a common though unimaginative one), the desktop seems to be one of the most popular these days.

Sony's CD-ROM title *The Haldeman Diaries* places the Nixon confidant's written works and even home videos on a metaphoric office desktop. So does Dr. Ruth's CD encyclopedia about sex—complete with Dr. Ruth staring out at you with a sympathetic but firm demeanor. Mindscape's *The Complete Reference Library* brings you the desktop along with the bookshelf—choose a book and see its contents on the slide projector-like screen. And Virgin's *One Tribe* has a room full of objects to click on—it's not so much a desktop as a complete living room metaphor.

Metaphors are tricky, though. Never assume that something is intuitive just because it looks like something else that's familiar. On how many "real" desktops can you drag your floppy disk to the trash can and have it ejected? Wouldn't you expect that action to erase the contents of your disk? And since when does the act of pointing at a lower piece of paper cause it to jump to the foreground? Metaphors are useful, but you'll often still need some explanation.

Metaphors are closely related to paradigms. The latter refers to several broad categories with related functionality and a similar look and feel. Chapters 6 and 7 deal exclusively with interactive media paradigms. These range from the basics—the Tutorial, Database, and Environment paradigms—to more emerging categories—Interactive Movies, Books, and Applications. In each, there are rules that define how a user "expects" a title in a particular category to work. And databases feel like databases, environments feel like environments—not just by functionality but by look, too. Start discussing now what type of paradigm you want your title to fit into. It will help guide you through the rest of this design phase.

Interface Design

Once you know what your program has to do, what your users get to do, and what metaphor or paradigm you're leaning toward, the fun begins in earnest. Interface design is where your program begins to take on a real life. It's the point at which you can begin to see it and touch it—if only on paper. But good interface design starts from a functional perspective, not an artistic one.

Chunk Model

Before you start drawing pretty borders and 3D buttons, do a Chunk Model. You know what your program has to do, so put it up on the screen—in empty rectangles. That's right, make a bunch of empty placeholders and start moving them around on the screen. This is not the time for artistic expression. You're tying to determine how the interface should work, not how it should appear. As you move these chunks around on screen, it will quickly be clear what needs to go where, how big certain features can be, and what the overall tactile feel of your title will be. Create a separate Chunk Model for each of your interActivities, and for every screen category you defined in your Functional Requirements.

Chunk Models are most useful for titles that don't make heavy use of environments, since those titles don't have a lot of pieces to move around; each screen is a discrete environment. In these cases, you're better off creating early storyboards—but try to keep the lessons of the Chunk Model in mind. Make the storyboards really loose. Use rectangles and nondescript ovals if you want. Don't fall into the trap that every storyboard must be a masterpiece.

Fleshing Out

As you're chunking or loose storyboarding, you'll be creating an interface. But the interface is not complete until it's been given a little bit of meat on its bones. So, go ahead and flesh out your Chunk Model a bit. Play with colors, textures, shapes, and concepts. Set a time limit, then go wild (but always remember to rein it back in). You want to make your interface look as good as it works.

Fleshing out has a functional purpose as well. Let's say you've decided you need three buttons at the bottom of the screen, each one with a text label. But you're not sure if all the text will fit once you've chosen a font or given the button a bit of a beveled age. So you go the extra step and add a dash more "look" to your interface's "feel." And although you can test your product's prototype with just a Chunk Model, a few fleshed-out screens will let testers comment on look and feel as well as functionality.

While you're at it, don't be afraid to look at other examples of stellar interfaces. Make sure the Producer has shared the competitive products assembled during the Analysis phase with the Interactive Design team. But don't stop there. You want to build a solid library of interactive media titles. Visit the World Wide Web and download screen shots. Only by knowing what's out there can you satisfy Interactive Media Guideline #3—Killer Design.

Style Sheet

Don't forget to make a Style Sheet. Define on paper the interface guidelines you think will be necessary so that other artists can maintain a consistent look and feel. Even if there's only one artist working on a project, it's still essential to get down in writing what you're trying to do, what tools to use, and what font and size to use for particular screens. Let your Style Sheet evolve with your project. When you get into defining how animations should look, define whether you're going for a Disney look, a stylized cartoon feel, or a watercolor impressionist approach.

You may find you need to beat the clock near the close of the project and bring in some pinch-hit artistic help. You also never know when your Art Director will be offered another job at double the salary—right at the most crucial phase of production. Attach the Style Sheet to the Functional Spec and disseminate it when the time is right.

Reinventing the Wheel

While you're designing, also think about whether you want a cookie-cutter-formula approach or a reinvent-the-wheel approach to your interface. As judgmental as these terms sound, there are benefits to both.

Cookie-cutter-formula approaches are the easy way out. They look at another product and say, "I want to be just like that when I grow up." These interfaces are not innovative, but that may not be the business model you're after now—or ever. Some companies, and titles, are meant to lead. Others identify a proven market (and a proven interface), and do it the same or just a little better. There are other advantages, as well. People will be familiar with a particular interface or genre, so it's an easier purchase decision. Look at all the copycats of Broderbund's Living Books. Check out all the *Myst* knock-offs.

You can also copy yourself. Let's say you came out with a great title with an award-winning interface. Now you want to tackle a different content area in the same general genre. If you make the interface just like the first one, it will save you time and money and your repeat customers will know exactly what to expect.

The reinvent-the-wheel approach sounds at first like a monumental waste of time. If the standards have been set, why spend months designing something new and completely unique, painstakingly screen by screen, if the same old thing would be just as pleasing? Well, the standards haven't been set. Interactive media is still evolving as an art form, and it's up to creative interface designers to push the envelope that notch further. Eventually, a standard way of doing things will emerge. In the meantime, it is our solemn responsibility not to just stand still, because if you stand still in an industry like this one, you're obsolete by the first maintenance revision.

In truth, there will never be a point when there's one way of doing things properly. Let's compare it with the movies, or even TV. Yes, there are certain standards that everyone uses. And most films are pretty formulaic—knock-offs of other successful flicks, not to mention the endless stream of sequels. But every once in a while, a young turk, an independent with a mind of his or her own, comes up with something quirky and wonderful. Quickly the copycats come—never as good as the original ("American Gothic" is no "Twin Peaks")—but the point is they inevitably come. And so, the industry evolves—ever so slightly.

Navigation Maps

A bunch of lovely interfaces don't mean squat unless they're sequenced in a meaningful way. A Navigation Map is a flowchart that shows how the various pieces of the interface fit together. It defines your program's interactive look and feel as much as the interActivities, as much as the Functional Requirements. This is the task where you determine how your users will get around your program. If you do it right, they'll barely notice they're navigating. Do it wrong, and they'll curse you for making them step back through 20 screens just to return Home.

The Navigation Map you create at this point is not screen-by-screen specific—that comes later during the Scripts, Storyboards, and Flowcharting task. This initial Navigation Map shows the general locations a user can go to, the overall superstructure. It is both a way of viewing your paradigm from a different angle and keeping track of all the disparate elements in your program. Indeed, the Navigation Map you create now may very likely do double duty later as your program's Index or Map function.

A Navigation Map almost always starts with a Main Interface screen and branches out from there. Often, there's an Introductory Sequence attached to it. Navigation Maps are made up of lots of boxes and lines. They look like a very interesting organizational chart. The simplest navigation structures can fit on a page. Figure 4.3 gives a generic example.

Figure 4.3

Navigation Maps always
start with a Main Menu
or Introductory
Sequence, then branch
off into places a user can
explore.

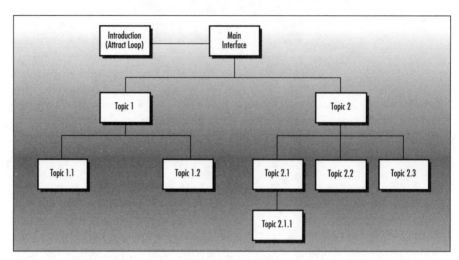

More complicated maps can span a book's worth of interconnected diagrams. The Navigation Map for *Explorers of the New World*, for example, shows each of the explorers' submaps under the Main Interface box, with each of their environments and interActivities listed below that. *Myst*'s Navigation Map probably showed a structure of the different worlds and all the key puzzles. An encyclopedia would show all the different functions (media gallery, index, search, timeline, and so on) branching off from a main boot-up screen.

These early Navigation Maps don't show every button or every function. They don't have a line that indicates where you can go from every screen. In Figure 4.3 above, you can probably go from Subtopic 2.1 directly back to the Main Interface, but the path isn't shown. Wait until you create your Scripts and Storyboard flowchart to add in all the lines and connect the dots.

Navigation Maps inherently imply that every program has at least somewhat of a hierarchical structure. It's true. You may be designing the most non-linear title to date, but from a programming point of view, screens have to be connected to each other. There has to be a starting point that the program opens to consistently. From there, you can get going in a multitude of directions, but already you're into a hierarchy. Keep in mind that Navigation Maps are concerned with the internal structure of your program. The more transparent that is, the better. The end user's experience may be, and probably should be, entirely different.

As you design your program's Navigation Maps, think about whether you want it to be heavily hierarchical or flat.

- Heavily hierarchical navigation takes the model in Figure 4.3 and keeps extending it. Topic 2.1 leads to Topic 2.1.1 which leads to Topic 2.1.1.1, *ad nauseam*. Each new topic is a new full-screen interface. If you want to trace back your route, you may find yourself in an endless staircase. As designers you'll certainly need to provide some controls that allow your user to jump around more easily.

- Flat navigation rarely goes beyond the first level. Often, when you click a hotspot, the resulting screen only covers part of the Main Interface behind it. Returning, then, is simply a matter of clicking the Main Interface behind, or if the Main Interface is obscured, clicking a one-level Return button. More examples of flat navigation can be found in Chapter 8.

Navigation Maps can be hotlinked to the actual program, especially if you're using a flowchart-based authoring system like IconAuthor or Authorware Professional. I like to print mine out and hang them on the wall for all to see. It quickly shows a client, or other team members, the overall structure of your program. The ins and outs of creating the best flowcharts are discussed in more detail in Chapter 9.

Paper Prototype

If you thought you could do all this design just by arguing back and forth in meetings, think again. It's time to prototype your design. Prototyping is "try it out" testing. You do it when you want to find out if something works before you commit too many resources to it. Since both the Information and Interactive Design phases have been pretty theoretical, your first prototype doesn't have to be a full-blown working masterpiece. You can even test it on paper. Here's how it works:

Have your Art Director, or someone with a decent sense of style, draw some quick interface examples on paper. If you've already fleshed things out on the computer, print those screens. Also print out your Navigation Map. Then lay the interface examples out on a big table. Walk the person you're testing it on through the screens, referring back and forth to the Navigation Map. You might want to have some sample content handy, maybe even a sample script (though to do the latter implies you've jumped forward to Pre-Production for some reason).

This process should elicit a basic gut reaction from your user. Take the results with a grain of salt—your testee hasn't gotten his or her hands on the program itself. What you've done is a pretty controlled experiment, with careful explanations in order to receive useful feedback. When the user has to go through your program solo, though, it may reveal a major muddle. Don't panic—if you're following the guidelines in this book, you should feel fairly confident that you're headed in the right direction.

Who should you test a Paper Prototype on? Mostly in-house people—just not the staff that's been directly working on the project. If you're running a one-title shop and everyone knows the project backwards and forwards, then get some colleagues from a neighboring firm. Trying out your design on real users is always admirable, but it's not necessary just yet. You haven't really "made" anything, and "real" users are much less forgiving than industry insiders.

■ Functional Spec Meetings

As you've be-bopped through Information and Interactive Design, the team has met a number of times, sharing information and influencing each other's direction. All of these meetings contribute to the creation of a Functional Spec. But at some point, the team has to sit down and formally agree on what's going into the (internally) published Specification. These meetings are run by the Producer, who should also be the scribe who creates the document. The Producer takes input from all sides and adds his or her own design vision. The group will break, the Producer will type up the latest Functional Spec document, then the team will reassemble, discuss, and revise this preliminary document.

Functional Spec meetings can be fast—a couple of two-hour afternoon sessions, or take forever—a month or more of nearly daily meetings to hack out every little detail. If the teams have been meeting regularly up to this point, the formal meetings should go pretty smoothly.

■ Functional Spec

The document that comes out of the Functional Spec meetings is called…oh, you know by now. What's in a Functional Spec?

- An Introduction and Table of Contents to what's in the document
- Your Marketing and Objective Summary right up front
- A screen-by-screen, or interface-by-interface, description of the product
- Sample graphics cut and pasted into the document
- Flowcharts, timelines, and maybe even a budget attached at the end

There are two basic types of Functional Specs.

Screen-by-Screen Specs

For programs where every screen has something happening on it that's significantly different—most of your graphic environment games fit here—the Functional Spec has a page listed for every single screen. These can get quite long. The Functional Spec starts at the beginning of the program and describes everything a user will experience in an average order.

First up is a description of the Installation screen and process. Next is the Splash Screen—where the program's title and publisher's logo usually go. If there's an Attract Loop that kicks in after a certain amount of down time, describe that here, too. Then it's on to the Opening Screen, and each individual screen to follow.

On each page, the following information should be listed:

- An overview of this screen—what is its purpose?

- How does one get to this screen?

- Where can one go from this screen?

- Narrative descriptions of each button, function, animated hotspot, or video on this screen (if the same functions are on separate screens, it's okay to repeat—just copy and paste)

- A description of the general style of the screen (attach a screen shot, if available, or the appropriate section from the Style Sheet here)

- Indications of what type of music or sound effects ought to play here

Interface-by-Interface Specs

For programs where many screens are identical functionally, but have different data within them—most of your reference products and encyclopedias fit here—the Functional Spec has a number of longer sections describing the details of each program interface rather than individual screens. Thus, there would be a section in the Functional Spec on the Media Gallery function of an encyclopedia, without listing a separate page for each media element. Specifics are then included in an Appendix or separate document.

In *PC/Computing How Multimedia Computers Work*, there was no point in having a separate page for each part of the computer to be animated—they all had the same functionality: Click a part on the screen and an animation played in a window. The details were therefore left to the scripts and storyboards (which were attached to the Functional Spec). The document itself was thus divided by interface—the Main Interface, the Ask the Experts section, the Help section, and the Tours section.

The same would be true for Living Book types of titles—each screen plays animations when you click a hotspot. The Functional Spec for *Arthur's*

Teacher Trouble, for example, probably consists of a page for each screen. The text that appears at the top of each screen would be shown on that page of the Spec, followed by a list of animations for that screen. The details of the animations would be in the storyboards, although the Functional Spec might include a brief description of the animations for a quick read. The Functional Spec would then include separate sections for any additional interfaces—such as the Living Books "Index" screen, the opening "Play" or "Read" screen, and the "Change a Language" screen.

Interface-by-Interface Functional Specs start off with the same linear progression—Installation, Splash, and Opening Screens. From there the Spec should include the same basic information as Screen-by-Screen Specs:

- An overview of this interface—what is its purpose?

- An explanation of how one gets to this interface

- An explanation of where one can go from this interface

- Narrative descriptions of common buttons, animated hotspots, functions, or videos in this interface (you don't have to worry about repeating similar functions as you do in the Screen-by-Screen Spec, because you've already grouped these functions as part of a common interface)

- A description of the general style of the interface

- Indications of what types of music or sound effects ought to play in this interface

At the end of either type of Functional Spec, include some additional statistical information. List, for example, all the environments, interActivities, places where video is needed, and animated hotspots in a series of closing appendices.

One more thing before we leave the Functional Specification: your cover page. Make a Sign-Off Sheet. Write down everyone who needs to see and approve this document, and get them to put pen to paper. It's hard to do, and it rarely occurs in totality, but you've got to try. It's not that things can't change once something's been signed off—they can and do, for the good of the product. But a signature indicates that the person has at least read what you're planning to do, or is giving you the green light even if he or she hasn't had time to read your document.

■ Marketing Demo

Clearly, a Functional Spec flows out of the Functional Spec meetings. But what's this Marketing Demo thing doing coming out of the same place, dangling like a befuddled pendulum and leading to nowhere? A Marketing

Demo is a quick—but very polished—demonstration program you produce at this point in the process to get buyers (or investors and publishers) hot and bothered. It's not a prototype—it's not meant to be tested. It's not even meant to be final—that's why there isn't anything leading from the Marketing Demo.

The Marketing Demo could be a kind of pseudo prototype, with examples of all the functionality you want to include in your final program. But it could just as easily be a movie trailer—a three-minute QuickTime flick that has nothing to do the final program but energizes sales. You can't create a Marketing Demo until you have your Functional Spec completed—you need a clear picture of what you're hyping. Once you have that, don't spend a lot of time on the demo. It's okay to make it small. But whatever you do, make it good. Polish up that puppy real shiny. Make it sing. Remember—this is all sales. You may never use that demo in-house again, but it will be shown over and over and over again to potential clients.

Marketing Demos are often created by the Art Director, since that person has been around for the Interactive Design phase and knows the product. But once you've finished the Functional Spec, you're ready to start assembling a fuller team. One of those early members might be the one to create the demo, too. In general, I like to keep it as a one-person task, not eating up too many other resources. The best sales piece cannot substitute for solid product delivered on time and on budget.

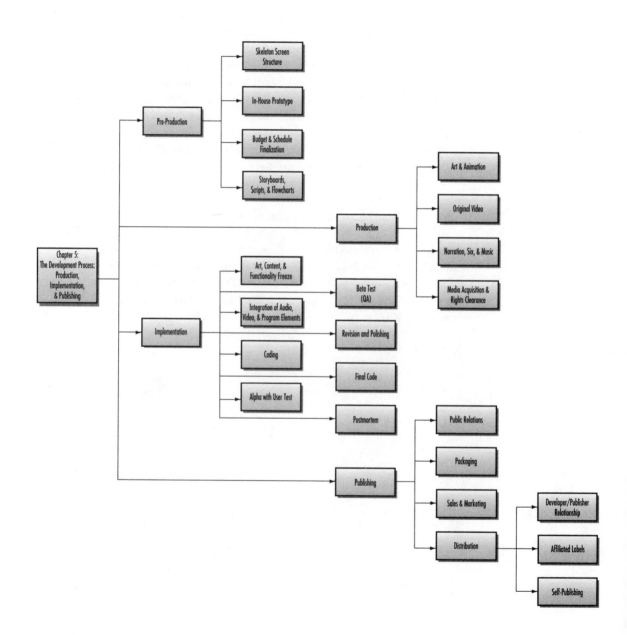

5

The Development Process: Production, Implementation, and Publishing

Phew... you've finished the gratifying, but tough, process of planning and designing what your product will look like. Now it's time to actually jump in and make it. What are the steps that go into the hands-on part of the development process? How will knowing what's to come after the design is said and done affect your original plan? This chapter takes a concise look at what happens when you've assembled your team and you're ready to really rock and roll.

There are three main parts:

1. Production—this is actually divided into two sections:

   - Pre-Production—this is the "design phase" of the production process, when you plan what you're going to do during production and assemble all the pieces and resources you'll need.

   - Actual Production—this is where everyone puts their collective noses to the grindstones and produces great interactive media.

2. Implementation—this phase kicks in after creation is "frozen" and all the pieces have to be put together. There are all sorts of technical terms in this phase—alphas, betas, and the like.

3. Publishing—once you've finished your product and reached "final code," what do you need to know about the publishing process? Good planning means creating mutually beneficial relationships with your public relations, marketing, and sales forces, not to mention the people who put together your packaging.

■ Pre-Production

Once you've got your design in place and you've thought long and hard about such things as audience, metaphors, interface, and paper prototypes, it's time for one last planning phase. If you're itching something awful to get going, don't worry—at least this phase is less theoretical. Pre-production consists of putting together real deliverables that will make your final product that much easier to create. There are four main pieces in the pre-production process.

Skeleton Screen Structure

Skeleton Screen Structures flow very directly out of your Functional Spec. If your Spec is complete, there should be at least a line or two jotted down for each proposed screen in your product. Some products have a billion screens; others have just one screen with an abundance of functionality. Either way, you can begin building a computer-based structure for your product long before you have the screens finalized.

It works like this: You designate one screen for each box in your navigation map and each media byte you have planned. The screen probably doesn't have anything in it except a label saying "Animation X goes here" or "This screen will contain the database interface." Then, using an authoring system or hard coding, you begin linking all those screens together. When it's all done, you'll have a massive interleaving set of screens with little or nothing on them. But you'll know how big your product is, how to navigate through it, and where any possible dead ends or inconsistencies that need to be plugged might lie.

This structure is called a *Skeleton Screen Structure* because it builds the skeleton of your product, although there isn't any real flesh on it yet. It's bony and it can walk, but you wouldn't want to meet it on a rainy day in London.

Skeleton Screen Structures vary depending on the product. The easiest ones to conceptualize—and the ones that probably work the best—are for fairly hierarchical program structures. These are programs where you're clicking on objects or even arrows to move through information. Each screen represents a different topic in your outline, and every screen sports an indicator of what will go there—an animation, a video, some text, a graphic, a sound effect.

The harder ones are for the more intuitive single-screen or flat interface programs. In the case of *PC/Computing How Multimedia Computers Work*, most of the information is accessed from one main screen. You click on objects, and a video/animation window appears on top of it. In this case, the skeleton looks less bony and more like a skull with multiple growths popping up at inopportune moments. Clicking in different places on the Skeleton Screen for the main interface brings up a variety of empty windows with labels such as "Mouse animation goes here" or "Talking expert goes here."

For a Living Book, the one-screen, animation pop-up metaphor is taken to the next level—the animation plays right on that screen with no video window at all. About the best you can do here is to create a screen that reads "Page One" with a lot of little pop-up placeholder boxes that will eventually represent complete animations.

Ironically, one way of looking at a Skeleton Screen Structure is that it's a living, breathing representation of the Navigation Maps that become an integral part of your Functional Spec. Who works on a Skeleton Screen Structure? Ideally, the programmer who'll be doing the final integration, since the Skeleton Screen is the foundation for the entire program. In rarer occasions, a Producer or even Artist can connect the thigh bone to the ankle bone—although this may serve more to facilitate the In-House Prototype described below than to build the basis for a technically complex completed program.

In-House Prototype

Somewhere in the netherworld following the completion of your Functional Spec and the simultaneous summing up of a Marketing Demo there lies an In-House Prototype. Most people confuse the terms *demo* and *prototype*, but they're very different. While the demo is there to sell your product to the outside world—clients, vendors, OEM accounts—the prototype is for your use and your use only. If the Skeleton Screen Structure is the living, breathing embodiment of the Functional Spec, the In-House Prototype infuses your original Paper Prototype with vitality.

In-House Prototypes can be very easy to construct. They're usually done by the project Programmer, though a technically savvy Producer might put together his or her own quick attempt. If you've done a solid Skeleton Screen Structure, you can basically add a little bit of content or some frilly dressing, and test it as is.

In-House Prototypes have to be simple. If they were as decked out as a full Marketing Demo, team members would get too attached. They'd be reluctant to change something—even if tests showed it didn't work with a majority of users. Here's another slogan to hang on your wall:

The more complete a screen is, the more impervious it is to change.

Since In-House Prototypes aren't meant to be shown far and wide, you can have some fun with them. Use staff members in place of actors you'll later hire. Add offbeat comments where serious text goes. You want to see at this early pre-production stage if people are going to get lost in your product. You want to see if your design makes sense, if it's the right direction. If you have a game idea, mock up a quick prototype now—if you haven't done it earlier while spec'ing the design. Otherwise you could get a game that just isn't fun.

Who tests an In-House Prototype? The same crowd that tested your Paper Prototype. In addition, try to show it to some "real" users, as well as the usual office cronies. At least bring in some folks from another department or team. Remember—you're under no obligation to pass it off to the sales staff as if it were a polished gem. Whoever you use, you want to see how they react to your creation, rather than how you—who have written the Functional Spec and knows everything there is to know about this puppy—will experience the prototype.

However, please don't go all out. Don't hire a screening room with two-way mirrors. Don't do controlled studies with a placebo group in the local mall. But test now, and test often. Then use what you discover. Don't be afraid to listen to your users.

Budget and Schedule Finalization

When you've finished your design, created your Skeleton, and done your Prototype testing, you should have a clear idea where you're going. If you've been meticulous in your planning, you probably also have a good idea of how much it's going to cost, and when you're going to get there. While you probably did a pretty good guestimate earlier in the game so that the boss or client knows the general ballpark you've been playing in (such as, "half a million, Christmas"), at this point you can come up with something final.

Your final budget and schedule will be closely tied together—especially if you use some decent project management software that lets you input dates and hours as resources. Clearly, the longer it takes, usually, the more it costs. The bottom line is affected more by human resources (and accompanying company overhead) than any other category, and that includes expensive hardware or media acquisition.

If you find that once you've fully spec'd a project, it looks like it's going to take twice as long as you planned, you can always throw twice as many people at it to bring it back in line—provided you budgeted for it in the first place. Otherwise, you'll have the unpleasant task of going to your client and asking for either more money or a reduced scope. If you ask for more money, the client fumes. If you ask for reduced scope, your artists and programmers grumble—they want it to be the best it can be. Because of all these hard decisions, it's the Producer, usually in conjunction with the client, who is in charge of the budget and scheduling task.

All this may be moot, since you already may be locked into your earlier date and budget. Hopefully, your early estimate was a broad one, so that your final budget and schedule fall within the initially publicized one. In no circumstances should you tell your client or management this, though! You'll do it for less. Fine—more profit for you. You can finish it quicker? Great—you can get started earlier on the next project. Or reward your team with a nice holiday.

You might be wondering how it is that you got to do all the work you've done so far without a firm budget in place from the get-go. The fixed guestimate routine described above is one way. Another is to negotiate an up-front advance for doing a feasibility test. In this case, some of the tasks listed earlier will need to be truncated while a prototype is created. The tasks are revisited later. It's not uncommon for a big publisher to advance $20,000 with no guarantee that they'll move forward on the project.

At Mindscape, our Finance Department developed an amazing spreadsheet that calculated everything a business-minded Producer needs to know. The Producer input the budget and estimated unit sales, price, and any royalties or content licensing fees, and the spreadsheet spit out a slew of data—including, most importantly, how close the proposed project met the company's target gross margin. As Producers, we would then adjust the budget, plead for higher numbers from the sales staff, or try to knock a few points off the royalties.

All this begs an important question: How do you get experience doing budgets and schedules? Unfortunately, all the book learning and computerized templates and spreadsheets in the world won't substitute for real life experience. The best way to know how long something takes is to do it a few times. And yet, every time you change jobs, the parameters change, too. Just because you could do a project of scope X in Y amount of time at company Z doesn't mean at company Q it will work the same. Your team members may be different. Corporate culture varies incredibly. At company X, the team is dedicated and stays every night until midnight. At company Q, everyone's out the door at 5 p.m.

Finally, don't forget to factor in a little hot fudge on a Sunday. You think it will take 6 months and $200,000? Add in a 25 percent fudge factor. That 6-month project will last closer to $7^1/_2$ months, and you won't be padding to ask for $250,000. Who doesn't need a fudge break, anyway?

Storyboards, Scripts, and Flowcharts

Now we're finally cooking! We're getting closer and closer to the moment everyone's been prepping for. But take it slow, because here's where you can really get nailed. You've got your plan, your budget approved, even your skeleton laid out. Your finger's on the trigger. Come on, gang, let's start making art. Let's record some music. The scripts? Oh, they'll come. We'll work in parallel. It will be fun!

Wrong. There's nothing fun at all about making changes to a well-loved animation or an expensively recorded aerial video of Brazil. But that's exactly what you'll have in store for you if you don't finish your scripts, storyboards, and flowcharts in advance of starting Production. The biggest mistake interactive media teams make—and I've made it myself—is starting to create images while a script is in flux.

To be fair to all the people who make this mistake, it's not usually our fault. And it's not our overanxiousness to get creative. It's the aforementioned budget and schedule. As nice as it would be if the Producer of a project could set a schedule and everyone would listen, in real life it's the client who says those five deadly words we dread to hear:

"I need it by Christmas."

And when the client says this, entire companies are sent scurrying, working into the late hours, compacting six months of work into three, all in pursuit of the holy grail of under-the-tree impulse buying. The most pronounced effect is that your well-drawn-out plan of finishing scripts—and even recording final narrations—before starting to animate is thrown to the wolves. If a project has multiple sections, section one gets written, section one gets animated, section two gets written, section two gets animated, and so on.

Sounds reasonable, except that what if you discover that something in section one would have worked better in section two? Changes. Or at the end of the first two sections, you realize that you've spent such a great amount of time and loving care that you've maxed out on disc real estate, and the remaining six sections have to be given a pauper's treatment? Oh, and then there are the inevitable delays. Your writer gets sick—it happens, you know. And suddenly the artists are without work for a few days or more. Or your fact checker goes out of town, but the art must continue. The fact checker comes home and, uh-oh, that's not the way that nuclear power plant inducer works. Changes.

All this doesn't mean you shouldn't plan it right. It just means that you shouldn't be surprised if things go awry in the process. And if you're aware of the potential pitfalls of the commercial software business, you'll at least be ready with an answer when the inevitable does occur.

Given all of the above, the final tasks that must occur—in a properly planned program—before full production happens are

1. Storyboards—before you start creating scripts for a visual media, you need to see what it's going to look like. As with the Paper Prototype, it's crucial to get it down on paper before you start committing expensive computer resources to development. Storyboards follow a fairly straight format where visuals and often sample text are shown side by side or top to bottom so that nonartists or writers can see what's about to be created. Rather than plunge into creating, a storyboard lets you get the bigger picture—this image will be followed by this image and this kind of a narration. Storyboards are especially crucial for organizing the steps in an animation. Artists and writers both can work on storyboards.

2. Scripts—the meat of the pre-production process lies in the script—which is far more than words. The best script formats mix visuals on one side with text on the other. Sounds like one of the storyboard formats, doesn't it? But in this case, it's the final text, not just example text. Scripts are not included within a Functional Spec, but they are a close partner, for without a script, a Functional Spec is just a shallow shell. Good scripts describe exactly what's going on, give the artists instructions or guidelines on what to draw, and discuss functionality.

3. Flowcharts—alongside the script in interactive media comes the flowchart. We've seen the importance of flowcharts for clearly mapping navigation as part of your design. Now, take your earlier flowchart and give it some teeth. Connect it to the script to show the interrelationships between plot or information lines in your program. Scripts must be carefully coded to match the flowcharts. A writer who can do a good flowchart is a true Information Designer.

Examples of scripts and flowcharts are shown in Chapter 9, "Tools You Can Use."

■ Production

The production process is really a series of parallel tasks held together with virtual silly putty by the Producer and Team Leader. Sometimes the tasks overlap, sometimes they continue on in their own unique rhythm. They'll come together very markedly in the Implementation phase. The four main tasks in the Production phase include the following.

Art and Animation

The heart of nearly every interactive media project is its art. There may be video, but the backgrounds, details, and objects that move and animate constitute the core of the interactive media experience. The roles of artists and animators (described here together because the same staff often performs both functions) were detailed in Chapter 3. As they move into production, these artists interpret what has been written in the scripts and storyboards to create original and hopefully stunning work.

Given the tools now available, it's easy to get carried away—to push pixels into the wee hours of the night, trying to get it perfect, playing havoc with a carefully crafted timeline. For this reason, the art and animation process needs to be closely monitored. Someone—usually the Producer or Team Leader—is required at critical junctions to say "that's good enough, let's move on."

This desire to stay on schedule needs to be balanced with a commitment to quality. A rush-it-out-the-door slash-and-burn attitude can backfire if the art creation process is truncated unnecessarily. You're interested in shipping the best interactive media titles, not garbage, on time. The latter can result if a project is overmanaged—where each animator, for example, is assigned an equal amount of development time for every animation no matter how big or small it should be. Or where artists are commanded to follow a storyboard or Functional Spec as if it embodied both the letter and the spirit of the law.

In truth, the process is more dynamic, varying under circumstances both in and out of the Team Leader's control. Free expression and interpretation of a script can lead to the most interesting, unique, and innovative solutions. The key is empowering the people creating the art by involving them in the brainstorming process. You don't have to include everyone on the art team way back as early as the Functional Spec meetings—things would probably get quite out of hand if this were the case—but forcing creative types to follow someone else's design will quickly lead to a lack of personal ownership and a 9 to 5 attitude even among the most talented.

At Mindscape, the artists had a center area devoted to performance art. Gumbys co-mingled with Barbie dolls. Dioramas of all sizes and shapes took on new meaning as the group process added knickknacks non-artists would have long before trashed. This playful atmosphere clearly contributed to the creation of more perfect pixels, so it was encouraged, not stifled. Creating art on deadline is a delicate balancing act between fostering a creative "art school" atmosphere and remembering that making interactive media is a business with real money and real deadlines on the line.

Original Video

Creating original video is a wholly different function than licensing video—which is part of the Media Acquisition process. When it comes to creating footage from scratch, there are two main activities:

1. Shooting the video—to get video to use in an interactive media title, you need to record it as you would any other video: direct to tape. The process and the people involved, are the same as if you were making a TV documentary—see Chapter 3 for more details on specific team member roles. There are some particular concerns that will affect how you shoot the video. For example, if you're shooting on a blue-screen set, you'll need to take care to set up your shots to fit your computer-generated backgrounds. More on that later.

2. Making it digital—once you've got the footage in the can, you need to digitize it, crop it, mix it with your art, animation, and sound, and compress it. Sometimes this happens at an outside service bureau. More often, it's an in-house function, since the tools to do it have become much more affordable. Mixing and matching video and artwork in-house also offers you a lot more flexibility, plus the ability to fix goofs more easily, with less expense, and—most importantly to some—with greater privacy. Indeed, digital video can help you save face.

Because the process of making movies for the computer spans traditional and digital domains, there are functions that cross over from one to the other. In a way, you're creating a *Theater in a Box*. That is, the usual language of film with close-ups, medium shots, cutaways, and so on becomes irrelevant in interactive media. Instead, the actors must deliver their lines as if they're standing on a stage—perfectly, with no opportunity to cut. If you were sitting in a theater audience, the director couldn't suddenly shift to a close-up. What you see is what you get. The theater stage has become the computer screen—unchanging, static—with the actor moving around in front of it.

But not all over it. Today's technology only allows for digital video windows of a certain size. QuickTime, for example, runs best at not much more than a 320-by-240 pixel window (that's the quarter of a screen we talked about before). Now, imagine that you've placed a box of those dimensions on your computer-generated stage. The actor can only move within that box.

If you want to see the whole actor, you shoot a long shot. But the actor can't get out of the box. If you want to see the actor's face, you shoot a medium shot. But since you can't see the actor's legs anymore, you have to situate the actor in the foreground, at a table, or peering in a window.

How is all this done? By shooting against a blue screen. It's the same process they use to do the weather on TV news. Also called *chroma-key*, the process involves the actor standing in front of a blue screen. He wears nothing with blue in it. The technicians press some buttons, and the tape that comes home from the studio features an actor surrounded by a sea of blueness. That tape, though—when digitized—then allows your in-house video people to place computer-generated backgrounds where the blue is. The backgrounds with the video are then lined up to perfectly match the bigger backgrounds on the computer screen. The result is that the actor appears to be walking on a stage, when really he's walking in a sea of blue in a quarter-screen video box. It's a pretty cool trick. The process is shown in Figure 5.1.

Fast forward ten minutes into the future: One of the main reasons the Theater in a Box metaphor has caught on so well is that it's simply not been possible to have large video characters moving around, given the 320-by-340 pixel window maximum in QuickTime and its less-than-kissing-cousin Video for Windows. But MPEG and Super Density drives (see Chapter 2) will change all that, allowing full-screen, full-motion video playback with additional, low cost hardware. This will mean the ability to do full screen "set changes"; that is, traditional movie cutting. Developers will undoubtedly still want to use blue screen—why build a full set when you can draw one? But the days of tiny characters limiting artistic vision are probably numbered.

Once the tape has arrived back home, your in-house video crew goes to work, digitizing the video footage, making sure the sound is right, cropping it to the right size, matching it with the backgrounds for Theater in a Box video, and compressing it with one of the algorithms described earlier for all types of video clips. The program of choice for matching video with backgrounds and then compressing it these days is Adobe Premiere. Other programs include Avid's VideoShop and more hardware-intensive solutions such as the Media 100 or a full nonlinear Avid editing system. Both can cost tens of thousands of dollars, whereas Premiere is under $1,000.

Narrations, Sfx, and Music

Most Sound Designers I know voice a familiar complaint. They want to start working on the score for their next masterpiece early. But the team always seems to get to the nitty gritty of sound design at the very end of the project. Then the musicians and technicians gets crunched and crazy and they yell a lot about unrealistic timelines and multiple overlapping deadlines. When it's all

Figure 5.1

An actor is shot against a blue screen. Background art is later placed in the blue, and the resulting movie is lined up with the "theater" background of the computer screen.

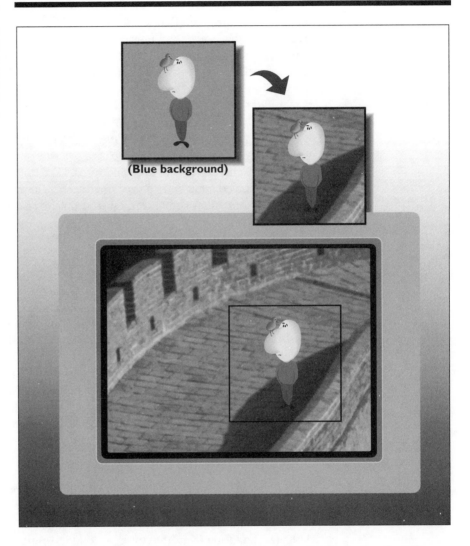

(Blue background)

over, though, the average sound designer will sigh and tell me there's really no other way to do it. And, oh yeah, they just love this job. What's going on here?

The recording of narrations, and the creation of sound effects and music, is probably the last step of the Production process. Narrations should be recorded early, but scripts have a way of getting changed up to the very end. "Scratch narrations"—where some in-house person with a better-than-average voice reads the text—can get done early in order to set some initial animation and video timing. But final narrations get pushed off until the narrations are written in indelible ink (or is that blood? It depends on the project).

Likewise, it would be great to start writing music for a title at the beginning, but it's hard to do that until you actually see what you're writing for. You can compose a general musical theme in advance and some generic sound effects, but timing it to an animation or adding that perfect punctuation or mood change to a video can only take place when all the elements are finalized.

Audio for interactive media is created, and played back, in two basic formats: MIDI, and sound files like WAV or AIFF.

MIDI stands for *Musical Instrument Digital Interface*. MIDI is the language of choice for sound pros. It's basically a way of creating music and storing it as computer code—all ones and zeros. That's what makes it digital. As such, it can be crammed into a very small space. The catch is that to play it back, your computer's sound card must be able to read the MIDI programming calls.

MPC sound cards, fortunately, are all MIDI ready. Macs are a less sure bet—surprising for a platform that's had built-in sound from the beginning. A lot of MIDI stuff as it's played back on the computer sounds pretty awful—computer game backgrounds and stuff. That's because it's supposed to repeat over and over again and remain independent of the game play. Synching up MIDI files and computer interaction isn't as easy as it sounds, and most interactive media developers opt to convert MIDI into files with names like WAV or AIFF.

WAV (for the PC) and *AIFF* (mostly for the Mac) store information digitally, but don't require any special hardware to play back. They're sound files, just like PICT is a file for a picture or AVI is a file for Video for Windows. So, why doesn't everyone use them? Because they're so flexible and independent, they take up more room. Indeed, the better they sound, the more room they fill.

There are a variety of flavors of digital sound files. *Bits* refer to the sample size that quantifies a sound's "resolution," so to speak—how much data is present in it. The number of samples that go by in a second is expressed in kilohertz. So, full CD-quality sound comes out at 16 bits with a frequency of 44 KHz. That also means that every second of sound requires 44K (for kilobytes) of storage on your hard disk or CD-ROM. The lower end, more standard to CD-ROM delivery, is represented by a measly 8-bit sound with a frequency resolution of only 22 KHz.

Narrations these days are either recorded directly to the computer or first on *DAT* (*Digital Audio Tape*), a format that—like PhotoCD—was supposed to make it big with consumers, but has become a standard for computer professionals. DAT, developed by Sony, records in perfect digital format—16 bit and 44 KHz. Sound that's recorded at the highest possible quality means you've got it saved for posterity—or if the technology ever allows for easy playback of 44 KHz sound from, say, an SD Digital Video Disc CD-ROM machine. Only if you start with the best can you hope to end up with a sweeter smelling fragrance.

Sound effects are probably my favorite part of the Sound Designer's work. It's just amazing how a toilet flush sounds running backwards with a lot of reverb. Cartoon sound effects must be carefully matched to the visuals, or else the crash-boom-bang occurs before the little bunny hits the bottom of the rabbit hole—kind of ruining the suspense. The Sound Designer's other bane of existence is that, after all his or her hard work synching things up and getting it as perfect as the art, the user that buys the CD-ROM then runs it on a painfully slow machine, which messes things up anyway. All the Sound Designer can do is wait patiently for the day when even quad-speed Pentiums are yesterday's technology.

Media Acquisition and Rights Clearance

Oy, Media Acquisition. It's one of those things no one likes to do but the lawyers tell us we have to. Wouldn't it be nice if you could just scan any picture you wanted and use it—no questions asked? Copy a musical piece and loop in the background? Unfortunately, there's this little thing called "intellectual property," and the intellectuals with the property get pretty testy if you don't pay them for their hard brain work. So, a lot of your Production time will be dedicated to making sure you really can use that Van Gogh painting—he's in the public domain now, isn't he?

Much of Media Acquisition is paperwork, with a little bit of detective work thrown in to keep the person doing it from going batty. Ah, but then there are the nuances that make it so much fun:

- If you've altered an image or musical piece so much it doesn't even resemble its starting point, do you need to notify the original creator and pay for it?

- How about if you've used an image for inspiration and you drew it yourself, but your inspiration looks mighty like the original?

- Then there are images you find from a variety of sources. You get to pick who to contact based on price. There's even the thrill of negotiation.

The questions above are great for images and even music, but video acquisition is so complex, you're best off reading the book on it. Mark Radcliffe and Dianne Brinson's *Multimedia Law Handbook* from Ladera Press is a great start. It has tons of examples of when you need to acquire the rights to a clip from the studio, the actors in the clip, the director, the writer, and so on.

With video as with images, you really are best off creating as much as you can from scratch. It's also a better way toward going down the road of making interactive media its own art form. The more you copy, the less original your piece is going to be, and the greater the chance it could have been done just as well in a different media format.

Media Acquisition has a nasty habit of starting too late—gee, is this getting to sound familiar? You really need your media in hand when you start production, but a lot of times, it's not until the script is done, or the artists have drawn their inspiration from that script, that it's clear which images you'll really need. The best way to operate is to be as aggressively proactive and forward thinking as you can. If you just think you might need an image of countryside in France, order it as soon as it comes to mind. You don't have to pay for images up front, but at least now you've got it, and if you use it, you can pay for it later. Keep careful track of all your images—many archive houses and museums may ask you to return even the PhotoCDs they create for you when the project's over.

There are some great sources of archival footage. Big firms like Archive New Media in New York are an excellent place to start. Most of the major television networks have libraries that license footage—NBC, CBS, WTN, BBC, to name a few. Some archives have "no manipulation" clauses. Others are exceedingly expensive, especially if you request something from a museum. Beware the British Museum or the Louvre—they'll charge you an arm and a leg and then tell you you can't use the image for more than two years without negotiating a new contract!

Music can be obtained from CD houses that specialize in creating catchy pieces that sound like things you hear on the radio or TV, but don't infringe on someone else's rights. There's even one company called Narration Tracks that creates musical backgrounds that are designed to be unobtrusive under a narration. Jasmine, Aris, and Correl all have "clip media" CDs with a variety of images, video and sound to choose from—all rights free.

■ Implementation

Implementation is all about putting the pieces together once they're made. By definition, at this point, your audio, video, art, and animation are all done. Intellectual property, if not paid for, is at least in the process of being acquired. The Implementation phase, accordingly, begins with a freeze, then proceeds through a series of milestones.

Art, Content, and Functionality Freeze

When all the pieces are finally together, tell your team to Stop! Desist! Freeze! Don't touch that stylus! Unless you freeze production at a certain point, you'll be playing cat and mouse until the last day of the project. Every time your programmers think they've got it done, a piece of artwork gets revised, or someone has a great idea about a new screen, or heaven forbid, an entirely new section. The most important skill here is to have someone (the Producer, the Team Leader) who can say no, and not bend under the pressure of "just another feature and we'll be able to sell another 20,000 copies!"

This is not to say you can't fix things if they're broken. A screen with the wrong artwork must be changed, art freeze or not. A terrible factual error caught at the last moment will affect even the best laid plans. But in your project management plan, write down a date for art freeze, and then try your hardest, within reason, to stick to it.

Integration of Audio, Video, and Program Elements

This step mostly consists of getting all the pieces collected. It's a physical process that is more daunting than it sounds. You may have hundreds, possibly thousands, of visuals, sound files, video clips, and pieces of text. If you were smart, you've been keeping close track of them all along. But now you have to bring them to one person, who will either integrate them into a program in a single location or distribute them to the programmers to work on different pieces.

If you're using a network (a way of connecting all the computers in your facility so they can talk to each other), all the pieces can be put up on the server (a dedicated machine that serves all the others), and a single working version of the program can live there as well. This facilitates more people working on the title at once. You can even have your testers working directly from the network, or burning test CDs from it.

Integration doesn't have to be an all-at-once process, though too often it is. If you're really planning ahead, you'll have been integrating on the fly, popping screens into your Skeleton Screen Structure, or adding real or virtual links to files that live elsewhere. Authoring systems make this easier. Some companies will use an authoring system to assemble material, then hand it over to the hard-core coders to do the dirty work.

Coding

This step varies depending on whether you're coding in C++ or using an authoring system. Coding in C++ requires a good networked environment, as described above, as most teams have more than a single programmer working on it at once. Assembly in an authoring system, on the other hand, can be done by one person alone, and in fact, many times it's better that way.

Most authoring systems are not easily networkable. I've seen different team members working on their individual pieces of a project, but usually, the scripting or programming that they add must be recopied by hand into the final version. It's often easier to do any "programming," as such, on a single Assembly Station (a computer dedicated to the sole task of assembling media pieces). Animation and sound changes can be done on different computers.

As with Integration, both hard coding and authoring system assembly can—and should—start long before the late stage that this step seems to indicate. Again, we return to the Skeleton Screen Structure. Done right, it's the backbone of your entire program, and will, by this point, already contain the programming for your title's basic navigation structure. Tougher programming tasks don't have to wait until the end, either. You're planning on including a custom database in that infotainment title? Start coding that section early, when your programmers are a little less crunched. You can put placeholder data in for now, then add the real McCoy when it's ready to be indexed.

Alpha with User Test

Now we're into milestones. An *alpha* is simply a stage in the development of the program. The alpha date is often used as a milestone for payment by the client or publisher. The alpha is also usually the first point in production that your product is assembled and coded enough to be able to burn a CD that you can actually send to someone and let it run by itself. (*Burning* a CD is the vernacular for taking your hard drive data and copying it to a CD-ROM.)

It used to be you'd have to send your hard drive data, usually on DAT (digital audio tape), out to a service bureau, which would burn the CD for you for a reasonable price. Nowadays, though, everyone has their own in-house CD "one-off" machines. These devices will create a limited CD from your data that plays back fine on any machine, but can't make a copy of itself. For that, you need a *glass master*—a more expensive mother CD that is ready to stamp out baby discs. Most interactive media development companies can now afford a one-off machine—they run anywhere from $6,000 to $15,000. Glass masters cost between $600 and $1,800 to make, but then the CDs that result are less that $1 each in large quantities.

No one expects an alpha to be perfect. By definition, it should include at least a sample of all the features you plan to include, but certainly not all the content. It gives the client a solid peek into what you're doing, early enough that changes can be made. Of course, your client, content owner, or upper management should be kept up to date throughout the product. It's just that, if the boss isn't physically in the same office, it's hard for him or her to inspect the work on a regular basis. And you're usually under such a tight schedule, you're not particularly interested in sending out samples that you know will be seen out-of-context and probably misinterpreted. So, time and time again, the alpha becomes the client's first serious look.

Alphas need to run, but again not perfectly. It's okay to have your client go through a more cumbersome process than usual of copying files and modifying the AUOTEXEC.BAT manually. The client knows you're busy.

When should an alpha be completed? Usually, alphas get pressed somewhere around 6–8 weeks before the completion of a project. In addition to getting client feedback, you should also do some user testing with the alpha. We've tested already with prototypes—both paper and computer based—but now you have something real to show, with a smidge of actual content and a dash of final screens. You may need to walk your users through the product a bit more than you would if it were really polished, but any feedback at any time is always a good thing.

For this user test, do use people outside the development team. They've been working so closely with the content that it's hard to be objective. And they may see things the average user will never notice—a stray pixel, a missed line that doesn't affect content but drives you crazy. For this user test, you may even get formal—call a company that specializes in getting together focus groups. Or at least try to assemble users from the target audience (it's not really fair to test a kids' title on their grandparents—they may not appreciate the snot and phlegm jokes the way the Nickelodeon young'uns would).

Beta Test—Quality Assurance

The next milestone after the alpha is the beta. Beta has a very clear definition, which the person paying you will never let you forget—if you don't meet the criteria, you don't get paid. *Beta* is defined as "all the functionality and all the content included with no known bugs."

When you press your beta disc using your one-off machine, you're sending out something you hope will be finished. If you've done a superb job of assembling or programming, there should be no bugs, no problems, no crashes. Out the door, it's time to get this puppy to market.

Not so fast. Because while you hope the product is a candidate for final code, you know in your heart of hearts that when it makes it to the tough cookies who live in the dungeons of Quality Assurance (QA) land, your product will be full of problems. But that's okay. Because pressing a beta initiates the formal QA process. The Quality Assurance department consists of the people you pay to play and break your product. Multiple copies of your disc are tested on multiple computer configurations by these professional testbusters. There are a couple types of testing they'll wind up doing:

1. Tests for content inconsistencies. The testers in this role will click every button (or environmental object) in the program with the goal of finding out if the next place the program goes makes sense. If not, they log it.

2. Tests for bugs and crashes. These testers need the patience of a digital Job, because they'll be clicking and logging and clicking and logging until the wee hours of the night. And every time a new version of the product comes in—even if it's a minuscule upgrade to correct for some small bug—they have to go back and do a full "regression." That is, they check everything all over again. Because you never know when one fix will break something else. The most repeated testing is for large reference products.

There is a bright side, though. Bug and crash testers can have fun trying weird combinations to induce crashes out of an otherwise reticent program. Hmmm, if you click this button while holding the Shift key and the Reset button simultaneously, I wonder what will happen....

Testing can occur in or out of house. Usually, there's at least one or two people in-house testing the product before it goes to the outside (read: more expensive) testing firm. If you're a developer and you're creating product for a specific publisher, the publisher usually has a big QA department, and they'll do the testing for you. Then, the Producer or Team Leader serves as an in-house liaison to the outside QA, passing on the latest-breaking news to the programmers or artists.

One of the questions that publishers love to ask their QA people is "is it true beta?" That means, does it fit the definition of beta closely enough that the developer gets an advance check? But it's also useful for scheduling. If it's not true beta, it means there's still functionality on its way or even, heaven forbid, new content or art! Once true beta is in, then it's only a matter of fixing bugs. Some general rules for how long that should take: At Mindscape, we allowed ideally 4–6 weeks for beta testing, usually 3–4 weeks, and at worst, 1–2 weeks of really grueling, all-night burn-outs.

Revision and Polishing

This is perhaps the most important step in your whole Implementation effort, but it is sadly honored almost entirely in the breech. Imagine this scenario: You've finished production, the product has been tested and passed the most scrupulous QA mousing. Wouldn't it be nice if you had a little time to make some revisions, to polish some of the rough edges? Especially if you've been racing against an unreal and irrational deadline imposed by the client, there's a good chance that you slapped the product together faster than you would have liked and there are little glitches you wish you could go back and fix. If you have a Revision and Polishing cycle built into your schedule, you may have that chance.

By the way, the worst glitches—the ones that are most in need of a Revision cycle—are those features the client said he or she just *must* have—but only after seeing the alpha. Sure, it wasn't in the Functional Spec that the client presumably signed off on, but the additional features really do make sense, and the client promises that those changes will make you extra royalties, so you agree. But the new feature looks rough, the graphics appear too slapped together.

A Revision and Polishing cycle doesn't have to be long. A week can be sufficient. But it's something you should insist on. You should put it in your project management timeline. But don't expect it to happen. Maybe those nice features will make it into Version 1.1 or Version 2.0. But you'll very likely be shipping a Version 1.0 that doesn't meet your own exacting standards. Live with it. That's business. Now go make the next one even better.

Final Code

Whether you got your Revision and Polishing cycle or not, when your product is finally ready, it's reached that milestone called Final Code. This is when you press your glass master, send it to the duplication plant, and say goodbye to your product for now. Don't worry—it will be back. It's a rare product that, when it hits the market and the even larger variety of computer configurations out there, doesn't reveal a few unexpected bugs that need fixing. If they're bad enough, you'll come out with a release update.

Final Code is a day to be celebrated. When the CD goes out, your team deserves a reward. Here are some of the ways you can show your appreciation:

1. A handshake and a pat on the back—that'll make everyone happy.

2. Better—some well-deserved time off. If your team, especially your programmers, has been putting in a week, a month, or more of night after night until 4:00 a.m., a little comp time keeps team members happy. If you do this, though, know that if any glaring bugs are discovered, your team may not be around to fix them.

3. More fun—a trip, a dinner, an event to help bonding and to let everyone know you're a fun person to work for (and you recognize hard work).

4. Most lucrative—a cash or stock bonus. Nothing satisfies like an extra month's pay or another 1,000 shares of stock with a short vesting cycle. You can bet the next time your team won't hesitate to put in long hours if they know that hard work pays.

Postmortem

When your team gets back from celebrating, it's time to hold a post-mortem. Yes, it's as morbid as it sounds. Everyone on the team is invited. This is where you dissect your product, and most importantly, the process that went into producing it. Postmortems typically involve

- Looking into every screen and discussing how it looks, how it works, and what could have been done differently or better

- Talking about the process—how the scheduling came about, how well it was adhered to, how the team worked together, and how well information flowed

Postmortems can get nasty. Especially when the end of a project is tense, some team members are looking for an opportunity to vent. They see this as their chance. Try your best to nip this inclination in the bud. You want a postmortem to be a learning experience.

Postmortems need to be highly structured so they don't disintegrate into name-calling. They shouldn't be held the day after a product ships. Give everyone a little cooling-down time. Even if it was the most harmonious team, they probably saw their children fewer hours near the end than they might have liked, and enough late nights can turn even the nicest artist into some Doom-flavored attack creature.

■ Publishing

The Publishing phase really kicks in once the product finishes but, like many of the tasks prior, has started long before. The four tasks that go into this phase are

1. Putting the package together

2. Letting everyone know that you've got a great product

3. Telling the right people

4. Getting the product to market

First things first, though.

Public Relations

Sure, you thought the first part of Publishing would be doing the package. If that were the case, though, your product would hit the shelves all dressed up but with no one to notice it. The first players to get involved are your Public Relations people. An initial press release announcing a deal or cooperative relationship may go out months or even years before your title hits the streets. Access Software's *Under a Killing Moon* had promotional kits, doo-dads, and "tschotkies" flooding magazine offices and stores from the moment they dreamed up the title.

Public relations is then involved all along the way, writing more press releases and taking your product (and hopefully, you) on the road to editors and magazine writers, even the TV circuit. Public relations focuses mostly on the press. Selling the public is left to the marketing and sales people.

At some point in the public relations process, they're going to need to show something. And one of the items PR people love to pass out is mockups of your packaging. So it's off to the next step....

Packaging

The packaging team needs to know as much about your title as possible, so they can start designing a box, writing the copy for the back of the box, and creating "sell sheets" that go out to potential buyers, both retail and OEM bundlers. Packaging people almost always live at the publishers. A developer may wind up designing the box for the publisher because their publisher likes their work, but it's not the same as having a dedicated team that knows all there is to know about candy boxes, jewel cases versus cardboard flip boxes, where to get color separations done the cheapest for large quantities, and the myriad other tasks that go into getting a box done.

Developers who have decided to self-publish their title will need to know as much as they can about package design. And it's not at all as easy as it looks. A beautiful box may not sell. Authentic hieroglyphic fonts for the title of your package may not be readable at a glance. Putting the name of the product at the top of the box at a time when stores have started stacking boxes so that only the bottom of the box shows won't help you move the minimum numbers you need. Hire a good team, then trust your packaging people. That's why they get paid the big bucks.

You can help them, though. You know your product better than anyone else. Who best to write some initial copy—both for the back of the box and press releases—than you, the developer? The box will need screen shots, too, so that potential buyers can get a feel for the product in the seven seconds they spend before going on. You could hand the CD to your packaging people and say "pick what you like." Or you could make some suggestions based on your intimate knowledge of your masterpiece.

The packaging process doesn't start after final code, either. It must begin months before. An initial concept is sketched out in multiple variations. The best are taken to a more formal treatment. Finally, a decision is made, and that box is created—and tested. If it doesn't play well in focus groups, it's back to the drawing board. Sometimes this happens after the product is out on the shelves, and it's the salespeople who've discovered it isn't selling because the box is wimpy. You can avoid all this by starting early, really early.

Boxes don't have to reflect their contents, either. The front of the box usually tries to go for the consumer's gut. The back previews the content.

And the side (or spine) is becoming the most important element as more and more products on the shelves crowd software boxes into a side-out presentation. You should get screen shots to packaging early—they can always be changed later, but at least they have them for placement.

While it's not something you can plan for in the development process, there is a raging debate about the size of the box. Right now, boxes are big, even though the CD-ROMs inside are small. That's because they're all competing for a slice of the consumer's mindshare. We're in a cereal box mentality—bigger must be better, even if it's filled with air. Some publishers give their boxes unusual shapes to make them stand out even more. The most prominent examples are Knowledge Adventure's octagonal boxes for *3D Dinosaur Adventure*, *Body Adventure*, and more. Broderbund's *Prince of Persia* looks kind of like an oriental tower. By the way, retailers hate these odd shapes—they don't stack well at all.

The problem with all these boxes is they're mostly empty. The most intuitive products don't need a manual—only a one-page QuickStart card. Yet there's nothing quite as unsatisfying as picking up a box that feels too light. Some publishers have gotten around this by stuffing their boxes with goodies. Knowledge Adventure's *Magic Theater* has a microphone; Interactive Publishing's *Teddy's Big Day* has a real stuffed bear that takes up most of the box. Future Vision Multimedia packs a heavy book, *How to Write Term Papers*, to fill up their oversized *InfoPedia* box. For the *Adventures of Nikko*, we included a box of crayons.

The Voyager Company has taken the opposite approach and put their product in a small book-sized box. There's no plastic jewel case inside, just a flap where the CD sits naked. It's environmentally friendly and fits Voyager's focus of creating booklike CD-ROMs that challenge the mind (their slogan is "Bring your Brain").

While you usually can't tell a publisher what type of box you want, you can pick your publisher by the type of box they usually use. Now, picking your publisher is probably only for the elite among us, but it's something to aspire to.

Sales and Marketing

I've lumped these two sometimes different categories together because they play off each other so much. Both functions are focused around moving more product off the shelf and into consumers' hands. Marketing dreams up promotions that create awareness of your title: Endcaps in stores (that's when you have a rack of just your title at the end of a store shelf). Contests to win free product. Doodads that hang from the ceiling announcing the arrival of the Next Big Thing. Packing the company's demo CD inside your package as a nice freebie.

How about coupons for discounts on future products? A fan club? The possibilities are endless. Depending on the company's promotional budget, they may want to even make up a videotape of your and other products to play in one of those endless loop set-ups at a trade show. Marketing is usually the address where print (and even TV) advertising gets devised. You'd be amazed how much a good ad campaign can contribute to a weak title's performance.

The sales staff is also interested in getting product to move—in an even more intense way. They're the street force, the men and women who arm themselves with product, literature, boxes, videos, sell sheets, and whatever else. They'll visit their key retail buyers and their best bundle connections, and they'll try to get your title in as many stores, catalogs, and computer boxes as possible. Sales will give you the fastest feedback, too:

- "The packaging is killing it."

- "No, it's the price—we've got to make this a real 'budget' title."

- "The ad campaign is all wrong. This encyclopedia should be marketed the same as *Mortal Kombat*."

Sales, like most of the roles in the publishing process, gets involved long before the selling process. They'll let you know what price your title should go out at and how many they think they can sell (they're usually conservative, because they have to commit to that number and their bonuses are linked to meeting their forecasts). All this, in turn, influences the budget, or what the publisher can offer a developer.

Distribution

Distribution is the last piece of the long and winding puzzle we've navigated together. Distribution is, as it sounds, how a product gets distributed into the stores, catalogs, and bundles that bring it to market. A publisher may or not have an in-house distribution capability. A developer working for a publisher never does. Some developers try to self-publish and rely on outside distributors to get their product into the channel. In each case, the "deal" is different.

Developer/Publisher Relationship

The deal that looks least lucrative on paper for the developer is the classic developer/publisher relationship where the publisher pays the developer a nice chunk of money as an "advance against royalty." The publisher takes on all responsibilities for distribution. The developer need only supply the hard disk with the code that will be made into the glass master.

The product then starts to sell. After it's made enough money to earn back its development advance, the developer starts to earn royalties. A small royalty of 10 percent or less is usually associated with this type of deal. Developers grumble that they'd rather be earning more on the back end—a higher royalty, that is—but the truth is, most products don't sell well enough to ever clear even a modest advance. A better strategy would be to load your profit into your advance, then finish the title for less than you forecast.

Affiliated Labels

Another popular distribution deal involves developing the product entirely on your own dime, then approaching a publisher about publishing and distributing it. This is the Affiliated Labels type of arrangement. The royalty is higher—up to 40 percent—but there is greater risk for the developer, who's absorbed the development costs and is now dependent entirely on sales in a fickle market to earn back his or her investment.

Self-Publishing

The final arrangement is the self-publishing deal. The small developer who takes this on supplies entirely finished goods to one of the big distributors. The distributor takes a cut, but it's less than either of the other two scenarios. If the product is hot, the developer keeps more. But the risk is enormous. Returns are the responsibility of the developer, who may press 10,000 CDs with expectation of sales on all of those, only to find that 5,000 are returned—either unbought or unloved.

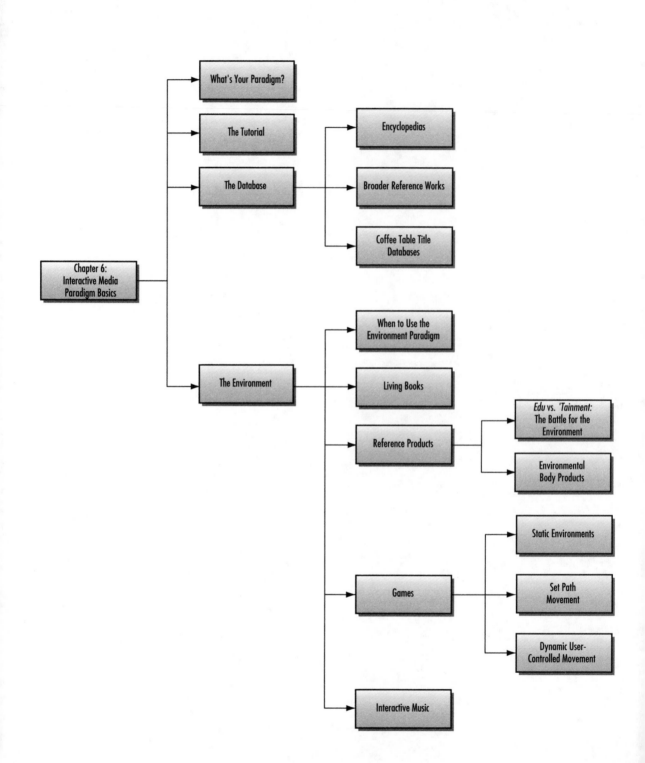

Interactive Media Paradigm Basics

IN THE FIRST CHAPTER, WE LOOKED AT THREE CENTRAL GUIDELINES that address when it's right (and when it's wrong) to invest your time, money, and REM sleep cycles in an interactive media title. On the assumption that your title idea passed these criteria, we ventured into the process, meeting some of the people you'll need on your team and delving into the development cycle. At this point, most of your planning should be over. But before you go too much further, take a step back. Take a look at what you've got so far.

How does what you're about to undertake fit into the big picture—the competitive view that considers the past, present, and future of interactive media titles? Are there patterns, similarities, or school-of-hard-knock lessons you can learn from? How can you take advantage of the wider universe of interactive media planning and design to create unique programs that are worthy of being produced? It's time to play a variation on an old game show. I call this one "What's your paradigm?"

■ What's Your Paradigm?

Interactive media paradigms are those larger constructs that define the category your title falls into from a design, not marketing, point of view. I'll cover six paradigms in this chapter and the next. The first three are what I call the biggies—the basic paradigms that encompass the vast majority of interactive media programs. These are

1. The Tutorial

2. The Database

3. The Environment

Why are paradigms so important? Because there are certain accepted rules that the different paradigms follow. Knowing which of these paradigms your title is leaning toward can help you tap into an already accepted body of knowledge. Interactive media titles are always trying to reinvent the wheel. Most of the time, that's good, especially since the wheel is still kind of square. But you don't have to beat your head against the wall unless you like the process of doing the beating at least as much as the feeling when you stop.

Paradigms are not exclusive. A program with a basic Database structure may include some Tutorials inside. An overall Environmental Paradigm product might sport a Database, accessible from a control panel or Main Interface button. Get to know your paradigms up front.

There's another, equally important reason to bone up on paradigm basics. If, for example, you've identified that the product you want to create has strong database tendencies, you can check the competition in the same paradigm. Even if a product you've identified is not a direct competitor (for example, you're making an encyclopedia so you check out all the other encyclopedias), someone somewhere in marketing or sales is going to be doing that kind of comparing. You want to be at least a step and a half ahead of him or her.

As we explore the world of paradigms, I'll be presenting a veritable ton of examples. Maybe you can even do your initial competitive analysis work here—saving yourself a trip to the mall!

■ The Tutorial

Tutorials can be summed up pretty simply. Titles that fit this paradigm teach you how to do something. They are one of the earliest forms of interactive media. CBT (Computer Based Training) programs almost always followed the tutorial paradigm. The stuff you learn if you study instructional design (like I did) in school tends to push you toward the Tutorial. That's because tutorials address specific learning objectives. They allow for tests and quizzes that measure a student's growth. They often go through a progression of linear steps, and that's okay—if you're the learner, you want to understand what's being taught as much as the program wants to teach you.

You know you've found a tutorial program when it has a structure that looks something like this:

Section 1

- Introduction—with note on "average time to complete this section"
- Information presentation itself
- Hands-on section
- Test

Section 2

- Pre-Test (if you don't pass, go back to Section 1)
- Information presentation
- Hands-on section
- Test

…and so on.

Tutorials have a bad reputation for being boring, but they don't have to be. The early CBT programs may have followed template formulas too literally. Every section looked exactly alike—seven information screens, always with a header in the upper left hand corner, a certain number of lines of text per block, graphics appropriately placed for maximum visibility, a slew of buttons. But there are some outstanding modern examples of tutorials that defy the conventionality of the past.

How to Shoot Video Like a Pro (Figure 6.1) is a tutorial paradigm CD title from Zelos Digital Learning. True to its name, its purpose is to make you a better amateur videographer. Because the program is aimed at the broad consumer market, it doesn't have tests you must pass to go on. But it does have the other basic features of the Tutorial. The title is divided neatly into categories—lighting, editing, audio, and so on.

Figure 6.1

How to Shoot Video Like a Pro uses the Tutorial paradigm to teach virtual videography.

Each section has the exact same setup—a little basic information followed by a try-it-yourself area—great for creating repeatability and perceived depth. You can use your mouse to adjust the virtual camera's zoom and watch what happens through the virtual viewfinder. While you're virtual viewfinding, a second, linked animation shows you what the camera is doing in schematic form. So, as your subject comes into focus in one window, you see how the camera is adjusting itself in the other.

Could this title have been done in another medium? Certainly there are videos that teach you how to use your camcorder. They're missing the hands-on component with instant feedback, though. *How to Shoot Video Like a Pro* may not be the ultimate reason to run out and buy an interactive media-ready computer. But if you already have one (and the subject interests you), it's around the same price as the video, so check it out. It's a very efficient example of the Tutorial paradigm in action.

If being a rock and roll star interests you more than learning to shoot videos, another Tutorial paradigm CD is your ticket. At the core of *So You Want to Be a Rock and Roll Star* (Figure 6.2) from Interactive Records are some basic instructions on how to play guitar and other instruments like the pros. Most people, however, will probably buy this title for the karaoke effect. They've recorded some classic oldies—"Sittin' by the Dock of the Bay" and others—and synched them up to groovy animations of musicians playing in different locations (on a pier by the dock of the bay, for example). Then you get to decide which tracks you want to hear.

Figure 6.2

So You Want to Be a Rock and Roll Star lets you learn while you play—in this case, the instruments on screen.

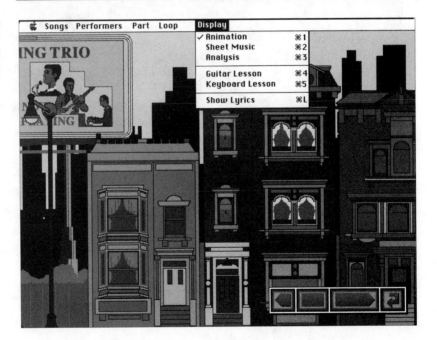

You want to play bass yourself instead of watching the cartoon bass player? Go for it. You want to warble with, or in place of, the computerized crooner? It's your title, you can do whatever you want as long as the doors are closed. *So You Want to Be a Rock and Roll Star* isn't textbook organized, but it gets its point across in a fun and engaging manner. You don't buy this title to sit back and listen to music. You buy it if you want to learn how to do something, and that's what Tutorials are all about.

There's no question about what your goal is when you buy one of the Wilson Learning business skills series titles (Figure 6.3). These CD-ROMs began as corporate training videodiscs—classic Tutorials—and their consumer counterparts bear striking resemblance to the originals. The idea here is to learn to negotiate better; or close that sale with more savvy; or improve your listening skills.

Figure 6.3

Wilson Learning has turned videodisc tutorials into CD-ROM consumer titles with products that teach interpersonal and business skills.

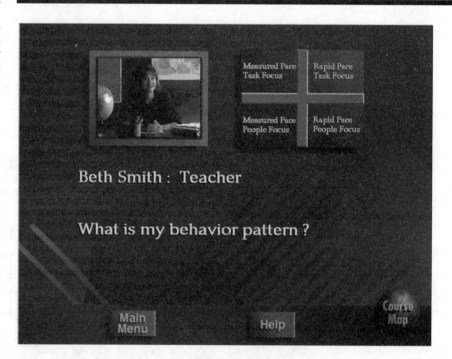

Through a series of video vignettes, you role-play your way to fame and glory. You've just gotten a big meeting with Client X. You come in and make your presentation. He tells you, politely, that he's not interested at this time. What do you do next?

A. Sulk out the door?

B. Put your feet up on his table and tell him why he's wrong while helping yourself to one if his cuban cigars?

C. Promise to keep in touch, send him more literature, perhaps see if someone else in the organization might be interested?

Obviously, the answer is B. And you're on a fast track to nowhere, buddy, if that's your answer. The Wilson Learning Series is so much a Tutorial that there are even quizzes and reviews as you move through the different levels. You can choose which topic to go to next, but once in a topic, it's a linear progression of skills.

Before you can sell shoes, you have to drive the car. So, along comes *License to Drive* from Janus Interactive, which promises to do for driver training what *Mortal Kombat* did to games. *License to Drive* is like the old driver simulation booths some of us used as teenagers—"except," reads the product's ad copy, "without the funky furniture and chewed-up pencils." Although they've jazzed up the "consequences" of bad driving, the program's self-stated goal is to help kids prepare for their driving test. So much so that it includes sample written tests you take after you've crashed and burned your car a few hundred times. Tutorial with an attitude? It doesn't get much funkier than this.

Need a breather? Spirit of St. Louis Software publishes a *Baseball Series Batting Clinic*. Any question of which paradigm you're in is dispelled by the title's Table of Contents: Hitting Videos, Hitting Mechanics, Hitting Technologies, Hitting Fundamentals, Hitting Drills, Lesson Review....

While CD-ROM and interactive media Tutorials are becoming more common, many software products these days come with a floppy-disk-based tutorial. These don't usually satisfy the "song and dance" criteria of interactive media; that is, while they may have some animation, they don't usually have audio—there simply isn't enough room on the floppy. But they do lead you through, step by step, how to use sophisticated software tools—everything from Claris Corporation's ClarisWorks to Microsoft Excel. If you're looking for examples of lower-tech tutorials and you're far from the nearest software boutique, see what came in the box of the productivity software you use every day. It's a great place to start.

■ The Database

Unlike the Tutorial, programs that fit the Database paradigm take a less didactic approach to the structure of information. Databases are probably the most common type of interactive media presentation. The idea is simple enough—take a wealth of interesting information and chop it up into small, easily searchable blocks. Graft a nice interface on the front, check to ensure interactive media appropriateness, and voilà—it's interactive media *au gratin*.

In a Database, getting at information is up to you, the user, and there are no time limits or learning objectives to follow. If there is a test, per se, it's for your own enjoyment and edification. Microsoft Encarta has a fun "test your knowledge" section, for example, but you don't have to pass anything to get to the next section.

You usually can tell you're in the land of Databases when:

- There are lots of buttons and a variety of ways to access information quickly.

- There are highlighted words and phrases that let you "hyperlink" to a related article, thought, or media element.

- There are no specific learning objectives present, as in a Tutorial.

Database paradigm titles fall into a number of categories.

Encyclopedias

First up are the big encyclopedias. Games, edutainment programs, and encyclopedias are the top selling titles in the interactive media business, so a lot of ink is spilled comparing their various features. For the record, Microsoft *Encarta* seems to win most of the reviewer polls, with Grolier's *New Multimedia Encyclopedia* (Figure 6.4) and Compton's *Interactive Encyclopedia* sparring for second place, and Future Vision's newcomer, *InfoPedia*, pulling up the rear.

Figure 6.4

Grolier's *New Multimedia Encyclopedia* has the best "old media" source and a brand-new single screen interface.

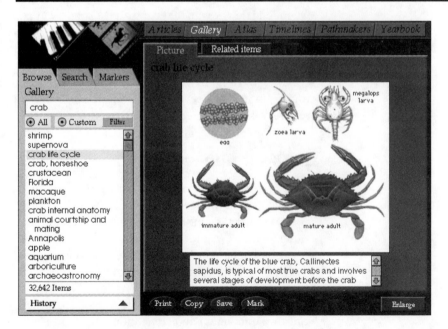

Each encyclopedia has its share of buttons. *Encarta* is the prettiest, with everything neatly arranged into various windows that appear on screen all the time. Grolier has a reputation for the best content: Its original source—the *Academic American*—is the most "adult" of the four. Compton's is based on its children's encyclopedia, and *Encarta* and *InfoPedia* both use *Funk and Wagnall's*, which has a reputation as a supermarket lightweight. While the latest version of Grolier's sports a spiffy all-on-one-screen interface, the previous versions forced users to wade through multiple overlapping windows.

Compton's solution to that problem was to extend the workspace—the last version of their Interactive Encyclopedia featured a large "virtual" desktop that was bigger than your viewing window; you moved around it using a small window in the corner. The latest edition of this top seller goes beyond the desktop entirely—it "stars" the authoritative Captain Picard (Patrick Stewart) from "Star Trek: The Next Generation" as the host of the title's context-sensitive Help.

Encyclopedias also demonstrate their innate database-ness through hypertext links. Throughout most encyclopedia entries you'll find highlighted (or underlined) words that you can click on to transport to another, related entry. Old-fashioned print encyclopedia users do this by flipping the pages and browsing, perhaps even stumbling upon an entry they didn't know they were interested in. Hyperlinking is about the closest CD-ROM encyclopedia users can get to this experience.

Broader Reference Works

After the encyclopedias, you have the broader reference works. These can be general, like *Microsoft Bookshelf*—which presents a wealth of "secondary" material (dictionary, thesaurus, book of quotes, atlas, and so on) wrapped up in a fast, intuitive interface—or more specialized, like Microsoft's *Cinemania*. *Cinemania* presents thousands of movie reviews (including a bunch from Roger Ebert of TV and print fame), cast listings, stills, and even video clips. It's comprehensive and focused but a little light in the video department, especially compared with all those thousands of text entries.

For my taste, I prefer a more concentrated work like Voyager's *Criterion Collection*, which includes fewer entries, almost all with clips. The *Criterion Collection* is a CD catalog to the videodisc collection of the same name also owned by Voyager (hence affording them a heck of a lot less headache getting clip rights). *Midnight Movie Madness*, a similarly focused title, is hosted by comedian Gilbert Gottfried and focuses on weird, wacky, and bad films showing at a theater or cable channel somewhere around midnight near you. Reference or entertainment? Either way, the result is solidly in the database paradigm.

Merriam Webster's Dictionary for Kids from Mindscape is a different kind of database—a database of words. The database elements in this title include arrows to scroll through the dictionary, and a nifty search function. For interactive media, Merriam Webster pronounces all 20,000-plus words, and includes a good number of animations and sound effects. The title also includes several games that reinforce the learning in a hip way.

Coffee Table Title Databases

Beyond encyclopedias and broader reference works, there are less hardcore databases and coffee table titles. Not as paradigmatically pure, the database in these types of titles tends to get disguised. You almost don't recognize it. Mindscape's *The San Diego Zoo Presents… The Animals!*, for example, wraps its database up in a tidy little environment—that of the world-famous Zoo with its different ecological areas. Once you're inside an area, though, there are tons of pictures and media elements, all button accessible, revealing the title's essential database nature.

In a classic database like an encyclopedia, there is a paltry media-to-text ratio. As with *Cinemania*, most of the tens (or even hundreds) of thousands of entries in the average encyclopedia are just text. You can do a specific search for the entries with animations, sounds, or videos, but if you were to look up *paper clip*, it's doubtful that it has earned its own video. One of the qualities that makes *The San Diego Zoo* such a database standout is that every animal gets a picture. And a much higher percentage of entries get a moving or audio media element. As with a coffee-table print title, the information is presented exquisitely, even if the overall quantity is less exhaustive than a hardcore encyclopedia.

David Macaulay's *The Way Things Work* from Dorling Kindersley Multimedia (Figure 6.5) is a database, too, but it's such a whizzy one that you're really inclined to forget that fact sometimes. You can choose from a variety of categories—machines, principles of science, history, inventors—then check out how specific "things" work. Each and every screen has a graphic and text. There are pop-up hypertext links. Many screens have extra audio information.

The best entries feature very useful (and funny) animations, showing how a gear box churns or how a toilet tank flushes. Sometimes you even click inside a graphic to start the animation. As tempting as it might be to classify this title as a modified environment paradigm, it's still a database. The biggest giveaway is the multiple layered windows each with its own close box in the upper left-hand corner.

■ The Environment

If you've been reading between the lines—heck, it isn't buried very deep—it would be hard to miss my drift that the creation of unique interactive media experiences that plunge the user into immersive near-virtual reality "environments" is a direction I think a great many interactive media titles could

Figure 6.5

David Macauley's *The Way Things Work* is a gorgeous graphic database with content that's true to its title.

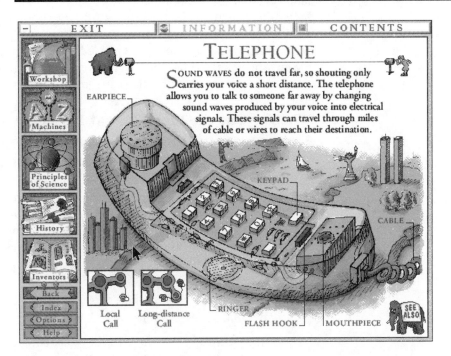

supremely benefit from. If I wear my biases pretty unabashedly on my sleeve, it's because I truly feel that letting a user learn, or have fun, by exploring a superbly rendered and compelling environment is just about the one thing that no other medium can provide. Can't do it in a book, except through your imagination. Can't do it at all on a video. So, I am tremendously enthusiastic about the increasing number of environment paradigm products I'm seeing these days.

This is the understatement of the year. Interactive media environments are all the rage. You'd probably be hard pressed to get someone in interactive media to condescend to talk to you if you're still hyping the values of Tutorials and Databases at the next Verbum Be-In. (The *Be-In* is an event that's been held in years past at the close of certain interactive media conferences. Sponsored by *Verbum* magazine, it combines a showcase for interactive media titles with psychedelic dancing and extemporaneous appearances by Timothy Leary and friends—really!)

We've already talked a little about environments as part of Chapter 1's Interactive Media Guideline #3—Killer Design. To recap: Environments plop you down in a virtual space where the name of the game—or edutainment adventure—is to click around and explore. The best titles feel so decidedly uncomputerlike that they create a cinematic experience that takes you far away from your word processor, with its (legitimate) tendency towards button-itis. Environmental interfaces are even showing up in what you'd think would be pretty straightforward reference products, like the *Random House Kid's Encyclopedia* from Knowledge Adventure. The best thing about the environment paradigm is that it prepares its designers for the day when they'll be able to work with true virtual reality as their front end.

When to Use the Environment Paradigm

There are two reasons for using an environment as your paradigm:

1. It's just another way to organize the information. Let's return to the database of birds we discussed jokingly in Chapter 1. If you recall, the issue there was whether the content—taken directly from a field guide to birds—was interactive media appropriate. Let's say you've added the necessary bells and whistles—lots of 3D bird animations with accompanying bird calls—and you've done your market research and determined there is enough of a basic interest. Now, how do you present your content? There are two ways:

   • As a database with scrolling lists that you click on to access interactive media presentations on each bird.

   • As an environment where the birds are sitting on the trees, perhaps gently animating in the breeze. You click on a bird and you get your interactive media presentation.

   The latter approach is probably more fun, but it's not crucial to the content. Some might argue that it's gratuitous at best, and at worst it actually hinders fast access of the information. Depending on what you're trying to create in your title and who your audience is, an environment might not be the best approach. The question is less blurred in the second case, when—

2. It's critical to the content. Here, there's no alternative to an environmental approach. Let's say you're Robin at Cyan about to design *Myst IX*. You've long since relinquished ultimate creative authority to the recently reorganized Broderbund Entertainment Group, a division of Microsoft. Bill Gates has decided he personally wants to design this interface. He figures a standard Microsoft application interface, with a button bar down the side or top, is the way to go. So he directs Cyan to structure this ninth (and final?) exploration of Myst Island like an interactive media spreadsheet. Each click takes you to another cell in the *Myst* matrix, where the clues are only a Windows 98 3D-button click away. Sounds like a blast to play.

Obviously, the environment is what *Myst* and its many copycats are all about. Here, the environment is critical to the content, and any questions about gratuitiousness should be addressed not to the creators of *Myst* but to future competitors who have stuffed in just "one more video" or "one more puzzle" so they can claim they have superior quantity where *Myst* "only" has quality. (Think I'm joking? I'll bet you'll see a box making just that claim very soon.)

How are environments used in the some of the best known titles today? Let's look at some of the major environmental categories.

Living Books

Broderbund may not have been the very first, but they made the concept of Living Books famous. From the moment *Just Grandma and Me* moused its way into the hearts of small fry and big kids alike, it seems that every children's product has had to have an environment full of "easter eggs"—hotspots hidden in a pretty cartoon world which, when clicked, trigger a fun animation. All of these titles share the same basic premise: A popular children's book is recreated for the computer (Living Book designers don't just scan in photos, they redraw the images to work better in digital format). Then hotspots are added that trigger the animations.

Each CD-ROM "book" is divided into computer "pages," with an arrow icon on either side of the screen allowing the user to move forward and back through the book. Each page shows the text from the book. Whenever a new page opens up, the text is automatically read aloud. Kids can repeat the entire text for a particular page, or just individual words, by clicking. This is supposed to be educational. It's not, but it's fun. Each product has an Index function, which allows you to get to any page you want quickly, and usually an option to see and hear the text in other languages (Spanish and Japanese are the options for *Just Grandma and Me*).

The "Living Books" moniker is now jointly owned by Broderbund and Random House, and the newly spun-off venture has its own offices, personnel, and sound studios a few miles south of Broderbund's suburban Northern California complex. The series is extensive, and keeps on going: *Just Grandma and Me, Arthur's Teacher Trouble, The Tortoise and the Hare*, and soon, very soon—Dr. Seuss on CD-ROM.

I won't kid you—I love these titles. The first time I saw that seashell don a top hat and tails and do a Fred Astaire jig, I got this warm, giggly feeling inside. When I show my interactive media classes the animation of Grandma getting goosed by a picket fence, there's always a riotous response. The humor is right on target, so to speak; the sound and music superb. But best of all, the environment is complete. You're right in it. There are so many hotspots, you can't wait to find the next. And everything you'd expect to react does.

Even more important, Broderbund's tech wizards have built these products so that the animations play almost instantly, even on low-end computers. This is crucial—today's kids (and adults) expect fast response, especially from a title with production values as high as a Saturday morning cartoon. Even a one-second delay while an animation gets itself in place to play spoils the environment effect. It feels like you're "opening" a document, which, in a sense, is exactly what you're doing.

Recess in Greece, from Morgan Interactive (Figure 6.6), is a worthy interpretation of the Living Books genre. Living Books excel in their simplicity—it's just the story being read to you, then you click around. In *Recess in Greece*, there's the story—you get to join the monkey Morgan as he is transported back to ancient Athens—but there are also puzzles to solve that teach you interesting asides about Greek gods and mythology. What attracted me to this product are the same basics that make Living Books fly off the shelves—fast response time, excellent animation, witty humor, and top quality audio.

Figure 6.6

Morgan Interactive's *Recess in Greece* adds puzzles and games to the Living Books myth.

Recess in Greece doesn't take itself too seriously. Hence, different gods appear as modern-day characters—a cowboy, an airhead, an Elvis. And the voicing is perfect—clearly not the programmer's sister and her cute but unprofessional kids. I know that the Living Books operation built a complete sound studio to handle all the sound and music needed in their titles; I'm not sure what Morgan Interactive did, but the effect is the same.

Mindscape's *The Adventures of Nikko* combines a couple of different paradigms—interactive storytelling with a much less sophisticated environmental interface. The premise in Nikko is that you make your own story. The first screen gives you a sentence with a space to fill in the blanks. You choose whether Nikko will be a prince or an elephant. Then, one day he meets a _____. The words *princess* and *frog* appear. You click one, the word glides gracefully up into the sentence blank, and the story line proceeds with, say, Nikko the elephant and his friend the frog.

In addition to the story line manipulation, each screen in *Nikko* is its own mini-clickable environment. But in *Nikko*, the effect is less than stellar. The environments are not packed with enough hotspots or animations. It's like opening your hotel room's mini-bar and finding only an RC Cola, a bag of stale airline peanuts, and a half-eaten Snickers bar. It just doesn't satisfy the way a full Living Books environment does, and the user isn't motivated to click everywhere.

In addition, because the product runs under DOS, the resolution is only half as clear as that of the average Windows or Mac product. While this allows for larger objects to be animated and move very quickly, the general feel of these 320-by-240 screens is old, like a run-down building just begging to be gentrified. It's too bad, because *Nikko*'s interactive story concept is very well done, and scores big points on the "uniqueness" factor—interactive stories absolutely positively cannot be done in any other medium.

If you're running a fast enough machine, Seventh Level's *Tuneland* is probably the most successful children's environment to date. It's not really a Living Book—there's no story line to follow, no text on screen. I'd describe *Tuneland* as a way cool interactive cartoon, in the very best sense of the word. You're plopped down in a country setting, where just about everything is clickable. There are no pages to turn; the product is entirely nonlinear.

Clicking the barn takes you into it; clicking the train station takes you for a ride to the mountains. Once in any of these mini-environments, clicking a hidden hotspot will trigger not just an animation, but a whole hoe-down. There's even an animated host—"played" by Howie Mandell—who you get to search for in every environment.

The title's producers hired some outstanding Hollywood talent and created totally hip-hopping versions of classic kids' songs. As the songs play, so do the animations (the title also comes with a CD utility that lets you run the songs by themselves). Seventh Level has developed its own proprietary technology, which allows lots of animation to happen on screen at once, all the time. In Living Books, animations are usually contained in a smallish area. In *Tuneland*, however, it seems like something is always happening all over the place. Hence, my description of it is as an interactive cartoon—and not the Hanna Barbera talking-heads variety, either.

There's only one hitch hindering *Tuneland*'s status as one of the most successful children's environments on the market, and it's a doozy: access time. Unlike Living Books, on a slower machine you can sit and wait for what seems like an eternity for one of *Tuneland*'s animations to kick in, or for a screen to change. When a slow machine is all I've got to demonstrate *Tuneland*, it usually racks up the yawns instead of the guffaws. And that's a real shame, because this title should really kick ass.

Reference Products

When an environment occupies center stage in a reference product, you have to ask yourself whether this is the best approach. And that all depends on how the people using the product want their information. Do they want to get what they need fast and that's it, or is the process of getting to the information half the fun? If you need to write a report for school on dune buggies, you'll want an interface that will let you quickly search, then call up the exact article you're looking for. You're in encyclopedia mode, where copy and pasteable text and graphics rule, and an environmental interface would be out of character.

But if your product is half reference, half edutainment, you might want to be infotained on your way to learning. In Future Vision's *Explorers of the New World*, the main navigational interface presents a series of maps with routes drawn out, each containing clickable hotspots along the journey.

This is not an environment. Rather, it's a very pretty, spatially pleasing database interface. But some of the hotspots plunge you into full-blown mini-environments: the court of Isabella and Ferdinand; an Aztec palace; a 3D rendered model of the ship where most of Magellan's men died of starvation. These environments, in turn, are filled with even more hotspots, each playing an animation with narration or video.

Now, it would be possible to arrange all the product's information—not just the maps—more like a database, with headings and subtopics and big bold buttons. But a lot of the fun in the title (and one of the Functional Spec's clear design goals) is the feeling that you're really "exploring" with the Explorers—that you've stepped into their world. Along the way, you learn all sorts of interesting, peripheral information—how a Moorish court appeared, for example, or what type of alcohol the natives drank (fermented cassava root, if you must know). Ambient sound and effects further the experience of really being in the New World.

Edu versus *'Tainment*: The Battle for the Environment

In truth, the decision about when an edutainment/reference product should go environmental depends on the balance between the *edu* and the *'tainment*. I said in Chapter 1 that most companies are in the entertainment business, not the education business—even if their products are socially redeeming. The question to ask is, what does the average consumer think about when he or she is buying an edutainment product?

First of all, that average consumer is probably a parent buying the CD for a child. This parent undoubtedly wants the child to learn something, to be culturally enriched. But what that parent is probably thinking in his or her heart is—my kid is hooked on Nintendo Power Rangers. If I can provide an alternative entertainment experience that will keep my child away from the tube—be it broadcast or 8-bit cartridge—and it just happens to have some edu in it, that would be the best. But *'tainment* is driving the purchase. In this case, the product should be as fun and engaging as possible. An environment approach may very well fit the bill.

That's very different than if the product is being purchased for its educational or straight reference value or its ability to assist a child user in writing a report for school. Then the goal is to get the information in as straightforward a fashion as possible. That dictates a very different, probably more database-y approach. In companies I've been at, the debate between whether a product should emphasize the *edu* or the *'tainment* is a very real and heated one. Before you get too far into a product yourself, decide which side of the philosophical fence you're on.

If you still want to straddle the border between *edu* and *'tainment*, you might want to give your users the option to get their information in different ways. The *Random House Kids Encyclopedia* does just that. The opening screen presents you with buttons like you'd see in a database, giving you your major categories to choose from. One option from the opening menu, however, is to go poking around in a neatly rendered 3D environment. The environment takes you to the same places as the buttons. But it's more fun. There are kid-vid guides along the way to help and entertain you. And the "world" they've created is totally cosmic, a surreal trip that keeps you coming back for more. If this sounds like a fun way to play while you learn, then Random House has hit upon a winning concept.

The Random House approach to letting you choose your mode of interaction is fairly in-your-face. Most other environmental reference programs provide the same functionality in a more subtle manner. There's usually an option to open up an Index or Map that organizes the information presented in the environment either alphabetically, hierarchically, or both. *PC/Computing How Multimedia Computers Work* (Figure 6.7) is a good example for a number of reasons.

As described in Chapter 1, the main interaction of this program is classic environment—a 3D computer on a desktop. You click a part of the computer to learn more, and an animation plays. For those users who don't want to poke around the motherboard in search of the network controller card, there's an Index that lets you scroll to *N* for network or *P* for power supply. There's also a map that shows the structure of the title hierarchically—which hotspots are connected to which view. Remember our discussion of different learner preferences in Chapter 4? The more options we give our users for how to get at information, the more chances we have of hitting the mark with more of the audience.

Figure 6.7

PC/Computing How Multimedia Computers Work has both an alphabetical Index and a hierarchical Map to orient users who aren't into poking 'round the power supply.

Environmental Body Products

The next in the Mindscape and Ziff-Davis Press "How It Works" book/CD series was *How Your Body Works*. In this title, the environment is even more fleshed out. Instead of just a computer on a desk, you're now transported to a mad scientist's laboratory. Beautiful 3D rendering organizes the information around clickable objects. Anatomy animations are accessed by clicking the x-ray panel. Information on disorders is in the file cabinet. Medical experts present their views when you click on the VCR. There's even a detailed list of medicines and how they work (where? in the medicine cabinet, of course).

How Your Body Works also uses its environment for some well-conceived fun. There are plenty of wacky objects to click on scattered around the lab, from exploding test tubes to chattering teeth. The original design for the product also included a pretty zany build-your-own Frankenstein monster game (it unfortunately wound up on the digital cutting room floor, replaced by an easier-to-program scavenger hunt).

A.D.A.M. Software's *A.D.A.M.—The Inside Story* doesn't give you the whole lab as an environment, just the body itself. While the overall interface is fairly button-y, when you roll your mouse over the naked body that occupies center stage, labels appear to identify the various body parts. You can zoom in, turn the body around, change its sex, and even change its race. Then get ready to dig in deeper—with *A.D.A.M.* you can peel away the layers for an up close and personal perspective. For the youngest (in age, if not at heart), there's even a fig leaf option that makes certain parts unavailable.

A.D.A.M.—The Inside Story is the consumer subset of a much more extensive, expensive program—just plain *A.D.A.M.*—which is aimed at the medical education and legal community. That product allows you to do computerized dissections, and to label and hyperlink any part or hotspot with a full encyclopedic entry. You can even introduce a wound to the body and watch how the infection spreads. The consumer version is more limited but uses the same technology, making it a very satisfying interactive media experience.

Other body products have jumped on the environment bandwagon. *BodyWorks* from Software Marketing Corporation also has a clickable body as its menu. So does Knowledge Adventure's *3D Body Adventure.* In Microsoft/Scholastic's *Magic Schoolbus Travels through the Body,* the user is placed inside the body via (take a guess)—a magic schoolbus! It's the same concept as the classic film *Incredible Voyage,* only toned down for kids.

It doesn't fit into the environment paradigm, but IVI Publishing's *Mayo Clinic* is probably the best known, most exhaustive body product of them all. It's a cross-referenced interactive database version of the 40-pound tome on many a bookshelf. While the animations and quick searching ability adds some value, I wonder whether, if someone were choking to death in your living room, would you really run to the computer, boot up the *Mayo Clinic,* type in **Heimlich Maneuver**, wait for the search to execute, click Play on the QuickTime video, and then return to your patient?

Games

Environments used in games can be divided into three subcategories:

1. Static Environments

2. Set Path Movement

3. Dynamic User-Controlled Movement

Static Environments

Static Environments are simple but effective. They sit there, fairly benignly, maybe with a little background movement, usually with plenty of sound. Broderbund's *Myst* (Figure 6.8) is probably the best known example. There are no fancy video tricks, few memory-intensive animations. Indeed, the program runs under HyperCard, which reveals a clue to its success. HyperCard has always done its best work at providing a way to link screens together in hyper-interesting ways. Sure, you can play video and animations in it, but there are better tools for that.

Figure 6.8

In *Myst*, movement occurs through static transitions: wipes, dissolves, and cold cuts.

The fact that *Myst* was built in HyperCard (on the Mac, at least—its original platform) often surprises people. They come away from the title somehow believing that they saw more, that there were more interactive media bells and whistles, that it must have been coded in C++, it's so sophisticated. But it's mostly click here, go there in this static environment. That *Myst* has become really the first megahit of the CD-ROM business says a lot about what can be done with less.

Set Path Movement

Set Path Movement in an Environment is what makes *The Seventh Guest* look so cool. The simple transitions of *Myst* are cashed in and exchanged for truly impressive moving walks up and down stairs, through doors, on the walls. Each is an animation created by the art and programming team. Once you've seen it, though, you've seen it—it's not going to change. The path is set. But it's fun while it lasts. *The Seventh Guest* initially hooks people through this cool look and feel. The games and puzzles are pretty good, too, though. The acting in the video, however, is something that even the game's creators at Trilobyte promise to improve for *The Eleventh Hour*, the program's sequel (Figure 6.9).

Figure 6.9

Click on a spot in *The Eleventh Hour*, the sequel to *The Seventh Guest*, and the whole scene moves around you—but only in a preprogrammed Set Path direction.

A title that takes the Set Path Movement concept in *The Seventh Guest* and *The Eleventh Hour* and makes it look even better is Mindscape's *Dragon Lore*. Here, the 3D world is some medieval land in another time or galaxy. You're this wolf-dragon thing, and you have to move around in the environment, picking up objects to open doors, feed the dog, chop wood—and that's just the opening scene for this two-CD set. When long Set Path Movements occur in *Dragon Lore*, the screen actually contracts to enable the animation to play better. The technique is okay, but I feel it takes you ever so slightly out of the carefully rendered world its designers have created for those short animated segments.

Dynamic User-Controlled Movement

Then there's *Doom*, which represents Dynamic User-Controlled Movement. In the previous two subcategories, nothing happens until you click the mouse. Then the screen shifts with either a static transition or a Set Path Movement. In *Doom* and games like it, the screen shifts as you move your mouse. You can turn "movement" mode on and off, but when it's active, you feel as if you're directing the motion. But because the animators can't create Set Paths in advance and capture them to an animation or movie file, the software has to extrapolate on the fly. This tends to make for a fairly chunky pixelated look when movement is occurring.

Most users don't mind. *Doom* is filled with enough rock 'em sock 'em unsocially redeeming action to keep its users most satisfied. With a joystick, this is a heart-thumping game that became a massive seller in a most unorthodox way. The game was originally offered free over online services—e-mail and the Internet. You'd get a little taste as a sample, but if you wanted to continue the story, you had to buy the retail package. Most people did.

A different implementation of Dynamic User-Controlled Movement can be found in two new and very promising technologies: QuickTime VR from Apple, and SurroundVideo from Microsoft. Although the two differ somewhat in execution, the idea is the same: A panoramic view is constructed from still photos (QuickTime VR has software that does the construction for you; Microsoft requires that you take the pictures using a special 360-degree camera).

Once assembled in the computer, though, you can navigate all around the view in any direction—including in and out—by moving the mouse around the screen. Because the technology is based on high-resolution photographs (computer-generated still graphics are okay, too), you don't lose significant resolution unless you zoom too far too fast. To sweeten the experience, sound can be dynamically linked to different spots in the view, so that you might hear a machine whirring in the background that gets louder as you move closer to it. Similarly, hotspots can be defined in the view, which, when clicked, transport you to an entirely different panoramic, interactive view. Apple's technology is the more robust, although Microsoft will undoubtedly get theirs into more consumers' hands.

The most breathtaking example of the use of the technology can be found in the *Star Trek Interactive Technical Manual* from Simon and Schuster Interactive. If you've ever dreamed about wandering the decks of the Enterprise NCC-1701D on your own, this title really makes it possible. Thousands of photographs taken before the Next Generation series shut down production were stitched together using QuickTime VR. The result is you can look at the Bridge from any angle, take a trip down the Turbo Lift, visit Sick Bay, the Transporter Room, Engineering…. I'll admit that I've been a fan of STTNG since the beginning, but this title is a mind-blowing experience as powerful as any in interactive media. Imagine what the technology could do for interactive surrogate travel!

Dynamic User-Controlled Movement can show up in the oddest places. Knowledge Adventure's *3D Body Adventure* includes a game that lets you move around inside the body with your mouse, zapping viruses and bacterial bad guys. It's not as much fun as *Doom*, and you don't really learn anything, but it's nice to see state-of-the-art environmental technology show up in reference products. Knowledge Adventure has used the technique in other products as well. Their *Science Adventure* features a kind of outdoor 3D museum where you navigate by moving your mouse, then click on what you want to learn more about.

Speaking of 3D museums, Apple came out with a prototype called *The Virtual Museum* a few years back, which let you move around a 3D space and click on paintings, sculptures, and all the politically correct pieces *Doom* would banish from this world and the next. The program was, unfortunately, never really developed into a commercial product. But Corbis Publishing did release *A Passion for Art*, which lets you roam around its own ideal museum. And Future Vision's *Artrageous* teaches about art by plopping you in a 3D world of towering paintbrushes and psychedelic tea kettles.

Interactive Music

For some reason, interactive rock and roll has adopted the environment paradigm whole-hog. Peter Gabriel's *Xplora 1* doesn't use a pure environment as its main structural device, but it has inside it a most innovative mini-environment—a walk through Mr. Gabriel's Real World Studios. The tour proceeds as a QuickTime movie plays automatically until it gets to a juncture—then you decide which way to go next. It's not totally smooth, but it represents a gallant attempt at pushing the environmental design envelope. *Xplora 1* also features some absolutely lovely menus, each more playful than the next; game-y elements embedded throughout (you can't get backstage unless you collect clues along the way); and a play-them-yourself section where you get to learn about musical instruments from around the world.

Prince Interactive (Figure 6.10), from the Graphix Zone, tries to be as gorgeously environmental as possible. You're plopped down in old whatever-his-name-is-now's fantasy mansion. You get to go exploring. The navigation is a little convoluted, but there are plenty of pay-offs along the way—particularly, snatches of songs and video clips from the Purple One. For more straightforward music appreciation, you can visit Prince's studio and click on the songs of your choice. For decadent diversions, there's his master bedroom and various unfortunately sexist remarks made along the way—but, hey, did you expect political correctness from a man who has spent a career defiling it?

Figure 6.10

If a lush environment with rude comments turns you on, *Prince Interactive* might be just your cup of purple tea.

Not content to rest on royalty, The Graphix Zone has most recently taken the environmental treatment to a more classic rock superstar. Bob Dylan's *Route 61 Interactive* (Figure 6.11) lets you hear all your favorite Dylan favorites while poking around a re-created Greenwich Village of the '50s and '60s.

David Bowie's *Jump* CD-ROM from Ion promotes the values of corporate rock and roll and voyeurism, all in the same package. In start contrast to Prince's lavish and decadent world, much of Bowie's land takes place in the cold, businesslike corridors of his publisher's studios. There are rooms to explore and windows from the office building across the street to peer into. Jump's highlight is the ability to mix your own music video—the music is set, but you choose the video clips.

Todd Rundgren actually did the mix-your-own-music CD the best— and the first—though few people caught it. His *No World Order* was originally released for CD-i; the PC version has just come out. *No World Order* is a truly

Figure 6.11

Route 61 Interactive features a re-created Greenwich Village where Dylan's songs are put into historical perspective.

innovative piece of interactive media art. Rundgren recorded little snippets of tunes that you put together depending on your mood (want it fast, slow, moody, blue—it's up to you). The are no visuals beyond some psychedelic animated inkblots, but the concept of not just remixing an existing piece, but making it up from near-scratch is absolutely art at its interactive media finest.

Does *No World Order* have replay value? And do consumers really want to work to get their music? Or has rock and roll (sadly) become more of a couch potato phenomena in the '90s? Well, if you're in the Todd is God school, this CD is heavenly. For the rest of us, though, I think the celestial jury has yet to decide.

The Residents have created a cult following on in-your-face weirdness. Calling their art "wacky" would be much too gentle. Their music and videos over the years have been nothing if not disturbing. Deformed creatures, bloodshot eyeballs, trancelike music with perverted lyrics. Did I mention I've been a big fan for years? Their entree into interactive music CD-ROMs is an animated adaptation of *Freak Show*, one of their most recent music CDs.

In *Freak Show* (Figure 6.12), you go wandering around behind the scenes at a circus side show. It's a complete and captivating environment. You get to meet such luminaries as Wanda the Worm Woman, Benny the Bump, and Harry the Headless something or another. As you probe deeper and deeper, you learn more that you ever thought you wanted to about these sideshow performers' secret lives. And, of course, you get to hear a song from the Residents about each. *Freak Show* is spooky and wonderful. It's marred only by the slowness of playback—it was created in Director and at times crawls when it should be jogging.

Figure 6.12

Freak Show is not just for lovers of the weird and disturbing music created by the Residents—it's also one of the most successful music environments created to date.

Is anyone out there still a fan of that dynamic duo known as Heart? If so, run, don't walk, as fast as you can away from the Heart interactive CD-ROM. Even an environment couldn't save this one. The graphics are atrocious, the paradigm some pseudo-database, and the music clips all truncated—would you rather hear a few full clips or lots of samples? Frankly, I'd rather hear neither, and that's probably the main problem with this title—it doesn't satisfy the Basic Interest criterion for anyone except maybe the program's designer. Come on, does anyone really want to see home movies of the Wilson sisters or hear interviews with them where we learn they were always musical from a very young age? Geez. This one is so bad I'm not even including a screen shot!

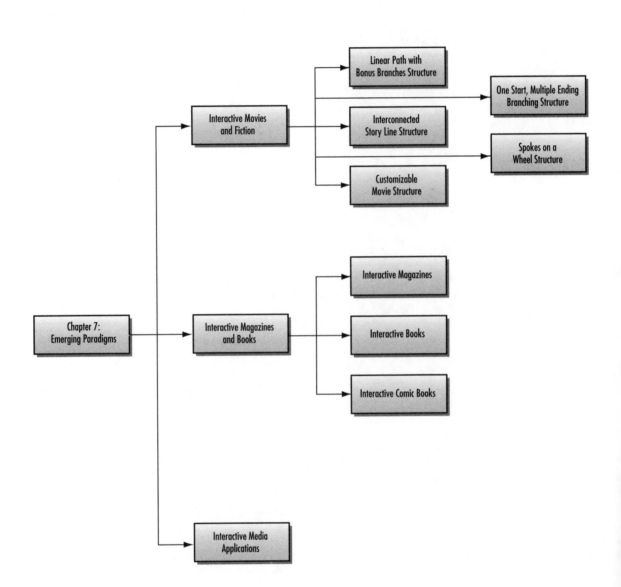

7

Emerging Paradigms

WHILE MOST INTERACTIVE MEDIA TITLES FALL SQUARELY INTO THE
basic paradigms of Tutorial, Database, and Environment described
in Chapter 6, increasingly developers are plying less charted
waters—experimenting with form, function and, naturally, paradigms. Making sense of these more avant garde and sophisticated
interactive media structures can be as challenging as the design
process itself. But knowing your paradigm, however obtuse, lets
you plan from strength.

There are three categories of what I call emerging paradigms. I'm sure by the time this is in print there will be more—so it goes with the cutting edge. In the meantime, here are the ones to be on the lookout for:

1. Interactive Movies and Fiction

2. Interactive Magazines and Books

3. Interactive Media Applications

■ Interactive Movies and Fiction

One of the goals of Guideline #3—Killer Design—presented in Chapter 1 is to foster the creation of interactive media environments that invoke a "cinematic experience." In such an experience, the layer of technology between the user and the computer is effectively neutralized in a digital suspension of disbelief. So what interactive media paradigm is better suited to implementing a totally engrossing cinematic experience than that of interactive movies and fiction?

Indeed, "big" media's (read: Hollywood's) fascination with interactive media is all about making movies and telling stories. When movie moguls Steven Spielberg, Jeffrey Katzen, and David Geffen linked up to form Dream-Works Interactive, it wasn't about educating disadvantaged urban youth. It was about creating money-making movies—the interactive way. Does Spielberg have a clue about how to make an interactive movie? That remains to be seen. His very involvement, however, is a positive step. It signifies the increasing involvement of world-class accomplished artists from "traditional" media in the new medium, pushing the design envelope just that much further.

But one need not look outside the interactive media arena to find computer-based pioneers who have begun to make their mark in interactive movie making. People like Greg Roach, founder and partner at Seattle-based Hyperbole Studios, have even taught workshops in the fine art of interactive fiction at conference seminars as well as at institutions such as San Francisco State University.

The best way to understand the big picture of interactive fiction and movies is by looking at their structures. There are a few varieties.

The Linear Path with Bonus Branches Structure

This is the simplest way to make an interactive movie program. Action begins at a single point and continues down a linear path until it reaches a conclusion. Along the way, however, there are branches that you can choose to explore. If you jump off on a branch, your return always rejoins the basic linear narrative. You may also choose to ignore the branch without any loss in the plotline. This structure is shown in Figure 7.1.

Figure 7.1

The Linear Path with
Bonus Branches
Structure gives you the
easiest way to feel like
you've "got it all"—you
either go forward or stop
and explore.

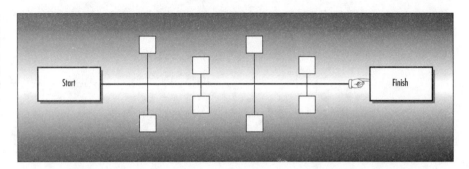

An example of the Linear Path with Bonus Branches Structure can be found in an interactive movie from Future Vision Multimedia—*Pathways Through Jerusalem.* This program lets you pick a tour guide from history—King David, Queen Helena (the mother of Constantine), Dirk the Crusader, Herod the Great, or Sulemein the Magnificent. Each then gives you his or her unique perspective on the great city beloved by many faiths.

Within a given guide's tour, the action unfolds as a linear movie. But at various points the movie pauses, and there are branches you can explore. If you do nothing, the movie picks up after a few seconds. Or you can click on a source, a discovery, a time morph. While most branches return you to the movie you'd been previously viewing, some branches let you jump off into another guide's tour, complicating the structure a bit.

A different mode allows you to click on any of 90 sites in the Old City of Jerusalem. Still, the average user will probably go through this program as a Linear Path, occasionally clicking Bonus Branches, but more frequently enjoying the irreverent dialogue, stunning visuals, and evocative music.

The Interconnected Story Line Structure

This interactive movie model has a set start and end point, but more than a single way to get from here to there. Often, this takes the form of multiple perspectives on the same story. Its format appears in Figure 7.2.

This structure was the basis behind one of the first and still best-known strictly interactive fiction titles—*The Madness of Roland,* from Hyperbole Studios (Figure 7.3). This story of a knight in days of yore was originally published in serial form as a HyperCard floppy-disk-based monthly. As the piece grew in size and sophistication, however, it made the transition to CD-ROM, and was recently even rereleased under the auspices of Time-Warner. Animation, more music, and actors' voicings were added to what began, quite simply, as a nonlinear interactive story.

Figure 7.2

The Interconnected Story Line Structure lets you go through the same story from different perspectives.

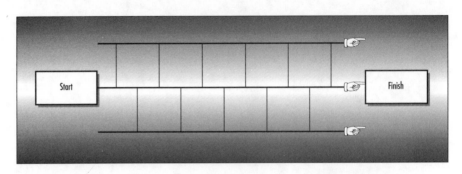

Figure 7.3

The Madness of Roland is a classic text-based example of interactive fiction.

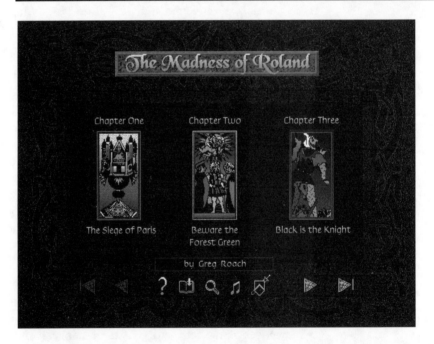

In *Roland*, each path is a different character's perspective on the events of the day. You can go through the title by only choosing one path. But then you're not getting the whole story, the richness of what the designers have set out for you. How you structure your experience is up to you—and that's half of the fun. You can traverse *Roland* one path at a time, straight. Or you can bop back and forth like a you're at a smörgasbord—a little of this path, a smidge of that, a smattering of the third, now back where you started....

I admire very much what *The Madness of Roland* attempts to do, and I have nothing but respect for designer Greg Roach. The title, unfortunately, suffers from a little too much teenage angst channeled into a Dungeons and Dragons type romantic/sci fi experience without enough shoot 'em up game play.

Fortunately, Hyperbole didn't rest on its laudable laurels. Their commercial follow up to *Roland* was *Quantum Gate*—a more ambitious, better implemented, and more profitable venture into true interactive movie making. The structure here is similar, but with a twist. Using a technique Hyperbole has dubbed "Virtual Cinema," in *Quantum Gate*, you are the central character. As you work your way through the program, you actually get to talk to the other characters and hear their responses.

This gives you the same multiple perspectives on a single storyline that is the base state for *Roland*. But you're also able to influence the outcome of the program, which fits better into the One Start, Multiple Ending Branching Structure described below. Indeed, in *Vortex*, Hyperbole's sequel to *Quantum Gate* (Figure 7.4), there are literally hundreds of pathways and dozens of endings.

Figure 7.4

Vortex: Quantum Gate II lets you in on its characters thoughts, as well as influence the program's outcome—a twist on its predecessor, *The Madness of Roland*.

The Customizable Movie Structure

This one looks a lot like the Interconnected Story Line Structure except for one crucial difference—the story lines are connected but not interconnected. How's that again? In the Interconnected Story Line Structure, you only get the full picture by jumping back and forth between the different strands. Each gives new information that adds richness to the production. The lines are intricately interconnected.

The Customizable Movie Structure, by contrast, presents the same basic plot, with only a few changes, on all of its forward lines. The lines are connected—you can pop hither and yon all you want. But it won't affect your narrative experience; the lines aren't interconnected in the same way. Instead, this structure, shown in Figure 7.5, places its unique power in the hands of the user to customize the interactive movie experience to his or her liking. The most interesting, even promising, way this can work is by allowing users to adjust a movie's ratings.

Figure 7.5

The Customizable Movie Structure lets developers take the sizzle out of Sharon Stone, or add Madonna to the Lion King.

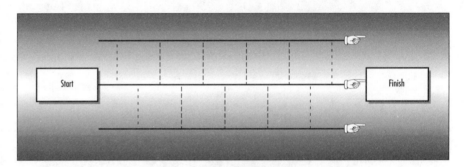

Using this premise, a completely linear movie, say *Fatal Attraction*, can be adjusted from PG to R to X. In Figure 7.5, the middle strand represents the way the movie was initially filmed. By reshooting the steamier, scarier scenes, you can translate *Fatal Attraction* into PG-rated family entertainment. Using the same technique, the movie can get dirtier and more violent—more bunnies in the microwave, perhaps? Cautious parents can set the ratings level at the start of the film and rest assured that their children won't be having stuffed animal nightmares that evening. Are there any interactive media titles like this on the market? Not yet, but where there is a Structure, there always comes a Way.

Adjusting ratings may seem far out, but there are titles that can take advantage of this type of flow right now—movies in multiple languages, where you can swap between Spanish, French, or Swahili at ease, for example. It's foreseeable that developers in the near future will allow users to experiment with variations in sound (turning sound effects on and off), subtitles, image quality, and a host of more mundane but ultimately useful controls.

The One Start, Multiple Ending Branching Structure

This is the classic interactive role-play structure, one that is frequently used in Tutorial paradigm programs. Don't let that scare you off. If you're a budding interactive media information designer, it's also probably the most fun to write. It works like this: You begin at a single starting point. As you progress through the narrative, the program stops and you're asked to make a choice. Will the hero take the girl or the chocolate? Will she choose the machine gun or the machete?

Depending on the choice, the program then branches in that direction. The story continues—on either path—until the program stops again and you're asked to make another choice. The line branches again. This kind of structure can get quite unwieldy. Eventually you have a structure that may have hundreds of endings. A small sample of it is shown in Figure 7.6.

Figure 7.6

The One Start, Multiple Ending Branching Structure is full of different pathways leading to different endings for the most effective replay value.

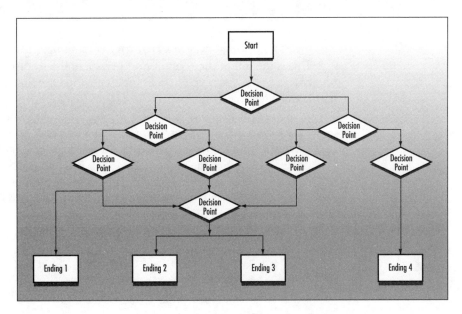

The One Start, Multiple Ending Branching Structure is like a maze, where some routes will get you out in a hurry and others lead to a quick dead end (and in interactive movie-cum-games, I really mean "dead" end). Along the way, however, the story lines can meet up, join together, and go their separate ways again. This requires a great deal of planning, both when you're writing the plot and when you're actually doing the filming. The result, however, is that you can save a lot of disc space through proper planning. Figure 7.7 demonstrates the concept.

In this ministructure, Line A branches into A1 and A2. A2 branches into A3 and A4, then A4 meets up with A1. When that happens, though, the characters in A4 must be aware of what has just happened in both the A4 substrand and the A1 main line. Not only that, but careful attention must be

Figure 7.7

This mini-branching
structure shows how plot
lines can reconverge to
save disc space.

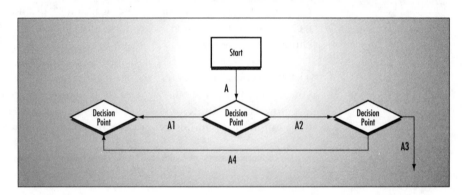

paid to *blocking*—where a character is standing, sitting, or placed on screen. This is the job of the "continuity" person in the traditional film business. It's crucial for interactive movies employing the One Start, Multiple Ending Branching Structure.

One of my favorite jobs was writing branching story lines for InfoUse's *Take Control: How to Stay Healthy and Safe From HIV and AIDS*, a role-playing drama for people with mental retardation (Figure 7.8). In Chapter 3, I described one of the vignettes, starring Bill and Barbara, a young couple deciding whether to have sex for the first time or not (remember the condom-in-the-doggie-dish failed attempt at humor?). The actual structure of that program was far more serious, though.

Bill and Barbara start out on the couch discussing whether to have sex. Barbara is the aggressor (we liked turning the tables on the usual stereotype). Bill isn't sure. The user is asked to decide if Bill should continue. If he says No, Barbara keeps up the pressure (just like real life). Bill has to decide again. A second No, and Barbara suggests watching TV instead. She goes and gets the popcorn.

Now, if Bill said Yes at the first junction, Barbara would get up and look for the condoms. Bill questions whether they need them at all, and the user can decide whether to have sex without condoms, not have sex at all, or keep looking. An "emcee" gives the appropriate feedback if the user opts for unsafe sex.

If the choice is to not have sex at all, the program loops back to the initial No path, and the couple ends up watching TV. This involved some elaborate blocking to get Bill and Barbara back onto the couch in the same position as before.

When it comes to games employing a branching structure, it's usually more along the lines of *Quantum Gate*, where you choose actual dialogue to

Figure 7.8

Take Control helps people with mental retardation stay safe from HIV and AIDS through a branching role play structure.

say to characters. This is also the case in Access Software's *Under A Killing Moon*, one of the most ambitious and well-implemented interactive movies to date.

Technologically, it's a tour de force—nearly full-screen video (not full motion, though) without any additional hardware required. From a design point of view, it mixes its paradigms freely. You start with a nice linear CD-ROM movie setting up the story—the usual futuristic thriller with a washed-up private eye saving the universe in mutant-filled post-apocalypse San Francisco. Got it?

In *Under A Killing Moon*, you're not the central character. Rather, you "help" the central character make decisions and navigate through his world. After the cinematic opening, you quickly progress to protagonist Tex Murphy's office. The interface shifts to environmental mode, and you can move around the office with your mouse, clicking on interesting items and taking others with you—"just in case." Outside, you can visit the local pool hall and have a conversation with the burly barkeep. You choose questions—and answers—from your on-screen control panel. The bartender responds differently to each, which in turn branches you to a different mini story line.

Under A Killing Moon doesn't completely fall in with the One Start, Multiple Ending Structure, because as you proceed through the title's four CD-ROMs, you're constantly propelled in a linear direction. The branches are mainly local, but they're very well implemented. This product deserves a studied look-through.

Spokes on a Wheel Structure

The last interactive movie/fiction structure doesn't have a starting point in the traditional linear sense we've explored so far. There is a place, a starting screen, that you come to first when you start up a program using this structure. From there, however, you can explore any number of discrete places, and these may use whatever model is appropriate. Figure 7.9 shows how this looks.

Figure 7.9

The Spokes on a Wheel Structure has a central starting point, but branches off into discrete places that may mix and match paradigms at will.

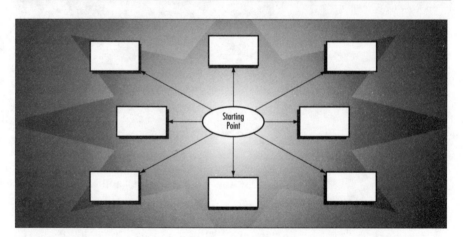

It's hard to think about interactive movies using this paradigm, because our familiarity with the term still leads us to think in a linear fashion. Indeed, all the interactive movies described earlier in this section have a set start and a definitive end (or endings). *Myst*, in some ways, fits the structure—you don't have to explore in any particular order, but by the time you're done with the program you've participated in a very cinematic experience.

InfoUse's *Ashtown*, on the other hand, takes full advantage of the structure without being much of a movie. In fact, the central interface—a main "town" environment with mini-environments to jump into—is almost a carbon copy of the Spokes on a Wheel flowchart. So, for that matter, is *Tuneland*. But neither of these titles sports a narrative—a necessary element for both interactive movie-making and fiction.

■ Interactive Magazines and Books

Whoa, what's going on here? A paradigm all about porting an old medium into the new? Doesn't that go against everything rallied for in Chapter 1's section on Interactive Media Approach? How can I even discuss such a thing and not lose a significant amount of face?

Before you get too judgmental on me, let me explain. My wrath pours out on those who take one medium and slap into another without paying sufficient attention to the uniqueness of the interactive media format. But if a magazine or book approach can be created in interactive media that truly takes advantage of the technology and state-of-the-art design, this constitutes a paradigm in its own right. The critical question to ask is: Does the interactive media magazine or the interactive media book contain enough added value over the original (if there is one) to justify its existence?

There are three basic types of interactive media magazines and books. Of these, titles can be subdivided into those that are based on an existing work and those that are created "from the ground up" for the digital generation. The three main categories are

1. Interactive Magazines

2. Interactive Books

3. Interactive Comic Books

Interactive Magazines

Newsweek InterActive, discussed first in Chapter 1, is a clear example of a magazine that is based on something we all have seen. The articles are new and specifically created for the digital version (that is, they're not just on-screen adaptations of articles from a recent print issue). But they still share a lot in common: The main way you go through *Newsweek InterActive* is to read it on screen. Some highlighted words let you Hyperlink to other places. Others bring up a graphic, an animation, or additional information in a window. There is a separate option that reads the article to you, presenting a narrated slide show along the way. And, of course, there's the extensive back end of related text and audio media material from old issues of *Newsweek*, *Newsweek On-Air* and the *Washington Post*.

Newsweek InterActive delivers an experience like reading the magazine, but at the end of the day it feels a bit skimpy. There are, after all, only two articles per issue. *Virtual World*, from Singapore's iMedia, never really got off the ground as much more than a demo, but its approach was a bit more fitting for the short attention span digital consumer: lots of shorter stories. Its main interface presents a fairly deep table of contents, appearing as you'd expect in a print magazine. *Virtual World* then lets you read the articles as text, paging through by clicking the left or right hand side of the screen. Graphics appear throughout, as do video icons that play a related video or animation clip in a window. *Virtual World* is not based on anything—it's an original interactive media creation, all about technology and, I suppose, virtuality.

Both *Newsweek InterActive* and *Virtual World* pay their respects to two spiritual forefathers—*Verbum Interactive* and *Nautilus*. *Verbum Interactive* was an early, ambitious attempt at pushing the design envelope in interactive media magazinedom. Created to be a quarterly digital adjunct to graphics magazine *Verbum* (the folks who sponsor the Verbum Be-In—see Chapter 3), it mixed text-based articles with performance art on a compact disc.

The main "read" of the title involves a number of articles that you page through. And, as with *Newsweek* and *Virtual World*, there are related animations (no real video—out in 1990, this is pre-QuickTime and AVI). The interface has a slightly different feel—there's a slider bar at the bottom of every page that lets you quickly zip through an article—and animations take up an entire screen, rather than playing in a window. But the basic parameters, the language of interactive magazines, was set even from this early juncture.

The most interesting feature in *Verbum Interactive* is decidedly unmagazinelike. It's cool enough to have been copied in nonmagazine titles. The title lets you attend a virtual roundtable featuring interactive media luminaries such as Marc Cantor, Stuart Alsop, and others. The panel members are arranged as if they're sitting at a long table. In fact, each was shot in distinctly separate spaces—sometimes halfway across the country from one another. But the backdrop is always the same, so when matted together, it gives the impression they're all sitting together. You can ask each one of them a number of questions, and they answer. This being pre-QuickTime, the video is actually animation playing back at a stifling 2, 3, maybe 4 frames per second. But the effect really works.

Verbum Interactive has other nice touches, too, that designers should pay attention to. At the beginning of the Roundtable, Verbum Editor Michael Gosney appears to give video help. He appears in a window at the center of the screen and, as he's describing the various functions on the screen, he points to them. The table of contents has a good feature too. It's designed as a pleasing stack of playing cards. Each "menu choice" gives a text preview of what's inside before you spend time waiting for that section to load. This is particularly important for this title, which, as I mentioned in Chapter 2 , is still one of the slowest loading programs around. But since it's a pioneer, we can afford to be a little less tough on it.

Nautilus has been around even longer than *Verbum*. It's not so much a magazine as a collection of essays, shareware, and other computer goodies. "Departments" on a recent CD include Desktop Media, Education, Entertainment, ComputerWare, and Industry Watch. Nautilus falls into the magazine category because it is "published" like a magazine, right on schedule every month as it has been for years now. The original interface was pretty clunky—you retrieved files to your hard disk through a button and folder approach. Lately, Nautilus has cleaned up its appearance. And it keeps on coming.

The next generation of interactive media magazines is represented by such titles as *Medio Magazine, Blender*, and *Substance:Digizine. Medio* is perhaps the most mainstream of this new crop, presenting interesting interactive articles on a variety of subjects. Its categories include entertainment, sports, finance, news, reference, "scene," and a kids' corner. There are video clips, photos, and stories from the Associated Press newswire.

Medio has become fairly well known, with prominent placement near the checkout counters of many software stores. Its future is a bit cloudy—recent layoffs threaten its continued existence, and the company has begun focusing more on its online version of the magazine. *Substance:Digizine*, on the other hand, continues to garner the trendy buzz, due to its irreverent Generation X approach to graphics and raw music. Up and coming digizine *Blender* is focused in a similar vein. For a much more studied approach, there's the niche market interactive media quarterly just published by JeMM—Jerusalem Multimedia—that covers political and religious topics related to Israel in an interactive format.

Interactive Books

The interactive book paradigm is practically owned by The Voyager Company, whose provocative slogan is "Bring Your Brain." They started out a few years back with an exciting technology for creating your own interactive books—Expanded Books, they call it. You can get the Voyager Expanded Books Toolkit, but most people prefer to buy pre-fab titles made with the technology.

What does the technology do? First of all, if you're a developer and you want to make your own Expanded Book, you simply need to "pour" the text of your title into the Toolkit, and it shows up with an interactive interface. Your users can then set electronic bookmarks, write notes in the margins, and copy and paste text. As with an interactive media encyclopedia, this is mostly useful if the book you've got on disk is something you need to quote from in a term paper. Beyond research functionality, though, you can also attach media elements.

Hence, Voyager's Expanded Book treatment of *Jurassic Park* includes drawings of dinosaurs and examples of how they might have sounded.

Marvin Minsky's Society of Mind (Figure 7.10) features the Professor narrating certain sections. Donald Norman's Expanded Book treatment of his interface design prowess finds the author walking around the screen in video and pointing out good and bad use of the technology. The Expanded Book version of Martin Gardner's *The Complete Annotated Alice* is full of Hyperlinks that will enlighten and inform you on the meaning of various symbols and surrealities in Lewis Carroll's classic. There's now a sizable bookshelf of titles in Expanded Book format.

Figure 7.10

Voyager's Expanded Books, such as *Minsky's Society of Mind*, add computer functionality and digital media to an existing text work.

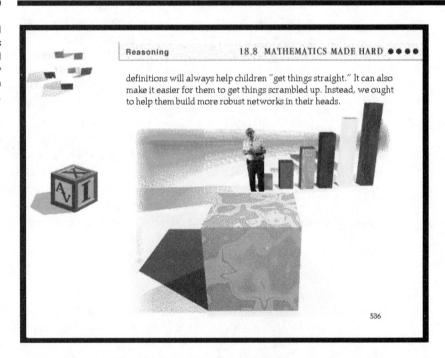

Is all this added functionality really useful? The electronic bookmarks aren't much of an advantage over placing a physical one in a paperback, although the interactive media elements can be fun. Fortunately, Voyager has remained true enough to the original print-based format that it doesn't try to convince you that you've bought something more than a book with a few bonus goodies. The packaging is minimal—a small cardboard package that looks like a slightly overstuffed paperback; the CD inside is in a simple paper sleeve. And they don't charge you much for the privilege, either—the basic Expanded Books are at a budget price, always under $20 retail.

There are more elaborate treatments of Expanded Books, though. The best of these is *Poetry in Motion*, which puts the text of some classic poems in one part of the screen, while a video window shows how the same poems are performed by their authors. What makes this so great is that poems are written to be heard, to be performed (that's why poets give readings). The juxtaposition of the video clips and the text is one of the most effective uses of interactive media technology I have seen. And watching Allen Ginsberg do a punk rock scream is a panic.

Interestingly, the Expanded Books are based on the HyperCard engine, and you need to install the run-time version of the program to play them. The aspect ratio of the basic titles fits the Apple PowerBook screen; run an Expanded Book on an old 9-inch Macintosh screen, and you lose part of the program. The programs were also originally intended to fit on a single floppy disk, presumably so you could "read" a title while commuting, particularly by train or plane.

Voyager may rule supreme, but it does not entirely own the Interactive Book paradigm. Microsoft has a Viewer technology that's been used in a number of successful titles, including *Jazz—A Multimedia History*, formerly published by Compton's New Media, and Microsoft's own *Cinemania*. The latter pushes the technology to the max, but most *Viewer*-based books are fairly pedestrian—scrolling text on screen, scroll bar with up and down arrows, the occasional graphic, animation, or video to liven things up.

Viewer sports similar controls to those in Voyager's Expanded Books, though in Viewer, they're less inspired, residing in standard Windows buttons at the top of each screen as well as in the menu bar. As such, titles created this way feel more like word processor documents than real books. Voyager, to its credit, has nicely translated the book metaphor to the screen. A bookmark in Voyager looks metallic. In a Viewer title, it's a checked menu item. Viewer titles are also harder for the layperson to create.

We touched on Living Books during our discussion of the Environment paradigm. A much more conventional, less environmental approach to the living book comes from Discis Knowledge Research (Figure 7.11), who have been putting classic stories on floppy disk for years now. Each screen has both the text of the story and a still picture corresponding to wherever the story is at. Clicking in the picture pops up a text label identifying a chair, a goblet, a princess. Screens are arranged to look like there's an open book lying there.

In conversations I've had with Discis staff, their educational philosophy is crystal clear: All that sophisticated animation and sound in the more well-known Living Books detracts from a child's ability to learn. Remember the Spinach to Popcorn scale? Discis books are decidedly green and leafy, and Discis is mighty proud of it.

Interactive Comic Books

Now wait a minute…. You're probably asking yourself—interactive comic books? What in the world is this substratum of an already questionable paradigm doing here? But it's hard to ignore facts on the ground. The truth is, there are already a number of titles out that fit nicely into this paradigm. And some of them are darn good.

The best known is an interactive media adaptation of Pulitzer Prize winner Art Spiegelman's *Maus*, a parable about a mouse in Nazi Germany (Figure 7.12). The original print version forced a rethinking of the place of comic books in literary society. Here was a moving, sometimes cynical, always deeply felt portrayal of the horrors of the Holocaust, told through cartoons. The CD-ROM—actually just a Voyager Expanded Book—doesn't mess with the original.

Like all good Expanded Books, the full comic book is scanned in and presented on CD-ROM. Extras include background into how the author created the work, including interviews with Spiegelman and his father, original sketches, and other source material. The result is a "collector's edition" of the original—and a significant adjunct to those using the program for scholarly purposes.

Figure 7.12

Maus on CD-ROM adds interviews with the author and additional background on the creation of the print-based comic book.

Maus the CD-ROM's attention to authenticity, though, impedes the experience a bit. The original comic is taller than what fits in the average computer screen. So, to read the comic on CD, you need to scroll up and down using the scroll bars. A bit of a pain, but the alternative would have been to scrunch the image to fit, much the way theatrical films are "adjusted" to make the transition from cinemascope to the square aspect ratio of broadcast television. The artist's vision is lost in the process. *Maus* avoids this, though the user has to work harder. (Maybe this is what Voyager really means by "Bring Your Brain.")

A more recent interactive comic book entry comes from Putnam New Media. It's Larry Gronich's *Cartoon History of the Universe*—a two-CD set based on one of a series of Gronich's Cartoon History comic books (Figure 7.13). But here, the original is not just slapped on CD, it's brought to life—Living Books style—and wrapped up in an elaborate and very cool interface.

You first enter into a postindustrial machine-heavy interface where you can choose from a number of mini-environments to explore (a Minoan Maze, the Ancient Athenian Acropolis). An animated host, kind of a nutty professor, is there to guide you—if you don't mind his annoyingly high-pitched squawk. Some environments take you to games—after you answer a series of amusing questions on ancient Egypt, you get to play in the Pyramid of Cheops.

Figure 7.13

The *Cartoon History of the Universe* brings Larry Gronich's print comic book to life, Living Books style.

The bulk of the program, though, is Gronich's comic strip, which leads you from Big Bang to the modern era. You choose which era to explore by clicking on a book in a nicely rendered 3D library. Each strip then appears on screen in panels, just as it does in print. But as you flip the pages, the Professor reads you the narration, and the characters act out what they're saying. Nice attention has been paid to voice-overs and characterization. The result is fun, funny, and definitely worth the price of admission.

At Bat, from JamBone Comics, is an original comic strip developed for the computer. The title is all about baseball and values—an unusual combination, maybe? Each screen is divided into panels. Flipping the pages automatically triggers an initial dialogue or animation. Then you're prompted (through flashing arrows) to click around to learn more. At various junctures, you can jump off to play games. I found the interface okay, albeit slow (our old friend Macromedia Director), but I wasn't too interested in the subject matter. If you're a baseball buff, consider checking this one out.

■ Interactive Media Applications

Every paradigm we've looked at so far has been best suited to the interactive media "title," that free-standing edu, info, or otherwise 'taining program that lets you look and play but not create something new. In Chapter 1, we even discussed the importance of thinking about *titles* rather than *applications* such as word processors or spreadsheets. And yet, there is a time and place for true interactive media applications —programs that use interactive media to let you really "do" something. There aren't many of these out there yet—this is truly an emerging paradigm. But there are a few that look promising.

First are the creation programs, like Knowledge Adventure's *Magic Theater* and Davidson's *Multimedia Workshop*, both of which let you create your own interactive media presentations. Using simple commands and click and drag functions, programs like these aim to be mini-authoring systems. I include them here, rather than in our earlier discussions of authoring system software, because they're not designed for the professional developer. They're sold on the same software store shelves as more traditional titles, and they loudly and clearly scream out "interactive media," even if you—the buyer—are the one supplying most of the media.

Broderbund's best-selling *Kid Pix*, by itself, doesn't really fall into the category of interactive media application. *Kid Pix* is a drawing program—like CorelDRAW or MacDraw—but with wacky sounds and zany drawing tools to appeal to even my two and four year olds. *Kid Pix Companion*—an adjunct program that needs the original Kid Pix to run—adds the ability to manipulate QuickTime videos, sequence slide shows, and import your own work.

A variation on this theme would be Maxis's *Klik 'N Play*—an interactive media application that lets you specifically create your own arcade-style games. You can use the stock characters and backgrounds they give you, or draw your own Marios and import them.

Paramount Interactive's *Rock Rap and Roll* is an interactive media application that lets you create your own music. The interface gives you a choice of different musical styles: techno, rock, salsa, and more. Each musical style has a number of preprogrammed rhythm tracks. You select the tracks you want, click Play, and then it's up to you to jam along by pressing keys on the keyboard that trigger various notes or sampled sounds. You can record and save your piece and play it for friends. The latest version of the application adds video to the mix, so you have something to watch while you're rockin' and rollin', but the original is so much fun, it's consistently been one of the interactive media applications I personally pull out and play with the most.

A recent entry, *MusicNet*, doesn't let you create anything. It uses interactive media to help you buy—in this case, the latest and hottest music CDs. *MusicNet* is a subscription CD. If you go for the bait, you'll get regular CD-ROMs delivered to your doorstep, each filled with a truckload of digital audio clips to preview. You take a listen, then you can order the audio CDs you like from the same folks who brought you the CD-ROM. There have been interactive media kiosks placed prominently in music stores that do the same thing, but this is one of the first to be sold to consumers at home.

Bringing music sampler CDs right to the consumer's home is a great way of increasing exposure for new and lesser known artists. It would be an even better concept for the CD-ROM business, where one of the biggest problems consumers encounter is the inability to preview relatively expensive titles before they buy.

The most ambitious interactive media application is much more than an application, it's practically a whole operating system. It's Microsoft *Bob*, and he, she, or it is designed to make it easier to work with computers. The interactive media chunk of *Bob* has mostly to do with the customizable guides who lead you around *Bob*, and the environmental interface that serves as *Bob*'s core experience (Microsoft calls it a "social interface").

As described in Chapter 4, *Bob* arranges standard Windows functions in an environment that looks like your (or somebody's) home office.

In the lower right hand corner of every screen is your "helper." You choose your guide's appearance, from a java drinking lizard to a frisky puppy. Each has its own personality, animations, and funky way of speaking (they don't actually speak, but their words appear on screen). Will Bob catch on? Is it just too precious? Or is the application the embodiment of many of the principles called for in *Interactive Media Essentials for Success*? Pick up a copy and judge for yourself.

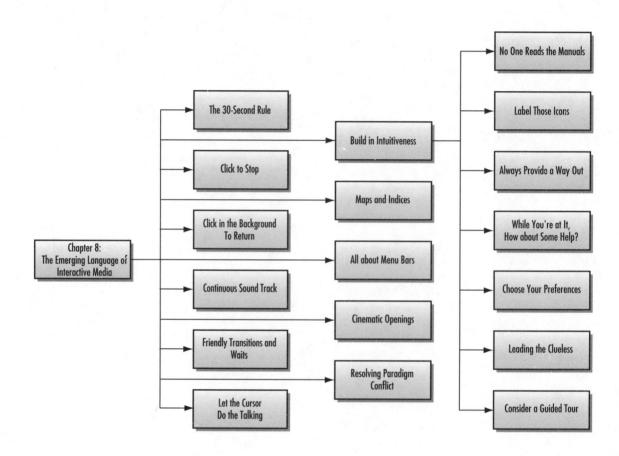

Chapter 8:
The Emerging Language of
Interactive Media

The 30-Second Rule

Click to Stop

Click in the Background
To Return

Continuous Sound Track

Friendly Transitions and
Waits

Let the Cursor
Do the Talking

Build in Intuitiveness

Maps and Indices

All about Menu Bars

Cinematic Openings

Resolving Paradigm
Conflict

No One Reads the Manuals

Label Those Icons

Always Provide a Way Out

While You're at It,
How about Some Help?

Choose Your Preferences

Leading the Clueless

Consider a Guided Tour

8

The Emerging Language of Interactive Media

Y OU'VE HAD A HARD MORNING. HECK, IT'S BEEN A TOUGH WEEK. your Information Designers aren't getting along with your Interactive Designers. The former have unearthed so much great content that they're insisting on some pretty lengthy animated and video presentations. The latter are equally insistent on chunking the material into 20–30 second MTV "media bytes." The Information Designers complain to you that a blip-blap-on-to-the-next-byte approach compromises the integrity of the material. The Interactive Designers are waving a 50-page report on the ever-shrinking attention span of the contemporary 11-year-old entitled "One Hand on the Joystick and One Foot Out the Door."

How did you get into such a pickle? Is one of these two equally competent teams right and the other wrong? Is there any way you could have set some guidelines up front so that things would be less ambiguous and your staff less cantankerous?

Interactive media has not been around all that long, but in its short existence it's already begun to develop its own language. Just as it took the cinema industry many years to settle on certain de facto standards and conventions, the language of interactive media is sure to evolve. Still, there are certain functions that users have come to expect from interactive media programs. This chapter discusses those conventions so that you don't have to learn the hard way.

■ The 30-Second Rule

The 30-Second Rule addresses the rambunctious debate between the Information and Interactive Designers presented in the example above by siding with the latter. Simply stated, it posits that no single media "byte" continue for more than 30 seconds without requiring some interaction from the user. This is a hard pill to swallow for some, but it's vitally important. The model is drawn from television. Certainly, networks like MTV have discovered the value of keeping things short and happening; viewers never get too restless with a bit they're not so fond of. Similarly, the classic Top 40 radio format of three-minute songs guarantees that if you don't like what you're hearing, there's a good chance you'll like the next song, so stick around.

Yet even with this fast-moving media material, viewers are zapping channels and pushing the old radio buttons with digital abandon. The trigger-happy nature of our society is only reinforced in the interactive arena by so-called "twitch titles"—games that require total concentration and a constant finger action on the joystick or mouse. Given this background, it's no wonder that the average CD-ROM user is similarly impatient. It almost doesn't matter whether or not an information byte is interesting. If it goes beyond 30 seconds—and even that seems high sometimes—the user will click to see something else.

Let's return to our initial debate for a moment. The Information Designers claim they can't break the information into small pieces—it just won't work that way. The linearity of the piece is crucial, they argue. But what if a particular media byte did run for, say, a couple of minutes? What would happen? *Click*—after 30 seconds, that average user would be checking something else out. The other 90 seconds of crucial material? Presented beautifully, but never seen. That defeats the Information Designer's *raison d'être*—to get the information to the user!

As with most of the guidelines you'll find in this chapter, there are exceptions to every rule. A particularly interesting video bit—say two Hollywood-quality actors having a fiery dialogue—can probably go on for a whole 45 seconds to a minute. An interactive movie—where the up-front design is for users to sit back and watch the piece with occasional decision points—can definitely break the 30-second rule by virtue of its unique focus. Older users who haven't been MTV'd to death might tolerate longer bits as well. And this guideline doesn't hold for text-only screens where there's no audio or motion presentation. But for most users, even 30 seconds can be long.

What kind of interaction is required after 30 seconds? Not a pause in the action with a gratuitous "click to go on" prompt. Instead, try to structure your program so that information is parsed into discrete information chunks where the whole story can be told in under half a minute. Those chunks might even be labeled so that users know what they're getting beforehand. The chunks are then grouped according to topic and placed on different screens, under different hotspots, in different environments, and so on.

In *PC/Computing How Multimedia Computers Work*, each clickable "part" of the computer on screen triggers an animated sequence. There was clearly more than 30 seconds worth of information on each, so we subdivided each animation into Basic, In-Depth, and Related sections. Some animations did go on longer than 30 seconds—those were battles with the Information Designer that I lost. And, as enamored as I am with the program's animation, my inclination is still to click and stop any animation that goes on beyond the 30-second limit.

■ Click to Stop

The 30-Second Rule works because of a related interactive media language standard: When you're viewing an animated or video sequence, if you click the mouse the sequence will stop. Exactly how it should stop is still emerging.

- In some programs, a click will make the animated sequence stop completely and disappear.

- In others, a click simply pauses the video—this is a QuickTime movie convention. A second click sometimes starts the movie playing again, while in other programs, you must use a play/pause button located on the movie's control bar.

- In yet other programs, a click outside the animation or video area stops and closes up the media byte, while a click inside the animation or video area pauses it, and possibly even restarts it.

Whichever option you choose when designing your product (this, by the way, comes under the category of Functional Requirements), you must include something. It is inconceivable and unforgivable for a program to insist on playing an animation or video to its conclusion, without giving the user a way out. The effect for the user is that the program has taken control of his or her computer. If that user wants out, and can't get out, he or she may very well hit the ALT+F4 combo to get out entirely. Now, that wasn't what you wanted, was it?

■ Click in the Background to Return

I'm particularly fond of the "flat" navigation structures described in Chapter 4, where the user has less of a chance of getting lost because the Main Interface is only one click away. When a new screen does appear, though, how does it relate to the previous screen? There are two options:

1. The new screen can completely cover the previous screen. If the program is really flat, clicking a basic return button will quickly get you back to the first level in a simple, intuitive way.

2. The new screen can lay on top of the old screen as a window. In this case, the background is still visible behind, and if you click on it, you go there. An example of this is shown in Figure 8.1.

This second concept might seem pretty basic, but imagine if the converse were true—if you could see the background but clicking it did nothing. The background then would simply be a piece of familiar looking art. Clicking in the background to return is becoming part of the language of interactive media. By following this guideline, you make your background art functional, not just window dressing.

■ Continuous Sound Track

Interactive media titles started out like silent movies. Sure, they'd play a bit of music or a sound effect at an appropriate juncture. The rest of the time, though, these early titles sat around waiting quietly for the user to click something. No more. Interactive media today is noisy. Users have come to expect, and developers are delivering, titles with Continuous Sound Tracks. The Continuous Sound Track concept comes from the movies, where there always seems to be a little something going on in the background, subtly adjusting the viewer's mood. In interactive media, sound and music should be present:

• After nothing has happened, or the user hasn't done anything, for a pre-specified amount of time

Figure 8.1

If you can see the background behind an information, animation, or video window, you should be able to click it to go back there.

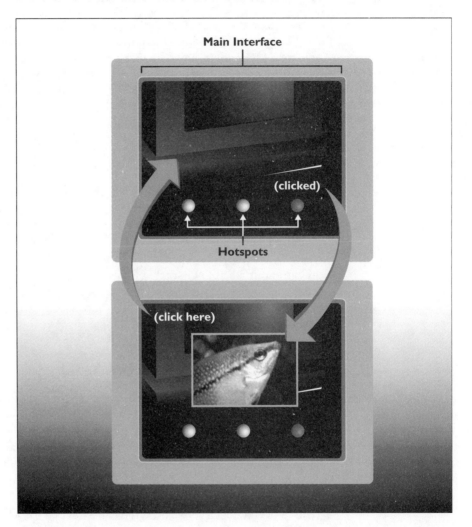

- During most animated or video sequences
- During transitions—this helps minimize the feeling that you're waiting

The basic rule for sound is that you should treat your title as if you're scoring a movie. Use sound to build excitement, to change the mood, to foreshadow and transition (a new scene's sound can start ever so slightly before the scene itself shows). And, as with the movies, there will be times when sound is not appropriate. In this case, the absence of sound is part of your Continuous Sound Track.

■ Friendly Transitions and Waits

It's inevitable that, even in the best designed and developed program, there will be some points where the user has to wait while the program is loading the next segment. It may not even be your fault—the user may be running your title on the slowest possible recommended system with half a dozen other applications still open in the background. The worst thing that can happen here is that nothing happens. The user clicks an animation, and waits and waits with no feedback that the system is working. On some computers, you can see the CD-ROM drive light flicker on and off while it's looking for data. But a lot of newer machines have dropped such niceties—a light left off is a penny saved.

The ubiquitous wristwatch for the Mac or hourglass for the PC is the standard language that says "Wait—I'll get to it in a minute." But there are more creative ways. A "hold on" musical theme gives users something to listen to at least—just like when you're holding in voice mail hell! Seventh Level's *Tuneland* plays music and includes a little animated character from the program itself to distract you. Living Books give you an animated transition stick figure. In the two-screen videodisc program *Take Control*, we put up a big "Please Wait" graphic while the videodisc would do its maximum five-second search for the right frame.

■ Let the Cursor Do the Talking

The cursor is a wonderfully expressive element in an interactive media program. Not only can it let the user know it's time to wait, but almost all titles with hotspots now execute a cursor change when the pointer rolls over something clickable. For many, this can be as simple as a change from an arrow to a hand. But you can get much more creative. In the haunted house CD-ROM, *The Seventh Guest*, the cursor looks like a skeleton hand. When you can click something, it beckons you in with an outstretched, animated finger. When you're over a nonclickable area, the hand waves a forbidding "no-no" gesture.

Animated cursors are used very nicely in Pineapple Multimedia's *Tales of the World*. The title includes a number of cartoon-y screens from around the world. The cursor tells you where to click and what you're going to get. For a song from Nigeria, the cursor might change to a musical instrument. For a recipe from Turkey, the cursor transforms into a cup filled with a steaming beverage. For the "tale" itself, the cursor appears as a book with pages turning.

Cursors can help with interscreen navigation, too. In an environment, the cursor can change to an arrow to let the user know the environment essentially "extends" beyond the borders of the current screen. Clicking in the corner causes a transition to the next screen. A slightly different cursor can indicate clicking will return you to a previous screen. In *Explorers of the New World*, we used the cursor in a novel way: After you click a hotspot, there is often a second level of in-depth information you receive by clicking on the same object a second time. You're alerted to this by a cursor change.

■ Build in Basic Intuitiveness

Unless the point of your program is to deliberately confuse your users (now wouldn't that make an interesting new paradigm…), there are a number of steps you can take to ensure your program is as intuitive as possible. Intuitiveness is not the same as simplicity. A CD-ROM game may be exceedingly deep and complicated, yet still be intuitive. Here are some tips to keep in mind.

No One Reads the Manuals

This is not entirely true, but no one should *have* to read the manuals. If you've designed an intuitive program, the average user should be able to install it (from the on-screen prompts), and then be up and running with maybe only some brief help or prompting at the beginning. If the user then runs into difficulties later, he or she may pick up the manual. But that initial experience with your program should be as transparent and friendly as you can make it.

Label Those Icons

This is a lesson from Interface Design 101. Icons are not intuitive. No matter how many interactive media programs have used an exit sign or question mark icon in the past, that icon in your program may not be immediately understandable to all of your users. And maybe you're using it in an ever so slightly different manner—this exit sign leads to an intermediary exit screen; another one immediately quits the program; a third closes down Windows and reboots your computer. Labels don't have to displayed permanently—they can pop up on a mouse roll-over. In that case, though, the pop-up has to respond quickly.

Always Provide a Way Out

This is probably my sole criticism with the environmental approach I have waxed so poetic on in the previous seven chapters. Full-screen environments, by their very definition, don't place an immediately obvious way to get out of a screen. And when you gotta go, you gotta go. All I'm looking for is a small, unobtrusive navigation or control panel area that includes a Quit button.

You might argue that there are some pretty standard ways to quit on both Mac and Windows platforms. But I've used plenty of programs where

Alt+F4 turned turkey on me. Another common quit convention, Command+Q, is a Mac convention, and on *Prince Interactive*, even that didn't work—it wanted just a plain Q!

While You're at It, How about Some Help?

If you've already added a control panel to your screen, maybe with pop-up-on-roll-over functionality, why not include a couple other useful buttons—Help is the first that comes to mind. It's not that users absolutely refuse to read the manuals if they're desperate. But a lot of times (especially in offices), the manual inexplicably disappears. Or a user is deeply entrenched in a particular scene, but can't figure out how to move on. Getting up and finding the manual becomes an extra chore. Including online Help is a great feature, and having it easily accessible is a thoughtful touch.

Help can range from a few simple text screens to context-sensitive narrations, pointers, and even video: Compton's *Interactive Encyclopedia* pops up Patrick Stewart from "Star Trek: The Next Generation" when you get lost. Help can act like Apple's Balloon Help—turn it on, then point your mouse at objects around the screen. An explanatory balloon appears whenever you roll over something Help recognizes.

Beyond Help, there are a few other buttons that are common to place on a control bar, control strip, or revealed menubar. These include

- A Return button (often displayed as a fishhook arrow icon)—this steps you back to the most recent screen.

- A Main Menu button—click here and you're instantly back at the top level.

- An Index button—this calls up the Index (see below).

Choose Your Preferences

Another button to add to your control panel that's often not included but is much welcomed and desired is a User Preferences dialog box. Here you can let your users adapt the program to their own style. Users like to have control over such areas as:

- Sound level

- Whether an opening video sequence should automatically play every time the program is started up

- Whether long animated transitions should occur in between screens

- Whether continuous music should always be present

Preferences can also allow your user (or different users) to customize how the title should appear—or where the title should open back up to—after the user quits and later returns.

You can use a Preferences option to your design advantage as well. Can't decide whether to label your hotspots or let the user discover them in exploratory fashion? Let that be a user option. Not sure if you should force users to sit through the credits each time they quit? Put it in the User Preferences. As more and more programs adopt this convention, it will surely become as much a part of interactive media's language as it is in traditional applications like word processors.

Leading the Clueless

Some of your users may be CD savvy; others may be encountering their first interactive title. And still more belong to that category affectionately known as the "interactive media clueless." No matter how many times they use a CD, they still aren't sure what to do—they don't learn languages well, including the language of interactive media. Don't patronize these users. Give them something to hold onto. Be nice to them. They just might buy your next CD.

How can you lead the clueless to water? An on-screen text prompt is one way—it's just a little more intrusive than a Help button. Microsoft Bob, despite my earlier disparaging comments, uses cartoon guides as Helpers nicely. Each guide lets you choose the most likely questions for a particular screen from a very clear menu. Flashing or animated sprites, which prompt the clueless toward your preferred next action, are effective too.

A very common method, even for the only moderately clueless, is the *Introductory Information Narration.* Whenever you come to a new section, a narration orients the user to this strange place: "Welcome to the world of small hairless mammals. Click on a rodent to learn more." But make sure it only plays the first time, through. If the user returns to the same screen again—no prompt.

Consider a Guided Tour

Whether or not your users are helplessly harried with no time for manual reading or are clinically clueless, just about everyone appreciates a snappy, to-the-point Guided Tour right up front. A Guided Tour should walk your users through all the major features of the program, paying particular attention to navigation and hidden functionality. Guided Tours work by taking control of the mouse and narrating a clear path through your program. First click on this, then click on that. Guided Tours can't skip around from topic to topic, because the cursor is simulating what your user will do.

Guided Tours should be brief—a couple of minutes maximum (it's okay—you can break the 30-second rule this time). They may be self-running or have a Table of Contents at the beginning. If the tour gets much longer than two minutes, though, consider building in a stop/start/pause function. Otherwise, a user may get halfway into a long tour, receive a phone call, and have to start over again from the top.

■ Maps and Indices

Here's another one for your control panel, but it adds more than just intuitiveness. A hierarchical visual map of your program, or an alphabetical text-based index provides a quick snapshot of what's in the program and a fast way to get anywhere quickly—just click the entry and you're instantly transported there. The best ones have a "You Are Here" flashing or highlighted locator built in. First time users may go straight to the Map or Index to see what's in the program. Sales staff looking to demo only the good parts will use it to bypass the dreck (not that there's any of that in your program, of course…).

Maps and Indices are not an either-or proposition. Each serves a slightly different purpose, and it's possible to include both in a program to provide for different users' aptitudes and information browsing styles. Maps are quick, but except in the simplest structures, they require that the user click a few times to navigate the hierarchy. They are best suited for environmental programs: You wouldn't want to get plopped down in a real-world foreign environment without a road map. Ditto for interactive media. An Index, on the other hand, is most useful when there are so many media bytes in a program that they're best displayed in a scrolling list with search capabilities.

■ All about Menu Bars

Every Mac or Windows office productivity application—word processors and spreadsheets, for example—has a fairly standard menu bar running across the top. For interactive media titles, some do, some don't. Reference products more often include a menu bar, while environments rarely do. In addition, depending on screen resolution, your title may or may not have a title bar at the top. Running under Windows 3.1, that title bar will include the Windows "ventilator" (the box in the upper left-hand corner that closes the program when double-clicked and pops up a menu when single-clicked). Windows 95 moves the "ventilator" to the right hand side. In either case, the ventilator can house menu-bar-like functions (Preferences and Credits can live here).

What does the language of interactive media say about menu bars? It doesn't yet. Since they are so reminiscent of mainstream applications, I tend to shy away from them. On the other hand, they can house some very useful functions—and that can even keep buttons out of an environment.

■ Cinematic Openings

Yes, this emerging language feature also comes from the movies. Every interactive media publisher these days has developed a spiffy animated logo sequence, and users have now come to expect these at the beginning of a program. It sets the tone and telegraphs a level of professionalism. A badly done opening screams out shovelware, so don't scrimp when it comes to this goodie. There can be up to four levels of opening logos:

1. The publisher's logo

2. The series logo (Living Books, IntelliQuest series, and so on) belonging to the publisher

3. The developer's logo

4. The program's title

Following these logos the program's opening plays, and it, too, should have a cinematic quality. You could pop right to the main interface with no fanfare, but how about a little Hollywood glitz to ratchet up the excitement? Microsoft *Encarta* has a very nice, politically correct montage of images and sounds. *PC/Computing How Multimedia Computers Work* opens like "Saturday Night Live," with a Don Pardo impersonator and two on-camera video hosts. *Explorers of the New World* kicks off with a dramatic compass spinning over a pre-Columbian map of the world, followed by video speeches from the great explorers themselves.

■ Resolving Paradigm Conflict

When you start sprinkling buttons like Help or Quit into an otherwise pure environment, you may encounter paradigm conflict. It's perfectly okay to mix paradigms in the same program (see Chapter 6). But how about on the same screen? Here's a tip if you're adding buttons (a feature of the database paradigm) to an environmental program: Don't make the buttons too glaringly obvious, unless that's your intention.

Buttons scream out "click me," whereas environments are more subtle—they tease you into prodding around with your mouse. So, in an environment with some very button-y looking buttons, guess which get clicked first?

Not the environmental objects. In fact, some users may not even realize there are objects in the background to click. This leads to serious navigation conflict.

In *PC/Computing How Multimedia Computers Work*, our 3D computer-on-a-desk environment has a drawer with a series of prominent buttons on it. The final button is labeled *Tours*. It wasn't intended to be a primary hotspot—indeed, the resulting animations are the least impressive in the program. But on user testing, we found that people tended to click the Tours button first.

In contrast, we thought the most logical way for users to exit the program would be to click the door. But with those big buttons up front, many users never even noticed the door in the back corner of the 3D room. We thought about labeling it, but it was supposed to be a home office—who puts an EXIT sign up at home? We eventually added EXIT to our prominent up front buttons. When it came time to do the follow-up, *How Your Body Works*, the setting was a more institutional lab, and the door was clearly labeled (there were also no buttons at all).

How about labels? Pure environments tend to sit there looking pretty while you move your mouse around to explore (the cursor usually changes to indicate there's something to click on). Database programs, on the other hand, have icons with labels. Can you have labels in an environment? If the labels stay up all the time, that's going to create some major paradigm confusion.

However, pop-up labels that appear when the mouse rolls over an object can work very nicely. It does transform your program into more of a reference environment than a purely fun exploratory environment, so keep that in mind. Both *PC/Computing How Multimedia Computers Work* and *How Your Body Works* use pop-up labels in their environments. Do take care that the labels don't look like buttons complete with 3D beveled edges. Users will be inclined to click the label, rather than the object, and you'll lose any environment feeling entirely.

From buttons and labels to logos and transitions, the language of interactive media is slowly emerging. For interactive media developers, a big part of the fun is being in the thick of those pioneers who are defining the standards, not just observing trends and developments from the sidelines. More than that, though, it's our obligation to guard against interactive ugliness and push this emerging language to its most intuitive and user friendly implementation.

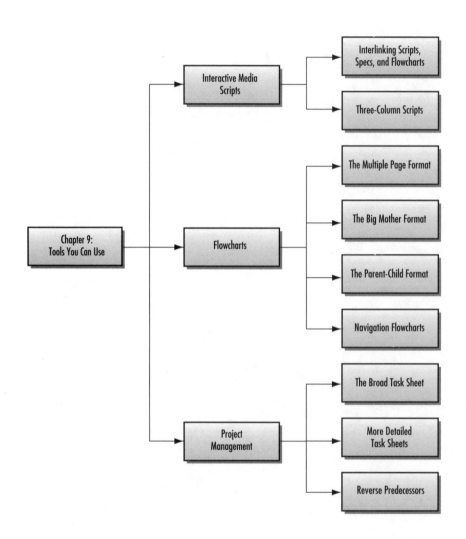

9

Tools You Can Use

OVER THE YEARS, I'VE DEVELOPED A NUMBER OF TOOLS THAT CAN aid the interactive media planner and designer. *Tools* might be the wrong term; they're more like templates you create yourself using normal off-the-shelf applications. To put together a Functional Spec, I rely on Microsoft Word. For flowcharts, there's not much better (on the Mac, at least) than Inspiration (from Inspiration Software). I prefer Microsoft Project for project management, but as with all of the above, you should use what you're most familiar with. In this chapter, I'll focus on tools you can use to aid the up-front planning and design process.

■ Interactive Media Scripts

The format for writing scripts for interactive media is very much like that of writing scripts in other media—with one big difference. Traditional media scripts need to specify what's being said and what's being seen. Interactive media scripts add what the user is doing and how the computer responds. This can be done in a variety of fancy formats, but I usually just write up a script in my word processor and add the extra information at the top of each section.

And there are plenty of sections. As we discussed earlier, writing interactive scripts means thinking in quick media bytes. A single script may have hundreds of mini divisions. And each needs a label—a name and a code—to make sense of the multiplying morass. This is particularly important since scripts don't guide the creation of the program—the Functional Spec does. But the Functional Spec can only do its magic if it is clearly cross-linked back to your scripts and flowcharts by the names and codes you set early on.

Giving your scripts a unique code name involves coming up with something that makes sense and that's consistent. A combination of letters, numbers, dashes, and periods will give you the flexibility you'll need. Use pneumonics, too. An *M* might be a good way to refer to a Main Screen. I've used *T* when I've had "Talk Show" environment screens. If you have a particular character, name that screen after her (*Sarah* gets screens that begin with *S*).

An *M* or a *T* or an *S* by itself looks kind of lonesome, though. I tend to add a dash and a number. Plain *S* becomes *S-1*. A screen following *S-1*, where the user has to make a prompted choice, might be *S-1Q* where the *Q* stands for *Question*. If your program is small, you can get away with simple combinations of ascending numbers, or additional number-letter combos. But bigger programs will need even more identification. Thus, a script in the dinosaurs subsection of your title might gain the prefix *BC* so that the Main Menu screen in this script becomes *BC-M-1*.

Interlinking Scripts, Specs, and Flowcharts

The relationship between the script, Functional Spec, and flowchart, as well as a coding system on the simpler side, is shown in Figure 9.1. Note that, were this a fully drawn flowchart, the name of the screen or section would be included along with the code in the flowchart box.

Interactive scripts never fully make sense unless they're read along with their accompanying Functional Spec and flowcharts. Yet, that's often exactly what happens. Either the client—or even members of the design team—winds up reading just the script, particularly when the team is in midst of a focused production task. In this case, it's important to repeat some of the information that's shown in the Spec right on the script itself. Each script section should

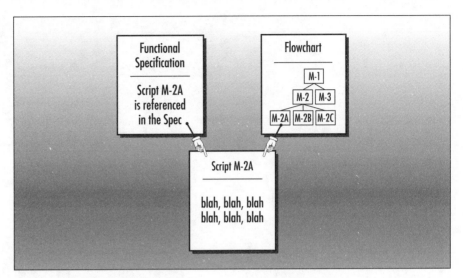

begin not only with the that section's code, but also with a narrative description of how it is interlinked with other scripts.

Let's look at a more in-depth example. Figure 9.2 shows the flowchart for a portion of a fictitious role-playing title. Notice the diamond symbols. This is a flowchart convention that indicates a screen where the user is prompted to make a specific choice. Diamonds are often a flowchart's best friend, and are particularly useful in role-playing titles.

Figure 9.3 shows the narrative headers only (not the complete script) for the relationship flowcharted in Figure 9.2. Ideally, each section with its header and code should be on a separate page (it makes it much easier to read), though if you're environmentally conscious or have very short sections, it's okay to bunch things up. Section narratives should answer three questions:

1. What is this screen all about?

2. How did I get here?

3. Where can I go from here?

These should be familiar from the discussion on what goes in a Functional Spec in Chapter 4. Go ahead and lift them verbatim from your Functional Spec. You don't need to find the perfect nuance here, just the most intuitive route through a lot of important information.

Figure 9.2

This flowchart is for a role-playing title called "Relationship Roulette."

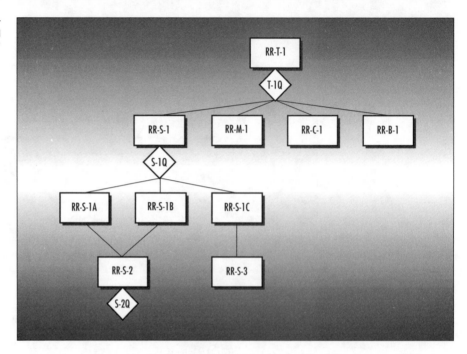

Figure 9.3

The narrative headers in an interactive script describe how the user will get there, what the user will do once there, and where the user can go next.

```
"Relationship Roulette" Script

RR-T-1
Talk Show Screen
This screen presents four couples to choose from -- Sarah and Sandy (RR-S-
1), Mindy and Steve (RR-M-1), Charles and Di (RR-C-1), and Brian and Jody
(RR-B-1). Users get here by clicking on the Talk Show icon from the Main
Menu (not shown in flowchart). Clicking on the icon for a particular couple
takes the user to that couple's screen.

Visual: Blah, blah, blah...
Music: Blah, blah, blah...
Narrator: Blah, blah, blah...

RR-S-1
Sarah and Sandy -- Introduction
This screen plays the video introduction to the Sarah and Sandy segment,
setting up their predicament. Users arrive here by clicking on Sarah and
Sandy's icon from the Talk Show screen (Script RR-T-1). Following the video,
users are presented with a choice screen (RR-S-1Q).
```

Figure 9.3
(Continued)

The narrative headers in
an interactive script
describe how the user
will get there, what the
user will do once there,
and where the user can
go next.

```
Visual: Blah, blah, blah...
Music: Blah, blah, blah...
Sarah: Blah, blah, blah...
Sandy: Blah, blah, blah...

RR-S-1Q
Sarah and Sandy -- Choice Screen 1
This screen allows users to choose a solution to the predicament presented
in Script RR-S-1. Users arrive here automatically at the conclusion of the
RR-S-1 video sequence. Depending on the user's choice, the program displays
either screen RR-S-1A, RR-S-1B, or RR-S-1C and its opening video.

Visual: Blah, blah, blah...
Music: Blah, blah, blah...
Narrator: Blah, blah, blah...

RR-S-1A
Sarah and Sandy -- Solution A
This screen presents Solution A to Sarah and Sandy's problem. Users arrive
here by clicking the Solution A button on Sarah and Sandy's Choice Screen 1
(RR-S-1Q). When the video segment is finished, the program automatically
goes to Screen RR-S-2.

Visual: Blah, blah, blah...
Music: Blah, blah, blah...
Sarah: Blah, blah, blah...
Sandy: Blah, blah, blah...
```

Three-Column Scripts

The script format described above is based on a standard traditional media script format. All we added were the codes and narrative headers. An alternative traditional media format for video scripts in particular is to write in two columns: Description of visuals goes on the left as well as any audio; dialogue, narration, music, and/or sound effects are presented on the right. For interactive media, a third column is added to describe what the computer—or the user—has to do at a given point. The narrative header information is divvied up between the first two columns.

Figure 9.4 shows a three-column script treatment of our "Relationship Roulette" fantasy title. The column for "visuals" is filled in here (it wasn't in the earlier example) so the format makes more sense.

Figure 9.4

A three-column format divides a script into three columns. Narrative header information goes into the first two columns.

```
"Relationship Roulette" Script

RR-T-1
Talk Show Screen
```

Computer	Visual	Audio
Users click on Talk Show (RR-T-1) icon from Main Menu (RR-M-1) to get here. Users may click on any of the four icons shown.	Four couples to choose from are shown -- Sarah and Sandy (RR-S-1), Mindy and Steve (RR-M-1), Charles and Di (RR-C-1) and Brian and Jody (RR-B-1).	Narrator: Blah, blah, blah...

```
RR-S-1
Sarah and Sandy -- Introduction
```

Computer	Visual	Audio
Users click on Sarah and Sandy icon (RR-S-1) from Main Menu (RR-M-1) to get here. Computer plays video segment, then automatically goes to RR-S-1Q Choice Screen.	Sarah and Sandy introductory video sequence plays	Sarah: Blah, blah, blah... Sandy: Blah, blah, blah...

```
RR-S-1Q
Sarah and Sandy -- Choice Screen 1
```

Computer	Visual	Audio
Screen automatically appears on conclusion of RR-S-1 video. User clicks on one of the three solutions presented to go to the corresponding next screen.	Narrator returns and summarizes Sarah and Sandy's predicament, then presents three possible Solutions - Solution A (RR-S-1A), Solution B (RR-S-1B), and Solution C (RR-S-1C).	Narrator: Blah, blah, blah... Music: Blah, blah, blah...

■ Flowcharts

We've already discussed flowchart basics—in this chapter and previously in Chapter 6. And hopefully you've become somewhat more comfortable with seeing flowcharts in the neighborhood—after all, they've headed up every chapter. When creating a flowchart, though, you have a number of different formats to choose from, and a variety of generally accepted symbols at your disposal.

Interactive designers use three basic formats for flowchart creation:

1. The multiple page format

2. The big mother format

3. The parent-child format

The Multiple Page Format

Flowcharts can get unwieldy quickly, with hundreds or sometimes thousands of boxes representing screens to be linked together. How can you, your design team, and the client take all this in? There are two ways to view a flowchart—on screen and on paper. If you choose to print out your flowchart, consider using the multiple page format.

The multiple page format places discrete, understandable chunks of flowchart on separate pages. Each page is linked to another using a symbol that looks like a fat, squat arrow. In the arrow is written the code that will be in the box at the top of the corresponding page. A single flowchart page may have multiple arrows. Every flowchart, except for the very first one, must have arrows for both

• Inputs—how you're getting to this flowchart from another flowchart

• Outputs—where you can go to from this flowchart

In Figure 9.5, Box BB-S-1 has two "fat arrows" underneath it, indicating that the flowchart continues with boxes BB-S-1A and BB-S-1B, respectively. The full boxes for BB-S-1A and BB-S-1B aren't included on the first flowchart page but on the two following pages, shown below the first flowchart "page" in Figure 9.5. The "fat arrows" are then repeated on these to indicate that the path to boxes BB-S-1A and BB-S-1B comes from box BB-S-1 on an earlier page.

Multiple page format flowcharts fit nicely into a three-ring binder and can be "read" in an almost sequential fashion. They're the best choice when you need to include a complicated flowchart in a report, proposal, or Functional Spec.

The Big Mother Format

If you like seeing the whole flowchart at once and you have an abundance of wall space, consider the big mother. Like the multiple page format, the big

Figure 9.5

The multiple page format is the easiest to print out and file in a three-ring binder.

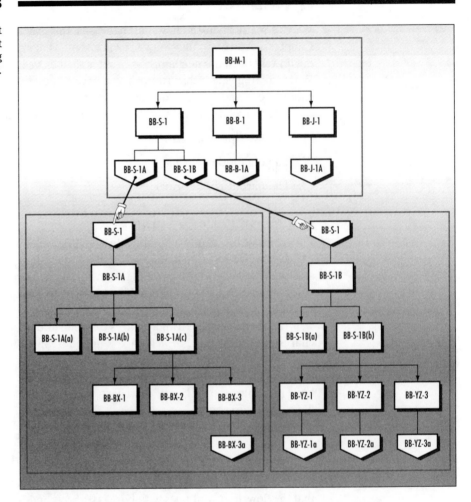

mother is also printed out, but its extra large size makes it harder to dissemi-nate. To make a big mother, arrange the flowchart on your computer screen as one enormous graphic. Skip the fat arrow icons—there are no separate page to connect. Take care that a single logical thought stays on a single page, and no symbols wind up straddling both sides of the border. Then print out the pages and tape them together.

Figure 9.6 shows a sample big mother. The box at the far left is the Main Map. That's followed by submaps, topics, environments, hotspots, animations, and videos. Everything is shown all at once, which requires three pages to tape together. This is a relatively tidy flowchart. I once had a big mother that required over 60 pages to print out!

Figure 9.6

If you have no shortage of wall space, the big mother lays out the entire program in one enormous image.

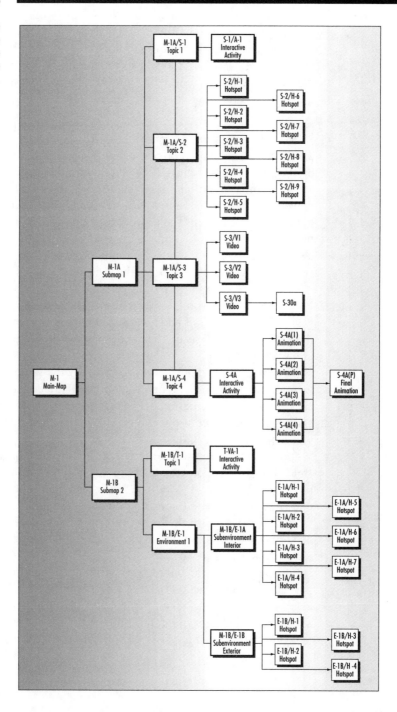

Plastered across your office wall or laid out on a conference table in front of your team, the big mother quickly gives everyone a picture of what's going in your program as a totality. You see how users can navigate your title, as well as potential dead ends. Big mothers for reference programs tend to be long and not deep, with lots of choices coming off of the Main Menu. Big mothers for environments can get fat in all directions. If you like to think in overall terms, the big mother is a winner.

The Parent-Child Format

This format can be used effectively only when you're viewing the flowchart on the computer screen itself. Most good flowcharting programs allow you to embed additional flowcharts in the boxes you see on the screen. The starting flowchart is called the parent. Any flowcharts that branch out from the parent are called children. The flowcharting program will give you some indication that a particular box on the chart has a child attached to it. Then, by clicking that box, you open up the child flowchart. Any box in a child flowchart can have its own children; they're called step-child flowcharts.

Figure 9.7 shows how parent-child flowcharts can work. Boxes M-1B/E-1A and M-1B/E-1B both have children attached. This is indicated by a gray square in the lower-left and lower-right corner, respectively. Double-clicking the gray squares opens up the children, which in Figure 9.7 are the boxes below the parent box.

The parent-child flowchart is essentially the same as the multiple page format, except that the fat arrow icons are handled electronically when you click on boxes in the parent. If you want to print out a parent-child flowchart, you can add your own fat arrow icon as a graphic rather than as an integral part of the program's logic.

Whether you're using a multiple page format, a big mother, or a parent-child relationship, don't try to create the graphics with an ordinary graphics or drawing program. The value of a dedicated flowcharting program is simple: The lines between the boxes you create are linked together logically, and when you move a box, the line moves with it. Combined with the ability to do sophisticated parent-child charts, the purchase price is earned back in a few billable hours of work.

Inspiration, a Mac-based flowcharting program that I rely on, has some particularly cute terms associated with parent-child relationships. If you decide to spin a child flowchart off from its parent into a stand-alone graphic file, you call that disowning the child. If you want to integrate a flowchart from another place into your existing parent, that's called adopting a child.

Figure 9.7

Parent-child relationships can be lovingly created using onscreen flowchart software.

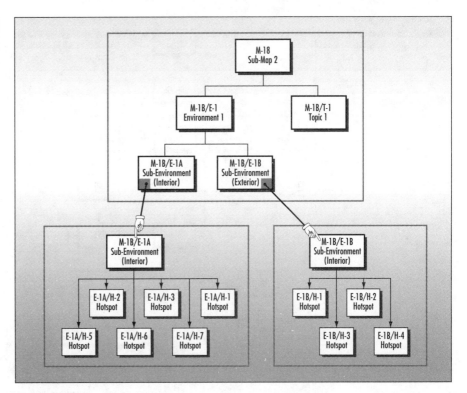

Navigation Flowcharts

As described in Chapters 4 and 5, there are two basic types of flowcharts—the content/conceptual flowchart and the navigation flowchart. The formats we looked at above are primarily content flowcharts. They show the logical progression of information and media bytes within the program. But they don't represent a clear navigation path, where you can trace every possible input and output.

Figure 9.8 shows a flowchart designed for navigation. The main difference between this and content flowcharts is that every possible path gets its own line. You may find it useful to use different line patterns and thickness. If you can get your hands on a color printer or plotter, that makes it even easier to figure out where all the lines are going.

Figure 9.8

A navigation flowchart
contains a line indicating
every possible input and
output.

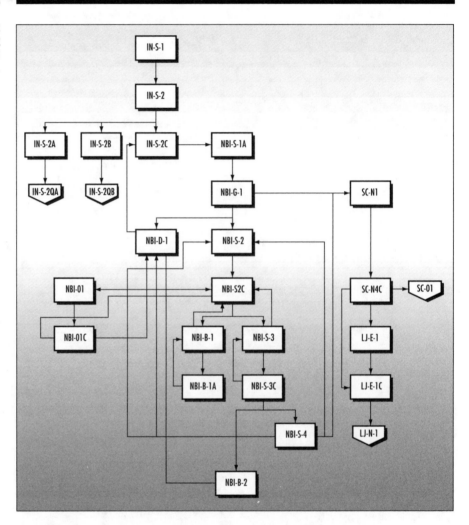

■ Project Management

Managing a large interactive media project is daunting, what with flowcharts, scripts, and Functional Specs all fighting for attention. How do you keep track of all the pieces, make sure that nothing gets missed, and keep things on time and on budget? Think about using a project management software tool. Project management software has gotten somewhat of a bad name, especially among start-up companies. Running the software, its critics claim, takes more time than actually managing the project. And time is always at a premium when you're trying to establish yourself.

But used gingerly, project management software can help you estimate an overall timetable for a project, and then provide formal or informal reports about where you are at any given moment. Project management software, of course, is only as good as its inputs. So, rather than providing a crash course on the intricacies of project management theory, I want to present what I've found are the best inputs—the crucial categories and columns to include in your project management task sheet.

The Broad Task Sheet

A task sheet lists all your project management data in a spreadsheet format. Usually, with the click of a button a task sheet can transform into a Gantt chart—a visual representation of that same information with vertical bars tracking tasks by date. The easiest way to start creating your task sheet is to review the development methodology described in Chapters 4 and 5 and input those steps into the "Tasks" line of the software. Then, start filling in the subsequent columns. Figure 9.9 shows some of the standard columns you'll need.

Figure 9.9

This project management task sheet shows tasks, duration, start and finish date, predecessors, resources, and notes.

ID#	Task Name	Duration	Start Date	Finish Date	Predecessors	Resources	Notes
1	I. Business Preliminaries						
2	High Concept, Basic Design, Name	5d	1-Jan	5-Jan			Project starts 1-Jan
3	Audience, Content & System Analysis	5d	8-Jan	12-Jan	1	Producer	
4	Competitive Analysis	10d	8-Jan	19-Jan	1	Producer	
5	Contract Negotiation	20d	1-Jan	26-Jan		Legal	With Content Holder
6	II. Information & Interactive Design						
7	Marketing & Objective Summary	5d	15-Jan	19-Jan	4-50%	Producer	Task begins during Task 4
8	Information Design	5d	22-Jan	1-Mar	7	Info Designer	Break for Xmas Holiday
9	Interface/Interactive Design	15d	12-Feb	1-Mar	8-50%	Art Director	Team comes together 1/2 way
10	Skeleton Screen Layout/Design Overview	10d	19-Feb	1-Mar	9-33%	Art Director	Task concurrent with 9
11	Scripts & Storyboards for Demo	5d	4-Mar	8-Mar	10	Art, Info Design	
12	Marketing Demo	10d	11-Mar	22-Mar	11	Art Director	
13	Finalized Functional Spec	10d	11-Mar	22-Mar	11	Producer	Concurrent with Marketing Demo
14	III. Pre-Production						
15	In-House Prototype	5d	25-Mar	29-Mar	13	Design Team	
16	User Test	5d	1-Apr	5-Apr	15	Producer	
17	Finalize Budget & Schedule (Go/No Go)	5d	8-Apr	12-Apr	16	Producer	
18	Initial Press Release	5d	8-Apr	12-Apr	16	PR	
19	Scripts & Storyboards						
20	Written	30d	25-Mar	3-May	13	Info Design	
21	Edited and Tech-Checked	10d	22-Apr	3-May	20-33%	Info Design	Diff member of Info team
22	IV. Production						
23	Art						
24	Interface Components	30d	25-Mar	3-May	13	Artists	These are "backgrounds"
25	2D Art	30d	25-Mar	3-May	13	Artists	
26	3D Art	30d	25-Mar	3-May	13	Artists	
27	Animation						
28	Storyboards	10d	6-May	17-May	21	Animators	
29	Scratch Audio	10d	6-May	17-May	21	Sound Designer	
30	Preliminary Animation	30d	17-May	28-Jun	28, 29	Animators	

What do all those columns in Figure 9.9 really mean?

- ID Number—this gives each row a discrete identity, just like the far left column of an Excel spreadsheet.

- Task Name—this is where you type in the name of the task to be completed.

- Duration— how long do you estimate it will take to complete this task? Write it down here. In Figure 9.9, "d" stands for "days."

- Start Date—when will this task start? You always need to input an initial starting date, but depending on how your tasks are linked, the software may calculate future start dates.

- Finish Date—project management software almost always calculates a finish date automatically, by adding duration to the start date.

- Predecessors—this is where project management software really struts its stuff. You can tell it to not start a particular task until a previous one is completed. In Figure 9.9, the numbers you see in the Predecessors column refer to the ID Numbers at the far left. So, Art Tasks 24, 25, and 26 can't start until Task 13 (the Functional Spec) is complete. Similarly, both Task 3 and 4 can't start until Task 1 is done. Predecessors can get quite sophisticated. For example, the predecessor 8–50% shown for task ID #9 means "don't start ID #9 until ID #8 is half completed." The more you can keep your tasks linked to each other as predecessors, the more the project management software will work for you, letting you know when a slip in one task will affect another task or, heaven forbid, the project ship date.

- Resources—who will complete each task? Listing the specific personnel to work on a task isn't necessary at the very beginning, but will become increasingly important when you start breaking down individual tasks, as described in the next section.

- Notes—always include a column for Notes, where you can keep track of the grittier details.

What tasks should you use as you fill in the broad task sheet? Figure 9.10 shows a sample list. Your own list will undoubtedly vary, but you can use this to get started.

Figure 9.10

These sample tasks can be used to get a broad task sheet going.

```
I. Business Preliminaries
   High Concept, Basic Design, Name
   Audience, Content, & System Analysis
   Competitive Analysis
   Contract Negotiation

II. Information & Interactive Design
   Marketing & Objective Summary
   Information Design
   Interface/Interactive Design
   Skeleton Screen Layout/Design Overview
```

Figure 9.10
(Continued)

These sample tasks can
be used to get a broad
task sheet going.

```
   Scripts & Storyboards for Marketing Demo
   Marketing Demo Completed
   Finalize Functional Spec

III. Pre-Production
   In-House Prototype
         User Test
   Finalize Budget & Schedule
   Initial Press Release
   Scripts & Storyboards
         Written
         Edited and Tech-Checked

IV. Production
   Art
         Interface Components
         2D Art
         3D Art
   Animation
         Storyboards
         Scratch Audio
         Preliminary Animation
   Video
         Choose Talent (Auditions)
         Pre-Production (Costumes, Sets, etc.)
         Shoot Video
   Media Acquisition
         License Text
         License Video
         License Stills
   Final Video
         Off-Line
         On-Line
         Digitize
         Link to Backgrounds
   Final Audio
         Choose Talent
         Record Narration
         Create Sfx
         Final Music
         Mix Narration & Music
   Final Animation
         Final Animation -- Timed to Audio
         Digitize to QuickTime

V. Integration and Authoring
   Art, Content, & Functionality Freeze
   Link and Edit Audio to Animation/Video
   Coding
```

Figure 9.10
(Continued)

These sample tasks can be used to get a broad task sheet going.

```
Alpha Date
User Test
Beta Date
QA Testing
Revision/Polishing
Final Code

VI. Marketing and Sales

VII. Ship Date

VIII. Postmortem
```

More Detailed Task Sheets

The task sheet shown in Figure 9.9 is useful for initial estimating, but it isn't so great when you need to get your hands dirty. Then, you'll want to start breaking down tasks into smaller components. Figure 9.11 shows a sample breakdown for the animation task. At this point, you'll want to write down exactly who's working on each task. The sample shown, for example, has two artists working on four animations. Notice how Animation 3 can't begin until Animation 1 is complete, since it's being worked on by the same animator.

Figure 9.11

The animation task shown previously in Figure 9.9 is broken down into smaller tasks.

ID#	Task Name			Duration	Start Date	Finish Date	Predecessors	Resources	Notes
1	Animation								
2		Animation 1						Artist 1	
3			Storyboard	2d	6-May	7-May			
4			Stratch Audio	1d	6-May	6-May			
5			Background	1d	8-May	8-May	3, 4		
6			Preliminary Animation	3d	9-May	13-May	5		
7		Animation 2						Artist 2	
8			Storyboard	2d	6-May	7-May			
9			Stratch Audio	1d	6-May	6-May			
10			Background	1d	8-May	8-May	8, 9		
11			Preliminary Animation	3d	9-May	13-May	10		
12		Animation 3						Artist 1	
13			Storyboard	2d	14-May	15-May	6		
14			Stratch Audio	1d	14-May	15-May	6		
15			Background	1d	16-May	16-May	13, 14		
16			Preliminary Animation	3d	17-May	21-May	15		
17		Animation 4						Artist 2	
18			Storyboard	2d	14-May	15-May	11		
19			Stratch Audio	1d	14-May	15-May			
20			Background	1d	16-May	16-May	18. 19		
21			Preliminary Animation	3d	17-May	21-May	20		

Reverse Predecessors

At the end of your task sheet (and at the end of the entire development process) are those pesky marketing and sales tasks. These can be estimated by doing *reverse predecessors*. If you know what your final code date estimate is, you'll know how early you need to start such tasks as preparing box art, the dreaded BOM (that's Bill of Materials—it refers to what items go into the physical box itself), and trade show sell sheets. These marketing and sales tasks are mostly applicable to publishers, but developers who are close partners in the publishing process will want to keep track of them as well.

Using reverse predecessors, you take advantage of most project management software's "minus" functionality. While earlier we subtracted, say, 50 percent from the finish date of a previous task to estimate the start date of some subsequent task, Figure 9.12 subtracts an actual number of weeks, indicated with a "w," from the ship date. Thus, Task 66 must begin 31 weeks prior to Task 78—the ship date (not shown).

Note that these dates vary wildly depending on the length of your product's development cycle. The sample shown is an extension of Figure 9.9—a CD title with 11 months for development starting on January 1. If your whole production cycle is 31 weeks or less, you obviously will have to pack more tasks into a quicker time frame.

Figure 9.12

The final tasks in product development can be estimated by calculating reverse predecessors from the ship date.

ID#	Task Name			Duration	Start Date	Finish Date	Predecessors	Resources	Notes
65	VI. Marketing and Sales								
66		Kick Off Meeting		1d	6-May	26-Mar	78-31w	Marketing/Sales	78 is Ship Date
67		Marketing Objectives		5d	15-Apr	19-Apr	78-28w	Marketing/Sales	
68		Title Approved		0d	13-May	13-May	78-24w	Everyone	
69		Bill of Materials Requested		1d	13-May	14-May	78-24w	Producer	
70		First Round Screen Shots		5d	27-May	31-May	78-22w	Marketing/Sales	
71		Packaging Focus Group		5d	10-Jun	14-Jun	78-20w	Marketing/Sales	
72		Announcement Sell Sheets		5d	10-Jun	14-Jun	78-20w	Marketing/Sales	
73		Back of Box Copy Sign-Off		0d	1-Jul	1-Jul	78-17w	Marketing/Sales	
74		Second Round Screen Shots		5d	8-Jul	12-Jul	78-16w	Marketing/Sales	
75		Final Sell Sheets		5d	30-Sep	4-Oct	78-4w	Marketing/Sales	
76		Documentation		1d	9-Sep	13-Sep	61	Tech Writer	61 is Beta Date
77		Shipping Press Release		5d	21-Oct	25-Oct	78-1w	Public Relations	

Once you've gotten to the point of plotting reverse predecessors, your project management task sheet should be just about done. But remember that solid planning is just the beginning of your development journey; now it's time to implement your design. Send us a postcard from the trenches! We'll be holding down the home front with an ample supply of fresh flowcharts and timely task sheets.

■ Appendix: Resources

Over the years since I first got the interactive media bug, interactive initiates have frequently asked me for advice on how to break into the industry. I usually refer them to a professional organization, like IICS, and maybe to an educational institution, such as San Francisco State University's Multimedia Studies Program. I always recommend subscribing to at least some of the plethora of interactive media magazines that have appeared in the past few years (this can be in print form or online over the World Wide Web). And it's never a bad idea to attend an interactive media conference or trade show—even if it's just to cruise the Exhibits Hall.

But whether you're a beginner or a long-term pro, you'll still want to keep up on the latest industry news, check out what's hot, and get a jump on the competition. This appendix is designed to serve as a resource for finding some of the above mentioned organizations, publications, and events. As with everything in this book, what I present includes my take on its relative worth. Balance out the pros and cons, and get yourself to moving to the interactive media beat.

■ Magazines

There are probably hundreds of print-based magazines that touch on interactive media in one form or another. General computer magazines increasingly include interactive media features and columns. Industry analysis newsletters give you inside information days or even weeks before the glossy magazines, but cost a premium—at around $400 per year for sometimes as few as 12 issues.

Many of the most interesting magazines are available "free to qualified professionals." You fill out a subscription form with your name, address, and lots of telling personal data—your job, the number of people working with you, and (most importantly) whether you recommend or actually purchase hardware or software. These freebies are good only in North America—something I discovered all too well when I relocated in 1994 to Jerusalem.

Whether you can get a magazine free, or you actually have to pay, you should be receiving at least a few publications a month, especially since reviews are such a central part of each—Digital Siskel may hate your competitor while Interactive Ebert may wax positively electronic over its questionable benefits. In the listing below, if a magazine has a World Wide Web presence, I've listed it. More in-depth web sites that go beyond recycling the text of last month's print issue are listed in the next section, specifically about online information sources.

A/V Video

Thick and glossy, its main focus is on traditional audio visual and video production. Mark Magel writes a good column on multimedia, though, and there are decent Mac-specific technical sections.

Monthly, free to qualified professionals.
Knowledge Industry Publications, Inc.
701 Westchester Avenue, White Plains, NY 10604
(914) 328–9157

Blaster

New, hip, CD-ROM 'zine for "screenagers," those teens who've grown up with a CD instead of a silver spoon in their mouths. Lots of game reviews, online links. From the folks who bring you Morph's Outpost (see below).

Monthly, $19.95/year.
Blast Publishing, Inc.
2223 Shattuck Avenue, Berkeley, CA 94704

CD-ROM Professional

Glossy magazine, all about CD-ROMs, with good European coverage (I found it in my local Jerusalem Tower Records). Changed editors recently to be more consumer focused.

Bi-monthly, $86/year.
Pemberton Press, Inc.
462 Danbury Road, Wilton, CT 06897
(203) 761–1466

CD-ROM Today

Fast becoming a must-read interactive media magazine, *CD-ROM Today* packs more reviews between its covers than virtually anyone else. Good articles, too. Special bonus—each issue includes a CD-ROM full of product demos so you try before you buy! Recently changed editors, staff, and moved to Silicon Valley from North Carolina.

Monthly, $94.95/year (including the CD-ROM).
Imagine Publishing, Inc.
1350 Old Bayshore Highway, Suite 210, Burlingame, CA 94010
(415) 696–1688

Computer Life

Mass market consumer magazine about all things computer—these days that means lots on interactive media. Designed to be a more accessible version of *Wired* magazine (*Wired* would beg to disagree).

Monthly, $24.97/year.
Ziff-Davis Publishing Company
135 Main Street, 14th Floor, San Francisco, CA 94105
(415) 357–5355
Online: http://www.zdnet.com/~complife/

Computer Pictures

Glossy magazine with focus on graphics and animations. Since these, in particular, are the bread and butter of interactive media production, this can be a very useful addition, especially since it's a snap to get on the freebie list.

Monthly, free to qualified professionals.
Knowledge Industry Publications, Inc.
701 Westchester Avenue, White Plains, NY 10604
(914) 328–9157

Consumer Entertainment News

Oversized newspaper-format magazine officially focusing on interactive media entertainment products (i.e., games). The publication's focus, however, has expanded to cover the entire range of interactive media titles as long as they have a consumer retail presence. Good articles on the business of wholesale and distribution, too.

Bi-weekly, free to qualified professionals.
GP Publications
1350 Old Bayshore Highway, Burlingame, CA 94010
(415) 696–1688

Converge

Technical resource with special columns on QuickTime, Video for Windows, Director, and more. Formerly called *The QuickTime Forum*. A straighter, though similar, read to *Morph's Outpost*.

Bi-monthly, $99/year.
Multi-Facet Communications, Inc.
110 West Iowa Avenue, Sunnyvale, CA 94086
(408) 749–0549

Digital Media: A Seybold Report

Comprehensive industry analysis newsletter from the respected Seybold Organization. Not quite as insightful since founding editor Denise Caruso moved to bigger pastures. Related to the Digital World annual conference in Los Angeles.

Monthly, $395/year.
Seybold Publications Division
444 De Haro Street, Suite 128, San Francisco, CA 94107
(415) 575–3775
Online: dmedia@netcom.com (see WWW site below)

Digital Video Magazine

All about how to capture, compress, and generally make the best out of digital video. A particular substrata within the greater interactive media universe.

Monthly, $29.97/year.
TechMedia Publishing, Inc.
80 Elm Street, Peterborough, NH 03458
(603) 924–0100

Electronic Entertainment

Quirky and fun glossy magazine focusing on interactive media entertainment. Lots of reviews and features as they relate to gaming software. Was edited by Gina Smith, who is now hosting an interactive media TV show.

Monthly, $18/year.
Infotainment World
951 Mariner's Island Boulevard, Suite 700, San Mateo, CA 94404
(415) 349–7781

FamilyPC

General consumer magazine for families who own PCs. Most of the software and interactive media reviews are for educational and edutainment products.

Monthly, $19.95/year.
Ziff-Davis Publishing Company
244 Main Street, Northampton, MA 01060
(800) 413–9749

HomePC

General consumer magazine for home PC users. Since so many home systems are interactive media-ready, though, there's plenty for the CD-ROM enthusiast or developer to read, (the reviews also tend to be kinder and less acerbic than, say, *Wired* or *New Media*).

> Monthly, $21.97/year.
> CMP Publications, Inc.
> 600 Community Drive, Manhasset, NY 11030
> (516) 562–7673

Instruction Delivery Systems

Glossy magazine on interactive media from an instructional point of view. Used to be free; now requires a fee or membership in its parent organization—the Society for Applied Learning Technology, which sponsors a series of educational interactive media conferences.

> Quarterly, $25/year.
> Communicative Technology Corporation
> 50 Culpepper Street, Warrenton, VA 22186
> (703) 439–1731

Internet World

Everything you ever wanted to know about the Internet. More from a developer than a user's point of view. Mecklermedia sponsors the Internet World conference, as well as a large and happening WWW site (see below).

> Monthly, $29/year.
> Mecklermedia Corporation
> 20 Ketchum Street, Westport, CT 06880
> (203) 226–6967

Mac Home Journal

Ladies Home Journal for propeller-heads? Not exactly. This is like *Family PC* or *Home PC* but strictly for Mac-ophiles. Reviews, comparisons, features. Education-heavy.

> Monthly, $19.95/year.
> 612 Howard Street, Sixth Floor, San Francisco, CA 94105
> (415) 957–1911

MacUser

Thick, all-Macintosh magazine with plenty of reviews and columns. Whether you go with this one or competitor *Macworld* (see below) depends mostly on which of the columnists you like better (*MacUser* has John Dvorak, *Macworld* has Guy Kawasaki).

> Monthly, $27/year.

Ziff-Davis Publishing Company
950 Tower Lane, 18th Floor, Foster City, CA 94404
(415) 378–5600

MacWeek

Latest breaking news, inside information months before anyone else. Corporate focus. You can get it all—except for the pictures—online now.

Weekly, free to qualified professionals (but very hard to convince them you're qualified).

Ziff-Davis Publishing Company
301 Howard Street, San Francisco, CA 94105
(415) 243–3500
Online: http://www.pc-computing.ziff.com/~macweek/

Macworld

Super-thick Macintosh review and product magazines with outspoken columnists. See earlier description on *MacUser* for pros and cons.

Monthly, $30/year (6 months free for attending any Macworld Expo).
Macworld Communications, Inc. (IDG)
501 Second Street, San Francisco, CA 94107
(800) 521–0600; (415) 243–0505 (editorial)

Morph's Outpost on the Digital Frontier

Morph is a gnome who lives on the interactive media edge and appears in cartoons in this irreverent and always lively publication. The magazine is mainly a technical developer's journal, but there's plenty to read for the more business-minded as well. One of my personal favorites (I love a magazine that refers to itself in the third person).

Monthly, $39.95/year.
Morph's Outpost, Inc.
5428 College Avenue, Oakland, CA 94618
(510) 601–8685

Multimedia Monitor

The oldest and once most respected of the expensive industry newsletters, the Monitor is still transitioning from its early days as the *Videodisc Monitor*. Conference reports (if you can't make it to the show yourself) are particularly valuable, as is its editorial commentary from industry veteran commentator Rockley Miller.

Monthly, $395/year.
Future Systems, Inc.

P.O.B. 26, Falls Church, VA 22040
(703) 241–1799

Multimedia Producer

For creators and developers of interactive media. Lots of "how I did this" type of articles; not as technical as *Morph's Outpost* or *Converge*. Originally an insert into both *A/V Video* and *Computer Pictures*.

Monthly, $40/year.
Knowledge Industry Publications, Inc.
701 Westchester Avenue, White Plains, NY 10604
(914) 328–9157

Multimedia Today

A glossy IBM products catalog with general articles at the beginning. Similar to the *World of Macintosh Multimedia*, except this one is produced at IBM itself.

Quarterly, free to qualified professionals.
Redgate Communications Corporation
660 Beachland Boulevard, Vero Beach, FL 32963
(800) 779–2062

Multimedia Week

Industry analysis newsletter. Late breaking news, trends—great if you can afford it. Was edited by Chris Sherman who broke off to start up *Multimedia Wire*—a fax and e-mail daily.

Weekly, $597/year.
Phillips Business Information, Inc.
7811 Montrose Road, Potomac, MD 20854
(301) 340–2100

Multimedia World

Slogan is "All Multimedia, All PC." This is a no-Macs-allowed club. Lots of hardware comparisons and industry news. Less title reviews. Hip, in a corporate sort of way. Began as an insert to *PC World Magazine*.

Monthly, $14.97/year.
PC World Communications, Inc.
501 Second Street, Suite 600, San Francisco, CA 94107
(415) 281–8650
Online: http://www.mmworld.com

New Media

Probably the most popular and widely read interactive media magazine. *New Media* has lots of reviews, a fold-out screen shot section, and good columns from the likes of Ted Nelson. There's even a very clever interactive media puzzle.

Monthly, $48/year (free to qualified professionals).
Hypermedia Communications
901 Mariner's Island Blvd, Suite 365, San Mateo, CA 94404
(415) 573–5170

PC Magazine

PC Magazine focuses on all things PC. Lots of hardware and software reviews. Interactive media stuff sprinkled in-between.

$49.97/year for 22 issues.
One Park Ave, New York, NY 10016
(800) 289–0429

PCWeek

Equivalent to *MacWeek* on the PC side. Lots of fast-breaking information. Has a corporate focus.

Weekly, free to qualified professionals.
Ziff-Davis Publishing Company
P.O. Box 1770, Riverton, NJ 08077
(609) 461–2100
e-mail: http://www.pc-computing.ziff.com/~pcweek

PC World

Like *Macworld* for the PC (or is *Macworld* like *PC World* for the Mac?). Hardware and software reviews for the whole computer, with interactive media info sprinkled in.

$19.95/year.
PC World Communications, Inc.
501 Second Street, Suite 600, San Francisco, CA 94107
(800) 521–0600

Publish

Glossy magazine focusing on desktop publishing. As with everything in this industry, more and more interactive media crossover.

Monthly, $39/year.
Integrated Media, Inc.

501 Second Street, San Francisco, CA 94107
(415) 243–0600

T.H.E. (Technical Horizons in Education) Journal

Glossy magazine, lots of ads and industry news, with a very specific education focus.

Monthly, free to qualified professionals.
150 El Camino Real, Suite 112, Tustin, CA 92680
(714) 730–4011

VRWorld

Everything you ever wanted to know about virtual reality. More for the developer than the user.

Bi-monthly, $29/year.
Mecklermedia Corporation
20 Ketchum Street, Westport, CT 06880
(203) 226–6967

Wired

The hippest interactive media read around. Totally innovative and fresh, with articles probing everything from the future of neurobiotics to the latest digital fetish. *Wired* is about digital culture. Don't look for hardware or software reviews. Get it anyway, and read it cover to cover.

Monthly, $39.95/year.
Wired Ventures, Ltd.
544 Second Street, San Francisco, CA 94107
(415) 904–0660
Online: info@wired.com (see below for WWW site)

World of Macintosh Multimedia

Mac-specific listing of all multimedia products plus Mac feature articles at the beginning.

Bi-monthly, $7.95/issue.
Redgate Communications Corporation
660 Beachland Boulevard, Vero Beach, FL 32963
(407) 231–6094

■ World Wide Web Information Sources

In the past year, the World Wide Web has exploded with sources of interactive media information. So far, most online sources are based on a print equivalent. You don't usually get the pretty pictures, but the text can be timely, lively... and usually free (beyond the charges you pay to your monthly service provider and any online connect charges, of course). Sure, there are advertisements peppered all around the Web, but you have to click to get the full treatment, making Web ads less intrusive than, say, Prodigy's quarter-screen screamers.

Some WWW info sites are relatively unambitious, simply featuring the text of the previous month's print magazine (those are listed with the magazine in the previous section). My favorite Web sites, though, provide daily or weekly interactive media updates on the latest technology, software product, deals, and industry trends—faster than I can get through any other media source. Then, there are a few sites that are entirely unique and interactive, sponsoring online exclusives, forums, and live chats.

Please note that this section lists only sources of interactive media information. There are hundreds, if not thousands, of totally cool sites operated by various interactive media developers and publishers to promote their wares. Also, remember that Web sites are much more volatile than snail mail addresses. There's not a universally accepted way on the Web to "forward mail" yet, and as companies are bought out, their sites often get transferred to the new parent.

If you're new to the Web, the language goes something like this: Every site has an URL (Unique Resource Locator). URLs always start with: http://. After that comes www. (for World Wide Web). Then you find the name of the company you're looking for, followed by the suffix .com (for company in America). Example: www.microsoft.com. Non-profit and government organizations often end in .org (example: www.iics.org). And companies overseas contain a different final letter combination (examples: co.uk for British sites, co.il for Israeli sites). After that comes a mess of gibberish that indicates the specific address where a particular web "page" can be found. *Digital Pulse* wins the prize for the most user-unfriendly address.

Computer Currents Interactive

In a number of cities around the U.S. (including the San Francisco Bay Area, Los Angeles, and Dallas), *Computer Currents* is a twice-monthly computer magazine with useful reviews and news. The Web version gives you back issues, resources, events, and more. Search for their annual Multimedia Resource Guide—you'll find the contact info for hundreds of interactive media companies in San Francisco's Multimedia Gulch.

http://ccurrents.infinite-access.com/cc/index.html

Computer News Daily

A collection of articles specifically on computer-related issues which appear in newspapers around the world and are syndicated by the *New York Times*. Includes daily news, features, and a weekly column by Bill Gates himself.

http://nytsyn.com:80/cgi-bin/times/lead/go

Digital Media: A Seybold Report Online

Can't afford the full print Digital Media? Go online. Billed as a "premium service," at least some of this site-in-construction will be free to the interactive media masses. Sections include Alliance Tracker, New Media Markets, contents of the print magazine online, fast breaking news, and more.

http://www.digmedia.com

Digital Pulse

Service from Time-Warner, which includes hardware and software reviews, kids interactive news, and links to print publications, including *InformationWeek*, *Time*, *InteractiveAge*, *HomePC*, *Technology Review*, and more. Part of the larger *Time* "Pathfinder" service.

http://www.pathfinder.com/@@aInhEgAAAAAAAOUS/pathfinder/pulse/pulsehome.html

HotWired

The Web companion to *Wired* magazine. *HotWired* sponsors live chats and forums, encourages submissions, and is totally irreverent like the print magazine. Online categories include Signal, World Beat, Piazza, Renaissance 2.0, Coin, and back issues of *Wired*.

http://www.hotwired.com

Index to Multimedia Information Sources

This site, updated by Simon Gibbs, provides an extremely useful service. Pointers to hundreds of interactive media sources are included in categories such as Bibliographies, CD Formats, Companies and Commercial Services, Conference Announcements, Conference Proceedings, Research, Software, Standards, and more.

http://viswiz.gmd.de/MultimediaInfo

MecklerWeb

A comprehensive site, set up by the Mecklermedia publishing concern, providing useful information and links to its print publications online. These include *Internet World*, *VRML World*, *iWorld*, and more.

http://www.mecklerweb.com/home.htm

Mercury Center

The *San Jose Mercury News* is the local paper in Silicon Valley. Mercury Center is a probably the best idea of what a good online newspaper of the future might look like, with feature stories, late breaking news, comics, local want ads, classifieds, and—the reason it's included here—an excellent computer and interactive media-heavy business section. It's not free, but at $4.95/month, it's a good deal, especially if you're out of town.

http://www.sjmercury.com

Morph's Outpost—Daily Spectrum

Morph has always been a good source of insider info. This site, written by *Morph* publisher Doug Millison, is so current, it's updated twice daily. The Maddog address is a complete *Morph* online site. *Daily Spectrum* appears in a more readable font and type size, however, at the MecklerWeb address.

http://www.mecklerweb.com:80/netday/morph/daily.htm
http://www.maddog.com

Multimedia Wire Web

Weekly interactive media insider news written by Chris Sherman, who was editor of *Multimedia Week*. The Web site is a tease for a much larger daily e-mail or fax which costs close to $400. This Web site includes links to companies, conferences, and associations.

http://www.mmwire.com

ZD-Net

Here's direct access to many Ziff-Davis magazines, including *Computer Gaming World, PC Magazine, Computer Life, PC/Computing, MacWeek, Family PC, Inter@ctive Week, Windows Sources,* and more.

http://www.ziff.com

■ Associations

Getting your information from print and electronic sources is great, but it's still basically passive. To really get interactive, you've got to hit the pavement. The best way to meet people, network, and feel a part of the action is to join—and become an active member in—a professional association. There are a number of associations devoted exclusively to interactive media. Other associations focus on a specific substrata—information design, for example—but cross over a lot into interactive media concerns.

Professional associations usually maintain a national office, but the real work gets done at the local level. To get involved, first go to a general meeting. Find out when the local steering committee or council meets. Attend a session. Professional associations are always looking for more volunteers. You may find yourself helping mail the newsletter. Or you could quickly be snatched up as a co-chair for a newly forming Special Interest Group. Your particular niche doesn't exist yet? Go out and create it yourself.

Professional associations eagerly embrace newcomers. And as you become known to the movers and shakers in an association as someone they can count on, you'll be in a better position to apply for a job opening at their company or ask them for a recommendation—even if you're still a beginner. As I mentioned in the Introduction to this book, it was primarily through the IICS professional association that I got started in the industry. I strongly recommend you doing the same.

Association for Educational Communications and Technology

This is a mostly college educators group, sponsoring an annual convention, local seminars, an awards program, and excellent periodicals and journals. If educational technology is your focus, consider the AECT. Not widely known in "consumer" interactive media circles.

(202) 466–4780

Association of Visual Communicators (AVC)

This group is on the down-swing; its main purpose these days is to sponsor the Cindy Awards—a 35-year old competition for corporate video and interactive titles. In its heyday, AVC's membership was composed of video and audio/visual professionals.

(619) 461–1600

Berkeley Macintosh User Group (BMUG)

If you're into Macs, and you're in the San Francisco Bay Area, BMUG's general meetings are like a Grateful Dead concert—frolicking, familiar, and ultimately safe to ask any question. BMUG puts out a great twice-yearly newsletter with hundreds of pages of opinionated articles. Meets on the University of California, Berkeley campus.

(510) 549–BMUG

Interactive Multimedia Association (IMA)

The preeminent interactive media association for hardware and software companies. Membership—including a few interactive media developers—stands at over 350 organizations. The IMA is active on a government lobbying level, and helps to set standards through its compatibility project and Intellectual Property Task Force. Sponsors the annual NAB/Multimedia World conference. Dues range from $300 for a small non-profit to $50,000 for a sponsor.

(410) 626–1380

http://www.ima.org

International Interactive Communications Society (IICS)

This is the world's largest professional association for interactive media developers, with 5000 members in 36 chapters around the globe. IICS focuses more on individual than company membership, and it excels at information exchange and networking. Each local chapter has a different flavor, but usually with a general meeting, SIGs, and a newsletter. There's also a national conference, awards ceremony, and discounts on other events and publications. Call or e-mail the national office for local chapter contacts.

(503) 579–IICS

http://www.iics.org *or* IICSHQ@aol.com

International Television Association (ITVA)

The professional association for makers of corporate and training videos. Meetings often spill into interactive media content areas, which makes this group worth attending selectively.

(214) 869–1112

Multimedia Developers Group (MDG)

Regional group which claims membership of most of the hottest interactive media developers located in San Francisco's now-famous Multimedia Gulch. MDG's offerings (and membership) somewhat overlaps IICS-SF, including monthly meetings, SIGs, and workshops. MDG events are higher priced but also classier. MDG focuses on company membership, while IICS goes after the individual developer.

(415) 553–2300

National Society for Performance and Instruction (NSPI)

The main professional association for information and instructional designers, whether they work in interactive media or not. Increasingly, meetings and lectures address interactive media applications.

(202) 408–7969

Optical Publishing Association (OPA)

Association for CD-ROM and other optical disc publishers. Good shared information, some excellent services, reports, and directories (including an annual listing of every CD out there), and the insightful analysis of founder Rich Bowers, who moderates a forum on CompuServe. No regular local meetings.

(614) 442–8805

Society for Technical Communicators (STC)

The main association for technical writers is moving slowly into interactive media as tech writers increasingly cross the digital frontier. Consider STC if you're a technical writer trying to branch out.

(202) 737–0035

Software Entrepreneurs Forum (SEF)

A local Silicon Valley group which sponsors meetings and lectures to promote software entrepreneurship. Over the years, most of the top speakers in the industry have appeared before the group.

(415) 854–7219

Software Publishers Association (SPA)

Major software organization, with membership of all the main computer publishers. The SPA occasionally publishes a standard or develops a policy relating to interactive media.

(202) 452–1600

■ Conferences

Once you get on a professional association's mailing list, you'll start to get a flood of "junk" mail. Notices and announcements about new publications, reports, meetings, and conferences will quickly fill up your mailbox. Conferences, in particular, are an excellent way to learn about interactive media. But sorting through the hundreds of conferences that come your way and deciding which to plunk down a few bucks on can be tough. There are a number of different types of conferences, each with their own pluses and minuses:

- Interactive media-specific conferences are all about interactive media. The lectures and seminars are about interactive media, the exhibits are about interactive media. These are probably the most focused places you can get a running start on the products and services currently available. Not to mention some serious schmoozing.

- General computer conferences have increasingly large interactive media elements. This is by virtue of the fact that interactive media hardware and software is the fastest growing segment of the computer industry. Accordingly, it's no surprise that the really big computer shows like Comdex or PC Expo are among the best places to learn the latest interactive media information.

- General noncomputer conferences are now adding interactive media tracks. The American Bookseller's Association now has a CD-ROM pavilion. So do conferences formerly devoted to selling video equipment or even syndicated television programs, like NATPE. These shows aren't worth going to unless you're interested in the general topic. (Warning: Don't go to a "Lawyers and Technology" show unless you like lawyers.)

Within the broad categories listed above, conferences can be subdivided once more:

- National conferences draw a crowd from all over the United States and often the world. They usually occur once a year either in a standard location or on a rotating basis in different locations. National conferences are priced high. If one happens to be in your town (if you live in San Francisco, Los Angeles, or New York, this is likely), you can usually get a pass to the Exhibit Hall for only $25–$75. Most of the seeing and schmoozing happens here anyway, so it's a good start. Professional associations sometimes receive a limited number of free Exhibit Hall passes which they distribute at monthly meetings.

- Local conferences are, as it sounds, local in nature. They cost less to get in, but that doesn't mean the caliber of the speakers is any less. You might not get a Bill Gates at the local Multimedia Expo, but it's still worthwhile to hear Mark Schlichting, the visionary behind Brøderbund's Living Books, discuss interface deconstruction. Local conferences have a nice homey feel, and can get more playful than a large well-established national one (Art Teco, for example, has its seminar emcees "work" the audience with hand-held microphones, like a bunch of hi-tech Phil Donahues).

The listing below includes the location and general time of year a conference is held. Call the number listed for the exact dates. A March conference one year might be an April one the next year, but the season usually remains constant. Nearly every conference runs between 3–5 days.

Art Teco

Developer's show sponsored by *Morph's Outpost on the Digital Frontier*. Attracts an arty crowd. Known for its irreverent approach and wild parties.
San Francisco—June
(510) 704–7171

CD-ROM Expo

All-CD-ROM show that's been eclipsed in recent years by shows with bigger sponsors on the West Coast and Las Vegas.

Boston—October
(508) 879–6700

CeBIT

The biggest European computer show with everything under the sun—including interactive media titles, hardware, and software.

Hanover, Germany—March
(609) 987–1202

Comdex

Biggest computer show in North America. Comdex has become THE show where major interactive media companies exhibit and make product announcements. An absolute must. Bring good walking shoes.

Las Vegas—November
(617) 449–6600

Consumer Electronics Show (CES)

Has been the pre-eminent show for video games and entertainment CD-ROMs, but vendors have pulled out recently for the newer E3. Unclear what its future will be.

Las Vegas—January, Chicago—June
(202) 457–4901

Digital Hollywood

A lower-priced version of Digital World (see following). Doesn't attract the big name vendors, but has a great lecture schedule. Similar to Multimedia Expo (by the same company) but with a Hollywood focus.

Beverly Hills—February
(212) 226–4141

Digital World

Classy, expensive, star-studded interactive media show. Formerly in Beverly Hills, Digital World has moved recently to the Los Angeles Convention Center due to its need for a larger exhibit hall. Connected with the print journal *Digital Media: A Seybold Report*.

Los Angeles—June
(800) 433–5200

Electronic Entertainment Expo (E3)

A newcomer that became an industry darling when it wrested one of the big video game makers away from its longtime home at CES. Mostly a games focus—from CD-ROM to carts. If you're vaguely connected to entertainment titles, you gotta be there.

Los Angeles—May
(800) 800–5474

ImageWorld/Video Expo

ImageWorld shows are regional and attract mostly a local crowd—including Exhibit Hall vendors. Began as a show called Video Expo, so the program is still video equipment heavy.

New York—September, San Jose—December
(800) 800–KIPI

Infocomm International

Formerly a video-focused show, Infocomm is branching into interactive media. Infocomm beefs up its speaking schedule by taking under its wing affiliated interactive media organizations that don't have enough resources to mount their own shows. At times, this has included IICS, AMI, AECT, and AVC's Cindy Awards. Famous for its projection screen shoot-out.

June in different locations around the country
(703) 273–7200

Interactive Healthcare

Interactive media titles, products, software, and hardware as they relate to healthcare and medical applications.

Alexandria, VA—June
(703) 354–8155

interMedia

Formerly called the Microsoft CD-ROM Expo. Has been the best (and only) all-CD-ROM show for years. Is now being eclipsed by bigger shows (Comdex, CES, and E3) which have large interactive media sections. Very expensive ($1000+)—but go to the Exhibit Hall at least.

San Jose—February/March
(203) 352–8254

Macromedia User Conference

Technical developer's show with a small exhibit hall devoted exclusively to Macromedia products. Awards and a developer's showcase. Nice friendly feeling.

   San Francisco—October
   (415) 252-2000

Milia

There are plenty of interactive media shows outside the United States and Canada, but this one recruits heavily from the U.S. community. Milia is billed as THE electronic publishing show of Europe. Attendance is small, but composed mostly of decision makers, so the people you meet are the people you want and need to meet. Plus a great location. Save up for it.

   Cannes, France—January
   (212) 689–4220

Multimedia Expo

Good entry to interactive media. Excellent speakers and a small, local exhibit hall. If this show pulls into your town, spring for the $25 entry fee to the exhibits. Or get a free pass from a local professional association meeting. Sponsored by the same organization as Digital Hollywood in Los Angeles.

   San Francisco—September, also in New York
   (212) 226–4141

Multimedia Live!

New show that unites local professional groups, publications, vendors, and developers in the San Francisco Bay Area.

   San Francisco—March
   (415) 453–1393

NAB/IMA Multimedia World

The National Association of Broadcasters conference focuses on new video equipment. The Interactive Multimedia Association sponsors a small but growing (in size and prestige) sub-conference focused on interactive media products and speakers. Go if you're already going.

   Las Vegas—April
   (800) 342–2460

National Educational Film and Video Festival (NEFVF)

An education-oriented show with a growing exhibit hall, an awards ceremony, and a small, still-homey feel. One of the only places you'll find a spirited discussion of interactive media Integrated Learning Systems.

Oakland, CA—May
(510) 465–6885

NATPE

If you go, you'll find it's clearly the weirdest show on the planet. This is where syndicated television vendors come to buy and sell everything from reruns of 90210 to the Susan Powter "Stop the Insanity" talk show. IICS has in the past two years sponsored interactive media breakfast seminars.

Various location around the country in January (recently in New Orleans and Anaheim)
(310) 453–4440

New Media Expo

Seminars and exhibit hall in Los Angeles. Makes its mark as more of a marketing- and business-oriented show versus one targeted at developers.

Los Angeles—March
(617) 449–6600

SALT

The Society for Applied Learning Technology sponsors one of the grand-daddies of conferences with an instructional and corporate training focus. Been around for 10+ years. Different conferences have different names:

Orlando Multimedia—February
Interactive Multimedia (Washington, D.C.)—August
(703) 347–0055

Seybold San Francisco Exposition

The pre-eminent desktop publishing show branches into interactive media. A free pass to the exhibit hall is easy to get and usually worth it.

San Francisco—September
(800) 433–5200

Siggraph

Siggraph is the graphics Special Interest Group of the Association for Computing Machinery (ACM). The show is heavy on 3D graphic hardware and software, with a little interactive media stuff thrown in for good measure.

Los Angeles—August
(312) 321–6830

Virtual Reality Conference and Exhibition

Everything about virtual reality—speakers, vendors, demos. If you've ever wanted to try out the latest VR games and toys, get a pass to the Exhibit Hall and go just to play. Sponsored by Mecklermedia, publishers of *VRWorld* magazine.

San Jose—May, New York—November
(800) 632–5537

Viscomm

Comprehensive graphic design and interactive media conference. Draws mostly a local crowd, but gets some very prestigious local speakers (the Interface Deconstruction seminar is a personal favorite).

San Francisco—June, New York—November
(212) 777–7200

■ Books

Books on interactive media are great for boning up on all the background you need to be conversant at digital techie parties. In contrast, interactive media magazines often assume a certain basic literacy, and professional associations—except for the ubiquitous "Introduction" seminars—can seem at first like entering another dimension. But the thick tomes that have appeared of late have plenty of room to explain even the most basic concepts in a patient, thorough manner.

The books I'm listing either focus on a particular specialty (for example, digital video or interface design), or they cover the entire range of interactive media tasks—from business and design through production and development. Since *Interactive Media Essentials for Success* focuses uniquely on just the planning and design phases of interactive media development, this list is really intended for your "advanced study." Build yourself a library now and you'll be able to lend out your collection when you're ready to mentor someone else!

Art of Human-Computer Interface Design

A collection of essays on interactive media interface design by various industry pundits, thinkers, and developers. Contents include essays on Creativity and Design, Users and Contexts, Technique and Technology, New Directions, and a collection of "Sermons." This is an invaluable book for anyone wanting a broad opening perspective on interactive media interface design.

edited by Brenda Laurel. Addison-Wesley Publishing Company, Inc. Reading, MA: 1990.

Business Week Guide to Multimedia Presentations

Another broad look at interactive media design, hardware, and software from the perspective of making a corporate or marketing presentation rather than a mass market consumer title. Specific chapters focus on graphics, sound, and video. Comes with a CD-ROM of interactive media application demos.

by Robert Lindstrom. Osborne McGraw Hill. Berkeley, CA: 1994.

Complete HyperCard 2.0 Handbook

HyperCard is probably the easiest interactive media authoring system to learn—and it's one of the least expensive to purchase. If you have a Mac and you're getting started with HyperCard, there's no better book than Danny Goodman's. Constantly updated, always clear, forever insightful.

by Danny Goodman. Bantam Books. Toronto: 1994.

Demystifying Multimedia

Dynamite overall introduction to interactive media with developer interviews, case studies, and detailed technological explanations. Produced by interactive media developer/publisher Vivid Studios, which has extensive first-hand experience. A textbook in some interactive media study programs.

by Vivid Studios. Apple Computer/Worldwide Multimedia Marketing. Cupertino, CA: 1993.

The Desktop Multimedia Bible

New Media Magazine contributing editor Jeff Burger has created his version of the "it's all here under one cover" interactive media bible. The name fits. Everything from business to production.

by Jeff Burger. Addison-Wesley Publishing Company, Inc. Reading, MA: 1992.

Graphic Design for Electronic Documents and User Interfaces

Use this as a companion to Brenda Laurel's book, and you'll be doing fine on interface design. Aaron Marcus has a hands-on, award-winning interface design firm in the San Francisco area. The best section of the book compares icons between the major operating systems—Mac, Windows, UNIX, OS/2, etc.

by Aaron Marcus. ACM Press. New York: 1992.

How to Digitize Video

A pretty technical tome, but I'm including it here because the authors, all members of The San Francisco Canyon Company, are some of the world's leading experts on digital video (they wrote QuickTime for Windows). They also know how to optimize a CD better than anyone. The book includes a CD-ROM with examples.

by Nels Johnson with Fred Gault and Mark Florence. John Wiley and Sons. New York: 1994.

HyperCard Stack Design Guidelines

The earliest HyperCard stacks were a holy mess. Apple had the foresight to publish this book to help novice designers add consistency and style to their stacks. Simple rules, like always put your buttons in the same place on each screen, or provide feedback when something is clicked. While state-of-the-art stack design in 1989 might seem almost quaint compared with today's sophisticated interactive media products, the basics are still quite valid.

by Apple Computer, Inc. Addison-Wesley Publishing Company, Inc. Reading, MA: 1989.

MacWeek Guide to Desktop Video

Good overall look at desktop video, from a technological, design, and planning side. Includes a CD-ROM of demos and QuickTime tools. Mac only (this is, after all, the *MacWeek* guide…)

by Eric Holsinger. Ziff-Davis Press. Emeryville, CA: 1993.

The Media Lab

The Massachusetts Institute of Technology's Media Lab is one of the world's foremost institutions for, as the book's subtitle states, "inventing the future." Under the direction of Nicholas Negroponte, the Lab has experimented with the future of everything from "personal newspapers" to virtual reality. Whole Earth Catalog editor and publisher Stuart Brand spent three months at the lab. These are his reflections.

by Stuart Brand. Penguin Books. New York: 1987.

Multimedia Law Handbook

Knowing the law as it intersects interactive media is important for the entire team—from the Media Acquisition person to the Producer. This book lays it out in simple terms for the layperson, with plenty of excellent examples. Everything from structuring the interactive media deal to clearing rights.

by J. Dianne Brinson and Mark F. Radcliffe. Ladera Press. Menlo Park, CA: 1994.

Multimedia Madness

Over 1000 pages focusing on interactive media hardware and software. Includes two CD-ROMs full of demos, presentations, photos, videos.

by Ron Wodaski. SAMS Publishing. Indianapolis, IN: [1995]

Multimedia: Making it Work

Along with Demystifying Multimedia, Tay Vaughn's book is probably the most complete, covering the whole range of interactive media activities. Long-time developer Tay adds his own personal insights (he wrote a column *for New Media* called "Ask The Captain.") The book comes with a CD-ROM of demos from Macromedia, which co-sponsors the book.

by Tay Vaughn. Osborne McGraw-Hill. Berkeley, CA: 1994.

A Practical Guide to Interactive Video Design

All about designing interactive videodiscs, this is an oldie but still a goodie. Particularly valuable is the section on flowchart symbols and conventions.

by Nick Iuppa. Knowledge Industry Publications, Inc. White Plains, NY: 1984.

Producer's Guide to Interactive Videodisc

Marty Perlmutter is one of the smartest guys in the business, with an extensive knowledge of interactive media and a sardonic wit. Both of these elements shine through in this book which focuses on videodisc production. The glossary at the end is particularly exhaustive.

by Martin Perlmutter. Knowledge Industry Publications, Inc. White Plains, NY: 1991.

QuickTime: Making Movies on Your Macintosh *and* Making Movies With Your PC

Bob Hone heads up Red Hill Studios, a small but impressive production facility I've worked with in the past. This pair of books—one for making Mac based digital movies, the other for PCs—is thorough and insightful. Better yet, he includes unique hands-on sections on editing specific types of digital movies—group discussions, product demonstrations—as well as basic video aesthetics as applied to interactive media technology.

QuickTime: Making Movies on Your Macintosh
by Robert Hone. Prima Publishing. Rocklin, CA: 1993.
Making Movies With Your PC
by Robert Hone and Margy Kuntz. Prima Publishing. Rocklin, CA: 1994.

■ Glossary: Jargon Watch

In order to survive in the increasingly cut-throat interactive media world, you really have to be able to "talk the talk"—to understand the nuances of techno-speak whenever it rears its acronym-laden head. So, if someone says they want you to work with a Jaguar, you shouldn't cry out in alarm. Similarly, if a client tells you to mess with his AUTOEXEC.BAT, that's not grounds for a harassment suit.

Understanding the lingo of interactive media is what this chapter is all about. I'll present the main terms you HAVE to know—and a few that would be nice to know, too—in clear, nontechnical language. When you're done, you should be able to mingle at the next techno-speak cocktail bash as well as talk to the hardest-core C++ coder.

3DO. An acronym for *3D Objects*, 3DO is the name of a hot set-top box from the 3DO Corporation. Introduced in 1993 with great fanfare, its super-fast 64-bit processing, double-speed CD-ROM drive, great graphics, and backing from Trip Hawkins—the man who built Electronic Arts into a powerhouse software publisher—made it an early favorite in the black box wars. That promise, however, is still waiting to be fulfilled.

286, 386, 486, 586 ... . These numbers refer to processor speeds for Intel microchips—the brains behind IBM PCs and compatibles. The greater the number, the faster and more powerful the chip. 386s (short for 80386) were the first chips with enough strength to run interactive media CD-ROMs. 486s are better and 586s (known as "Pentium" chips) really sing.

680x0. This is the family name for Motorola's microchip, used primarily in Apple's Macintosh computer. It comes in four varieties, roughly paralleling the power of the x86 chips from Intel: the 68030—like the Intel 386—was the first with sufficient juice to run interactive media. The 68040 powers up many Quadras. Apple's equivalent to Intel's Pentium is an entirely new type of chip called the PowerPC (see below).

Analog. Sound that comes from a tape or LP is recorded as a "wave." The up and down motion of this wave is known as *analog*, in contrast to *digital*, which translates those waves to ones and zeros. Speakers always translate back to analog, since that is what the human ear can hear.

AUTOEXEC.BAT. This is a DOS term, dreaded by all sensible human beings. The AUTOEXEC.BAT is a file that helps the DOS operating system know what to do. Many Windows 3.1 titles need to modify the AUTOEXEC.BAT to run properly. It's common, but considered bad form, for an interactive media title to do this on your computer without asking first.

AVI. An acronym for Audio Video Interleaved, this is Microsoft's file format extension enabling ordinary PCs to play digital movies without any additional hardware. AVI refers to the way the sound and visual tracks are woven together so they play in sync. Microsoft Video for Windows files usually end with the three-letter tag ".AVI."

C++. When a program is hard coded, rather than created in a more layman-friendly authoring system, C++ is the programming language of choice. It's "object oriented," which means that programmers can build re-usable pieces of code attached to specific objects. C++ development requires hiring knowledge-able—and expensive—programmers.

CAV. An acronym standing for Constant Angular Velocity, this term refers to videodiscs that are formatted so that each disk revolution is equal to exactly one frame. This makes for extremely accurate frame-by-frame searches. CAV disks can hold 54,000 still frames on a side, which translates into 30 minutes of motion video.

CDTV. Commodore Computer's "Commodore Dynamic Total Vision" was one of the first set-top boxes to hit the market. It was badly designed, never had many titles available, and didn't have the marketing muscle of a CD-i or 3DO. It died a fairly painless death not all that long after its release.

CD-i. Compact Disc Interactive from Phillips is a set-top box that comes in a variety of configurations—a standard consumer "black box," a professional version with a floppy disk and keyboard, and a portable unit—the CD-iMan. Designed in the mid-80s, CD-i debuted late, and was pronounced by many industry pundits as dead on arrival. Defying its critics, the system continues to hang on, especially in Europe.

CD-ROM. The technology focus of most of this book, CD-ROM stands for Compact Disc—Read Only Memory. CD-ROM discs are exactly the same physically as the CD audio discs. The "ROM" indicates that, instead of just music, CD-ROMs can hold any kind of digital data, such as text, audio, video, or animation. CD-ROMs act like big floppy disks (holding up to 650MB), except they can't record data—they will only play back.

CinePak.   This is a popular compression algorithm used to stuff big digital movies into a smaller space. CinePak was originally called CompactVideo, and was developed by SuperMac. It works best with video, rather than animation, files.

CLV.   An acronym standing for Constant Linear Velocity, this term refers to videodiscs that are formatted for maximum storage. Each revolution of a CLV disk can hold between one and three frames depending on whether the laser is at the fat or the skinny part of the disk. While this makes a CLV search less precise, CLV disks can hold up to 60 minutes of motion video per side, making them ideal for linear movie playback.

Compression.   When a file—usually a digital movie—is too big to fit on a disk or to play back smoothly, it needs to be compressed. This can be done through hardware or software. Indeo, MPEG and Cinepak are specific compression algorithms which encode, and later decode, the data.

CONFIG.SYS.   Dreaded only slightly less than the AUTOEXEC.BAT, this is a file that is also needed by DOS to run. It essentially "configures your system." Unlike the AUTOEXEC.BAT, interactive media programs don't usually alter the CONFIG.SYS file themselves. But users sometimes have to go in and do CONFIG.SYS surgery when an interactive media program that's supposed to run flawlessly doesn't.

Digital.   All computer data is digital—be it pictures, music, or video. This simply means that the data is translated into ones and zeroes, rather than analog "waves." Digital data can be arranged in any order that fits on a disk (the computer does this automatically), while analog data (from an audio or videotape, for example) must have a beginning, middle, and end point.

DAT.   Digital Audio Tape is a format devised by Sony to replace traditional analog audio cassettes with digital cassettes. The new format tapes have the crystal clarity of audio CDs and you can record on them. Though they never caught on with consumers, DAT has successfully transitioned into a standard for sound professionals, and is a common medium for backing up a computer's hard drive.

DCC.   A competing format to Sony's DAT, Phillip's Digital Compact Cassette also records digital music and data. The quality isn't as high as DAT, but DCC recorders will play existing analog cassettes.
(Sony's format, in contrast, is an entirely different size, requiring the consumers to convert their music libraries, or buy all new tapes.)

Director. This program from interactive media powerhouse Macromedia is the most widely used authoring system for consumer applications. Director adds a user-friendly layer of interactive media functionality, shielding non-programmers from the complexities of developing in C++ code. Director programs play on both Macs and PCs, some set-top boxes, and—soon—over the World Wide Web.

Double-speed vs. Single-speed. The first CD-ROMs spun at a particular speed. When technology improved, a new kind of CD-ROM appeared that spun twice as fast and transferred data to the computer faster as well (not quite twice as fast, though). Double-speed drives can play single-speed disks, but not vice-versa. Quad and even 8X-speed CD-ROM drives are now replacing double-speed drives as standard equipment on new PCs.

DVI. Digital Video Interactive was the first CD-ROM format to play full-screen, full-motion video. Unlike solutions such as QuickTime or Video for Windows, DVI requires special hardware in the computer. Video footage must be sent to a DVI encoding facility to be put on the CD. DVI boards are mostly found these days in IBM's UltiMedia systems.

DVD. The Digital Video Disk is a promising new technology which allows up to ten gigabytes of data to be crammed onto a CD-ROM. There are two types of DVD disks—one from Toshiba (nicknamed the SD, for Super Density, and positioned for use in set-top boxes) and another from Sony/Phillips (positioned as a desktop computer add-on). The disks spin faster than traditional CD-ROMs and have better video quality.

HyperCard. The grand-daddy of consumer authoring systems, Apple's Hyper-Card continues to thrive, especially in educational settings. HyperCard uses a stack of cards metaphor, and has an easy-to-use English language-like authoring language called HyperTalk. The most recent upgrade finally added color. For the Macintosh only.

HyperMedia. Interactive media programs (as well as "pages" on the World Wide Web) excel at providing links between one section and another. Whenever you see a highlighted media item or a highlighted word, you click it, and you're instantly taken to a new section. Purely text-based titles are often called Hyper-Text. Going between sections is known as HyperLinking.

Indeo. This compression algorithm from Intel is very popular for shrinking Video for Windows movies. It is based on the software-only encoding portion of the Intel's hardware-intensive full-motion video DVI standard. A popular hardware digitizer that works well with Indeo is Intel's Smart Video Recorder.

ISO 9660.   The International Standards Organization (ISO) came up with the "9660" format for organizing files that is now standard on all CD-ROMs. ISO 9660 is sometimes known as "High Sierra."

Jaguar.   Atari introduced this new cartridge and CD-ROM set-top box in time for Christmas 1994. It features fast 64-bit processing, great graphics, and some good titles. Jaguar is somewhat of a comeback for Atari, once king of the game hill, but long since eclipsed by the makers of Mario and Sonic the Hedgehog.

JPEG.   An acronym for Joint Photography Experts Group, this compression algorithm is a good choice when you need to reduce the size of still images. JPEG keeps track of each compressed photograph or graphic individually, in contrast to MPEG (see below), which primarily accounts for data differences between frames.

Laserdisc.   This is Pioneer's trademarked name for "videodisc." Pioneer's recently introduced combination videodisc/CD-ROM/cartridge machine is called LaserActive.

Magneto-Optical Drive.   MO drives combine magnetic and optical storage techniques on one disk. They are the heftiest of all removable, re-writeable media technologies—up to 1.3 gigabytes can be stored on a single drive, dynamite for backing up an entire hard disk or even a CD-ROM in progress.

MIDI.   An acronym for Musical Instrument Digital Interface, MIDI is a language for recording and playing back music digitally from a computer or another MIDI device (such as a keyboard). The notes are stored as ones and zeros, so MIDI files are quite small. But, when played back through a MIDI sound board, the music sounds almost as good as the day it was composed.

MiniDisc.   Sony introduced the MiniDisc with hopes of re-creating Walkman success. The MiniDisc records and plays digital audio—though not quite as crystal-clearly as regular CD audio disks. Like Sony's other great digital hope—DAT—the format hasn't caught on with consumers, though some interactive media developers are using it for data storage. MiniDiscs hold up to 128MB of data.

MPC.   A computer with the "Multimedia Personal Computer" label is guaranteed to adhere to certain minimum standards set by the Multimedia PC Marketing

Council. If you put an MPC-labeled sound board or CD-ROM drive in an MPC-compliant computer, the two pieces should work together. This is the closest the PC world has come to the plug-and-play convenience of the Macintosh. There are now MPC2 and MPC3 standards as well.

MPEG.   An acronym for "Motion Picture Experts Group," this compression algorithm is ideal for compressing large digital video movies down to small size. MPEG can stuff at a 100:1 ratio and more by only measuring what data has changed from frame to frame. The similarly named JPEG, in contrast, keeps track of each frame separately, then compresses.

Multisession.   The first CD-ROMs could only be written to once. That is, once you recorded onto the disk, that was it—you had to use it. Multisession technology now lets you write data at one time, and add more to it later. For the user, you can pretty much count on any double-speed CD-ROM drives being able to read multisession CD-ROM disks.

Network.   Computers in a developer's office are usually "networked" together so they can talk to each other. This means that when you want to transfer a file, you don't have to put it on floppy disk and walk it to the next computer. Instead, you can simply copy it over the network cables. A Local Area Network (LAN) operates inside an office. Larger networks help make e-mail possible.

OEM.   An acronym for Original Equipment Manufacturer, an OEM deal—in interactive media terms—refers to a title you receive "bundled" for free when you buy a new piece of hardware, such as a new CD-ROM drive or full computer set-up. In classic manufacturing terms, a hard drive made by Sony placed in an Apple computer is an OEM deal, where Sony here is the Original Equipment Manufacturer.

OS/2 Warp.   IBM decided a few years back to create its own sophisticated competitor to DOS. OS/2 (Operating System/2) has been around since the late 1980s, but only recently has it been simple enough (and small enough) to be useful for real consumers. This latest version has been given the cooler surname of "Warp."

Pentium.   This is the trademarked name for what was originally known as the Intel 586. It is currently the fastest offering in Intel's line of x86 chips for personal computers. The name Pentium arose to prevent rival chip makers from using the generic 586 moniker. (Intel unsuccessfully tried to prevent in court smaller chipmaker AMD from selling their own "386" chip.)

PhotoCD.   Kodak created this format to allow consumers to "develop" their family photos straight to CD-ROM from 35mm film. The local photo finisher was supposed to ask "do you want prints, slides, or a CD?" Instead, the format has become a standard way of moving around archival footage for interactive media developers. The format is supported by most set-top boxes and CD-ROM-based desktop computers.

Photoshop.   This is probably the most important painting tool used by interactive media artists. Almost anything can be created and manipulated using this program from Adobe. Photoshop images are then animated in a program like Director, or handed off to the programmers who sequence them in hard code.

Premiere.   Probably the most widely used digital video editing program, Adobe's Premiere allows Mac and PC users to sequence, cut and paste, and apply effects to pre-digitized video and audio segments. The video is digitized using a digitizing board such as VideoVision or VideoSpigot, and is then compressed using a compression algorithm like Indeo or Cinepak.

PICO.   Sega introduced the toy-like PICO cartridge player in 1994 and has had moderate success with it. The system places a plastic book on top of the cartridge. Flipping the pages of this book triggers different images and interactive activities, which appear on a connected TV screen. Small data storage, limited interactive media elements—this is for the small fry only.

Pippin.   Apple's foray into the set-top box race, the Pippin's main advantage is it can play Macintosh CD-ROM titles with only minor modification. This gives early Pippin adopters an enormous pool of titles to choose from. The system specs are exciting, but its initial price, at $500-plus, is prohibitive for a set-top box.

PlayStation.   Sony keeps cranking them out. This is their answer to Nintendo, Sega, 3DO, and CD-i—a CD-ROM based set-top box with great graphics and fast processing. It's just hitting the market now, so it's hard to say how it will sell.

PowerPC.   An advanced microchip, the PowerPC is used in Apple's latest Power Macintosh line and will be available in IBM computers by mid-1996. For the Mac, the chip replaces the 680x0 series, and maintains (some say exceeds) parity with Intel's Pentium chips. The chip resulted from the still-startling alliance between IBM and Apple.

ProAudio Spectrum.   Along with the SoundBlaster sound card (described below), the ProAudio Spectrum sound card is a de-facto standard for interactive media-ready PC sound. Made by MediaVision, minimum specs on a PC product often call for "ProAudio Spectrum, SoundBlaster, or compatible."

QuickTime.   A revolution when it was introduced, QuickTime was the first mass-market technology allowing digital video to be "tossed around" as easily as a graphics or sound file. QuickTime is simply an extension to the Macintosh's operating system; it allows the computer to recognize a file with the extension ".MOV" as a movie. QuickTime is up to version 2.0 with quarter-screen size. QuickTime for Windows allows the same QuickTime-ready movie to be played cross-platform.

QuickTime VR.   QTVR is an extension to the basic QuickTime technology that allows developers to build 360-degree panoramic environments. Using the mouse, users can then walk around in this environment, and click on objects that look interesting for an instant magnification. The Star Trek Technical Manual was the first consumer title using the QTVR technology.

RealMagic.   The first popularly-priced MPEG card to hit the market, the Real-Magic board brought full-screen, full-motion video down to under $500. Manufacturer Sigma Designs also funded a number of developers to convert their existing titles to run on the RealMagic board.

Red Book, Green Book, Yellow Book … .   There are many "books" for defining how a CD-ROM encodes its data. The Red Book defines how regular audio CDs line up their ones and zeroes. Other "books" that define standards for data structure include the Yellow Book (CD-ROM), Green Book (CD-i), Orange Book (WORM—Write Once, Read Many Times), and White Book (VideoCDs). Red Book audio cannot be played at the same time as Yellow Book CD-ROM data except in a format called CD-ROM-XA, which interleaves the data and audio tracks.

Repurposed.   When content in one media format is taken and converted to interactive media, this is called "repurposing." The earliest videodiscs were full of repurposed linear videos—sometimes with very little extra interactive structure. CD-ROM developers in search of a quick buck continue the trend of repurposing existing media clips in a less-than-original way.

Saturn.   Sega upped the ante on its first CD-ROM-based system—the SegaCD—by introducing the Saturn. All the usual comments for a killer set-top box apply: super-fast graphics and processing power, double-speed CD-ROM drive. Plus the marketing muscle of Sega. A kind-of "Saturn Lite" is known as 32X.

Set-Top Box.   In contrast to a traditional desktop computer, set-top boxes play interactive media titles on the TV set. The name comes from where most of these black boxes are placed. Set-top boxes may play CD-ROMs directly into the TV—like 3DO or CD-i—or bring interactive media content over the phone or cable lines from a central computer.

Shovelware.   Take a load of unrelated images, videos, sounds, or otherwise mixed and matched content, shovel it onto a CD, and sell it cheap—that's the basic recipe for what is disparagingly known as shovelware.

SoundBlaster.   This popular sound card from Creative Labs is found in many interactive media-ready PCs. Minimum specs on a computer will often require a SoundBlaster or compatible card. There's the basic SoundBlaster, as well as Pro and SoundBlaster 16 versions. For video, check out the VideoBlaster, also available from Creative Labs.

SurroundVideo.   Microsoft's response to Apple's QuickTime VR, Surround-Video provides the same basic functionality: the ability to walk around in a 360-degree panoramic view. The biggest difference is for developers: QTVR will "stitch together" a panorama from individual photos or frames. SurroundVideo requires that you capture the images with a special panoramic camera.

SyQuest.   Probably the most popular removable cartridge on the market, a SyQuest drive allows interactive media developers to move very large files around. SyQuests act like an enormous floppy disk—you can read and write to them, and they hold either 44 or 88MB megabytes per disk (a new 128MB cart is just becoming available).

System 6, 7, and 8 ... .   The equivalent of DOS or Windows for the Macintosh world, this is the name of the Mac's operating system. Some older Macs still run System 6; most have upgraded to System 7. System 8 (code-named Copland) is due out in early 1996, and should best Windows 95 in terms of interactive media features.

UltiMedia.   No, this isn't multimedia without the "m." It's the name of a high-end IBM interactive media system, usually delivered with a built-in DVI Action-Media board for full-motion, full-screen video. The UltiMedia is based on the IBM PS/2 architecture.

Ultra64.   Nintendo and Silicon Graphics teamed up to create the next genera-tion game system with the usual litany of super-fast graphics and processing power (the "64" is for 64-bit processing). The system uses cartridges, not CD-ROMs, as the delivery media.

Vaporware.   Software products are often announced, then nary a sight is seen of them for months or sometimes even years. Those products which seem to exist only on a more ethereal level are known as vaporware.

Video for Windows.   Microsoft's answer to QuickTime has been playing techni-cal and functional catch up since the day it was born. Still, because of guaranteed Microsoft compatibility, Video for Windows digital movies are used everywhere in the interactive media universe. See the description on AVI for discussion on VfW's file format.

Videodisc.   12-inch videodiscs can hold tens of thousands of still frame images, or up to 60 minutes of analog motion video. There are three commonly accepted "levels" of videodisc use, ranging from stand-alone with a remote control to com-plete control by the computer. While videodiscs have resurged in popularity in spe-cialty movie stores, they have been supplanted by CD-ROM as the interactive media of choice.

VideoSpigot.   This hardware and software video digitizing combination, origi-nally developed by SuperMac, allows users to "pour" video into their applications. It was one of the first low-cost video digitizing boards. A "pro" version allows for simultaneous capture of audio and video.

VideoVision.   A higher-cost hardware solution for digitizing video and captur-ing audio to a Macintosh. This has been the hardware of choice in the $10,000 range. The very high end belongs to non-linear digital video editing systems like the Avid and Media 100.

VIS.   An acronym for Video Information System, VIS was an early casualty of the set-top box wars. Introduced by Tandy (the Radio Shack People), VIS ran on a 286 computer with Modular Windows. Titles were supposed to port easily from

Windows, but didn't. That, plus the unit's terminally slow speed, sealed an early death.

Windows.   Saddled with the ugly interface and funky functionality of DOS, Microsoft created Windows, a shell program that essentially sits on top of DOS and adds a pleasing graphic look—as legally reminiscent of the Macintosh as the courts would allow. Windows 3.1 was the first version to truly take off. Windows 95 makes interactive media much easier and replaces DOS as the computer's operating system. Windows NT is found mostly running in office networks.

World Wide Web.   The WWW is the hyperlinked, text and graphic-based part of the Internet. Nowadays, it seems like everybody is creating a "home page," which can then be linked to any other home page using a standard called HTML—HyperText Markup Language. The "Web" can now play audio in real time and—soon—animation and video.

XCMD.   Short for eXternal-Command, an XCMD is a small self-contained program that can be used to extend the functionality of an authoring system such as Director or HyperCard. XCMDs are written in C++, then compiled, so they run fast and efficiently. XOBJ—short for X-OBJECT—and XFCN—short for X-FUNCTION—are variations.

■ Index